Undermining Capitalism

Undermining

Joel Krieger

Capitalism

State Ownership and the Dialectic of Control in the British Coal Industry

Princeton University Press, Princeton, N.J.

095 483

HD
9551.6
· K74
1983

For my mother, Lucille Krieger
and my father, Philip Krieger

CONTENTS

LIST OF TABLES

ACKNOWLEDGMENTS

Few research projects and probably fewer books derived from dissertations could be accomplished without the generous assistance and encouragement of many persons and institutions. Because of the need for extended research overseas and access to sources above and below ground which could easily have been barred to me, I think my debts of gratitude are unusually great.

I owe a special debt to the National Coal Board and to the National Union of Mineworkers not merely for making this study possible, but also for helping me on a daily basis to accomplish my research. I wish to thank the many employees of the NCB and members of the NUM who assisted me with rare generosity both of time and spirit. While there are many more people deserving thanks than I can mention here, I am particularly grateful to A. Matthaei and Derek Broadbent at Hobart House, Dr. Alan Griffin in Nottingham, and G. L. Atkinson, J. Foley, Vic Hildreth, and Ernie Mackley in Durham (on the NCB side); and to Walter Malt and the lodge secretaries and officials in the Durham collieries I visited, and Len Clark, Joe Whelan, and the branch secretaries and officials in the Nottingham collieries I visited. Bill Dowding, research officer for the Durham Miners' Association (DMA), provided invaluable assistance as did the many pitmen who encouraged, kidded, and instructed me at each colliery.

I was very fortunate in having Samuel H. Beer as my advisor in the Government Department at Harvard where this work began. He encouraged me and helped me with remarkable skill, knowing when patience and support were needed and when nothing but a hammering on some of my arguments would do. For his energy, dedication, and wise counsel, I am very grateful.

I am indebted to friends and colleagues in Britain and America who encouraged me in my research and helped me with critical advice, especially Suzanne Berger, Stephen Bornstein, John Carney, A. W. Coats, Sam Cohn, Ellen Comisso, Dave, Maureen, and Emma Douglass, David Held, Ray Hudson, Peter Lange, Jim Lewis, Charles Maier, Martín Sanchez-Jankowski, David Stark, and Rosemary Taylor. I would also like to thank Mrs. Iris Sloggatt for her unique assistance, Jane Szurek for extremely helpful research, and Sandy Thatcher at Princeton University Press for demonstrating in full the rare qualities of a fine editor. I owe thanks to Kris Glen for, inter alia, critical literary advice in the closing stages of the project.

Finally, I wish to express my gratitude to the several institutions, organizations, and departments which helped me either financially or in equally important but less tangible ways to accomplish my research: Cambridge University, Faculty of Economics; Durham University, Regional Policy Research Unit; the University of Nottingham, Department of Economic and Social History; Wellesley College; Harvard's Center for European Studies; the Council for European Studies; the Krupp Foundation; the Social Science Research Council; the American Council of Learned Societies; and Columbia's Institute on Western Europe.

Undermining Capitalism

CHAPTER ONE

STATE OWNERSHIP, THE NCB, AND CONTRADICTIONS OF BUREAUCRATIC MANAGEMENT

When the party label Social Democrat still referred mainly to German Marxists, and the Labour Party was occupied with working through the special meaning and purpose of socialism for Britain, the issue of nationalization was at the core of party debate. In 1952, Roy Jenkins, now a leader of Britain's own Social Democratic Party, but then representing a strong mainstream position within the Labour Party, explained what state ownership in Britain was all about.

> A substantial extension of public ownership is . . . an essential prerequisite of greater equality of earned incomes and an inevitable concomitant of greater equality in the ownership of property. . . . The measures of nationalisation which we saw between 1945 and 1950 were largely *planning* measures. They were put forward as proposals which were necessary to ensure adequate governmental control over the whole economy, and the industries which were chosen were mostly those through which this function could best be exercised. As a result, they were necessarily measures which involved whole industries and which imposed a centralised structure upon them. All the main line railway companies had to be taken and it would not have done to have substituted catering for coal.[1]

In their efforts, Jenkins and the other "revisionists" who sought to enshrine "equality" rather than ownership and control of "the means of production and distribution" as the central orthodoxy of British socialism, were programmatically successful. Whatever the battles about the meaning of socialism and the related leadership struggles in the Labour Party during the Bevanite period, a moderate, highly compensatory, industry-dominated, capitalist rationalizing model of nationalization has held sway in postwar Britain. But the revisionists, and the "fundamentalists" as well, badly misjudged the consequences and enduring meaning of the practice of state ownership. Accordingly, they missed something significant about the evolutionary prospects of contemporary capitalism.

Cast within a matrix of capitalist forces, the publicly owned enterprises were not to afford governmental control of the "whole economy." Moreover, equality could not be administered through the wages (incomes) policies of the nationalized industries, despite, as we shall see, the most sophisticated and sincere management efforts. Worst of all, no centralized structure could be imposed successfully on far-flung, regionally diverse industries with long, vital, and divided histories and workers who held these histories dear. Remarkably, both the moderate center and the Marxist outreaches of the Labour Party—and the broader socialist movement beyond—failed to appreciate the self-limiting character of capitalist nationalization. Nor did they anticipate its contradictory consequences and, despite current signs that old debates about the meaning of British socialism never die, the disputes of the '50s do not wear well on new reading.

While stressing the revisionist dogma of equality, Jenkins tried also to absorb the fundamentalist concern for planning, ownership, and control. Both camps were to be disappointed. State ownership has not generated equality of any recognizable kind and it does not represent public control from the commanding heights for transformative purposes. Nationalization does not, as a classical strain of social democracy suggests, mean that leading industries can be wrested progressively from the control of capitalists and the state turned piecemeal to the interests of socialism. For one thing, capitalists have been quite content to offload moribund industries onto the state under extremely favorable terms, and for another, nationalized industries have operated by principles (for example, "buy dear and sell cheap") and strategies (notably in hard-nosed industrial relations bargaining) which give the advantage to capitalist elites and reproduce the norms of class society. Nevertheless, despite the implementation of state ownership on exceedingly capitalist terms, nationalization undermines capitalism in unforeseen ways, without ever offering an alternative example of industrial organization and economic coordination. As it turns out, I agree with Jenkins only that when considering the problems of state ownership in Britain, "it would not have done to have substituted catering for coal."

In what follows, I will use the history of the nationalized British coal industry to illustrate what to me seems a fundamental truth about contemporary capitalism, namely, that even the most subtle and far-reaching efforts at rationalizing capitalism are likely to come undone. In this book, I look at the premier effort of the National Coal Board (NCB) to do exactly what a sophisticated management operating a troubled industry as part of a capitalist-rationalizing state is supposed to do. The management should rationalize production and, as Jenkins tells us, use public ownership to promote the equalization of incomes, all through the imposition of a centralized structure.

After nearly two decades of sporadic negotiation, the NCB and the National Union of Mineworkers (NUM) agreed upon the implementation of a national uniform wage for faceworkers, the 1966 National Power Loading Agreement (NPLA). Both sides believed that the agreement would inaugurate a period of industrial harmony and provide the basis for improved productivity which was required to stabilize the industry. I argue that the NPLA failed, despite painstaking planning and artful management execution, because it unleashed a surprising battle for control of production and ultimately reordered the inner life of work relations and industrial conflict down the pit. I argue that a new "dialectic of control" at the coal face, generated by the NPLA, triggered regionally distinctive responses from miners, who reacted to the imposition of national uniformity with a high degree of flexibility and self-conscious strategy. They responded in ways which were encouraged by disparate patterns of work relations and conditioned by the miners' concrete work situations—the history of the pit, the geology, the technology, and the organization of labor under which they worked. Specifically, I looked at Durham, with its history of thin seams and low productivity, its union moderation offset by Geordie determination to "fight the gaffers" with unusual workers' control strategies, and at Nottingham, the high-producing area of the post-1926 breakaway union, with its traditions of competitive, hierarchical, and disciplined productivity.

It turns out that the cornerstone of NCB strategy, which was to stabilize the industry's prospects by imposing uniformity and rationalizing wage structures, proved unsuccessful in both regions, as the efforts proved incompatible *in different ways* with the values and practices of both Durham and Nottingham miners. While the specific problems faced by the NCB in implementing the NPLA—ambiguous productivity results and the first two national strikes since 1926—are no doubt linked to British coal, per se, the consequences of the failure of the NPLA are likely to be of more general significance.

These observations concerning the contrast between British socialist theories about public ownership and the practical consequences of such ownership are preliminary, and I shall return for another look at these issues much later. For now, I merely want to introduce the possibility that the Coal Board's problems are not unlike those that may attend the management of other state-owned enterprises. Even more central here, they signal fundamental contradictions which in general diminish the capacities of centralized state bureaucracies to administer policy effectively. Accordingly, the fate of British coal may tell us something important about the contradictory and self-limiting practices of the contemporary state, and the ways in which capitalist rationalization is endemically undermined.

NATIONALIZATION AND WAGES POLICY

Born in the era of competitive capitalist ownership, regional divisions persist within the modern nationalized industry to scuttle the best plans of the NCB's management team, which is attempting (with uncertain results) to plan, centralize, and coordinate the business of mining coal in Britain. Thus, decentralizing tendencies and potential sources of localized conflict have been a fundamental genetic fact of the industry. Recognizing this, from the start the new management sought to impose a centralized structure on a fragmented industry.

Along with the formal transfer of ownership on 1 January 1947 of 1,400 colleries, 225,000 acres of farmland, 85 brickworks, 55 coke-oven and by-products plants, 140,000 housing units, and assorted shops, hotels, milk rounds, and swimming pools[2]—the National Coal Board also inherited a confusing complex of local wage agreements from the capitalist owners. For work directly at the coal face—hewing, putting, pulling, caunchwork*—men were typically paid by results (piece rates). But there was no consistency among the pay levels. The same job, even under comparable geological and technological conditions, more likely than not received a different compensation on a face in South Wales and a face in Scotland. Indeed, two men performing the same task on the same coal face in a given colliery might also receive a different level of pay, since "anomalous conditions"—for example, the presence of water or a faulting condition—led to a custom of bargaining on the spot over the specific piece-rate level. The "spot bargain" in turn would not only be determined by the working conditions (such that a higher rate of compensation per "piece" might offset the lower production potential of work

* See Glossary for definitions of mining terms.

under poor conditions), but also would vary according to the balance of labor-management power in the particular colliery.[3] Thus the variety of pay levels and wage agreements was endless, and the situation constantly in flux. Adding to the irregularities of the wages system, there was no clear job ladder with consistent definitions of task or with uniform salary scales. This note of uncertainty and irrationality frustrated a vigorous management team bent on applying every potential advantage of centralized structure toward the end of harmonizing industrial relations and increasing productivity.

Failing in a series of attempts to rationalize a piece-rate wage formula, from the late 1950s onward the NCB and the miners' representatives, the National Union of Mineworkers, focused their attention on the negotiation of a uniform time-based (daywage) agreement. Finally, after years of NCB irresolution followed by a curious reversal in NUM policy, the National Power Loading Agreement (NPLA) was signed in June 1966. Stipulating a five-year transition to a uniform national daywage for face workers on mechanized (i.e., power loaded) coal faces, the agreement transformed the inner workings of the industry.

At the beginning the NPLA was considered a great victory for the NUM and the mineworkers, who resented the age-old practices of victimization, relaxed safety standards, and competitive productivity which accompanied a piece-rate wage form. But the path-breaking agreement was, in the end, pressed by the NCB on a divided union. A time-based wage suited the management needs of an industry which was rapidly mechanizing its operations, thereby replacing worker initiative with machine running time as the ostensible determinant of productivity. Moreover, in return for a uniform wage, which could be affected neither by machine breakdown nor poor geological conditions, nor by variable laboring effort, the NCB won the right to establish full management control over the direction of the labor process.[4] The NPLA was a monument of the NCB's efforts to rationalize the industry by applying the advantages of centralized administration. The NCB viewed the daywage agreement as the critical instrument with which to force modernity on an industry encrusted with fragmenting distinctions—regions with diverse labor histories and varied patterns of geological and technological resources—and decentralized habits.

MANAGEMENT STRATEGIES AND THE PITFALLS OF RATIONALITY

By the time I began my research in the summer of 1974, attitudes about the NPLA had changed. Coal Board officials, and more than a few of their NUM counterparts, were calling the daywage agreement a disaster.[5] The NPLA was not only responsible, at least indirectly, for the national strikes of 1972 and 1974, but it contributed to declining productivity. It was presented as an article of faith throughout the industry that new incentive agreements based on productivity (subsequently introduced in the winter of 1978) offered the only hope for generating renewed vitality within the industry. From both the NUM and the NCB I invariably received the same persistent advice. If I wanted to study what was really going on in the industry, I ought to look at the effects of wage structures and try to understand the importance of the transition from payment by results to daywage in the 1966-1971 period.

Although skeptical at first that a single policy innovation could have such far-reaching consequences, the unanimous claims of miners and managers that the NPLA had transformed work relations, industrial relations, and patterns of productivity were persuasive. These claims were enough to draw me into much deeper research about the management strategies and processes of deliberation which led to the NPLA and about the subsequent effects of this agreement; the results of my investigation comprise this study.

As I began to consider the behavior of the Board in negotiating the sweeping rationalization of wage structures,

I discovered a critical unresolved issue which made me question the wisdom of miners and managers and reflect further on the implications of NCB management strategy. From the time I began my research to this day, the NCB has stuck to a simple story about the consequences of the national daywage agreement. The elimination of material incentives for high productivity led, according to the official interpretation, to reduced worker initiative and hence to disappointing trends in productivity. The claim, while it obviously had some basis, aroused my suspicion. Every regional employee of the NCB industrial relations staff in Durham could detail for me the effects on productivity of time-based wages as compared to a straight payment-by-results scheme or a complex time-based wage plus productivity bonus scheme. Then why couldn't the Hobart House wage structure brain trust anticipate the obvious results a decade earlier? Why had the NCB introduced the "disastrous" wage structure in the first place?

If the NCB were simply staffed by incompetents or if they had been forced to the decision by the power of the NUM, then the administrative processes would concern only those with a special interest in the industry. But if, on the contrary, the NCB had employed sophisticated planning strategies and if, as I was led to believe, they had artfully managed and directed the lengthy negotiations— then broader issues were at stake. Were there structural reasons why results which were unforeseen by management would scuttle the most carefully planned strategy of a centralized bureaucracy? Were there, for example, tendencies toward deconsolidation which unavoidably limited the centralizing efforts of national, nationalized management? Was there something beyond the specifics of NCB policy and the British coal industry which made the best laid plans of rationalization go awry and appear, by their consequences, irrational? Initial research into the history of negotiations and NCB management strategy confirmed my growing suspicions that the answer to each of these questions might be affirmative. If so, more was at stake than the failure of NCB policy. By looking at the causes behind the destruction of the wages strategy which lay outside the NCB proper, I could explore the transmission of policy initiatives from centralized bureaucracies to the groups directly affected by their administrative practices. By this focus—on the connection between state policy formulation and the response of those who are the object of particular bureaucratic initiatives—I could hope to illuminate problems of centralized bureaucratic management under capitalism which have fallen in the cracks among state theory, studies of bureaucracy and organization, and accounts of the behavior of diverse groups, interests, and classes that both influence and respond to the policies inaugurated by state agencies. I was convinced that the implementation of the NPLA in the British coal industry posed serious questions about the problems and processes of state bureaucratic management which warranted further investigation.

The NCB Bureaucracy and the NPLA Negotiations

For two months during the autumn of 1976, I visited NCB headquarters as a guest of the Industrial Relations Department. At Hobart House I was provided with documents which revealed the inner decision-making network of the Coal Board; its rationale for critical wage policy decisions; the influence on policy articulation of communication with other nationalized industries and various government ministries; and the inner strategy and day-to-day evolution of critical negotiations with the NUM.[6] This documentary evidence confirmed decisively that the NPLA was the consequence neither of management incompetence nor NUM pressure. On the contrary, the record suggests a competent, rational, and aware bureaucracy, carefully and cautiously considering the options available to centralized management in a regionally diverse and economically troubled industry, and effectively directing the pace and the outcome of the negotiations.

The NCB entered the negotiations for rationalization of the wage structure with its eyes open and, from the point of view of its management responsibilities, with admirable caution. Pressed by Arthur Horner, secretary of the NUM, in a speech in Rothesay in 1947 to accept that in time all miners would be paid the same rate for a job from Land's End to John O'Groats, the Board refused to offer any assurances.[7] For the NCB, reasonably enough, Horner's basic challenge was posed with a slightly different twist: what wage structure would ensure maximum *productivity* from Land's End to John O'Groats?

At first, the NCB management simply did not know the answer and, probably very wisely, thought that a single best wage structure might be impossible in such a regionally distinctive industry. A series of draft reports and memoranda which were circulated between 1949 and 1951 within a half-dozen NCB committees concerned with wage policy, reveal an eminently sensible and coherent set of management concerns.[8] During this period, the NCB wage policy was governed by the desire for a contented labor force which could be maintained at the proper level of manpower* with the necessary skills, and paid as little as possible. The Board needed a rational and explicit wage policy as a central element in the overall fiscal planning of the industry. Moreover, a policy was required to guide annual negotiations, and especially to brake the runaway wage drift which in the coal industry took the form of continual applications for the upward revision of piece-work price lists. With inadequate manpower a consistent headache in the expanding coalfields, and the increasing presence of alternative employment—the manufacture of equipment

* The effort to reproduce, whenever possible and appropriate, the living dialogue and common usage of persons working in the British coal industry has led unavoidably to the inclusion of gender-specific terms like "manning." There are in fact no women working down the pit and I encountered none in the decision-making ranks of the NCB. Accordingly, masculine terms in all cases refer to men and I have otherwise avoided suspect usage.

for power plants, mining machinery, general machine tools—destabilizing the manpower supply in the contracting coalfields, the NCB wished particularly to shape a wage policy around systematic manpower planning. This, and its concern to meet the burgeoning demand for coal from the Central Electricity Generating Board (CEGB), in particular, conditioned the Board's strategy.

The conclusions reached by the NCB were clear. For all categories of workers, the central consideration was the probable effect of wage rates and differentials on recruitment, attendance, and effort. An increase in wages to dayworkers was likely to have a positive effect on these three factors. But no precipitous action should be taken, since fiddling with differentials might have dangerous unintended effects on the efforts of the higher paid classes of laborers employed on the face and on regionally diverse manpower requirements. Pieceworkers' wages were considered high enough to attract recruits and were pitched at the proper level for men already in the industry. Increases were considered more likely to harm than enhance attendance and effort. Therefore, increases to pieceworkers should be avoided except to compensate for instances where an increase in daywage rates might inadvertently reduce the differential to a level which was too low to attract workers to the more dangerous and arduous work at the coal face.[9]

Thus, as the NCB entered serious negotiations with the NUM in 1951 over the rationalization of wage structures in the coal industry, the watchword was caution. The NUM could be relied on in the long run to try to secure uniformity since, as the Board recognized, this was one of the principles enunciated in their standing orders (constitution) and consistently reaffirmed by prominent members of the national executive.[10] In the short run, the NUM could be expected to claim increases in earnings, regardless of the character of the wage structure. While the claim for increased wages could not be resisted, particularly during that expansionary period, it could perhaps be channeled into the most productive districts.

Any claim for national uniformity was another matter.[11] The principle of a reduction of differentials which lurked behind any proposal for wage structure rationalization, whether between regions or between classes of workers, was firmly rejected by the Board. With the related problems of production and manpower uppermost in their thinking, the appropriate NCB committees resisted any specific recommendations, whether from the NUM or from individual staff members, which would alter the existing patchwork quilt of pay differentials and relativities. The Board was determined to pay wages which were adequate to attract workers to the industry and to keep them in pits within given regional concentrations. Above all, they wished to retain differentials which were wide enough to encourage men to take on the directly productive jobs, but not so wide as to promote discontent—which could be translated into reduced productive efficiency—either among pitmen elsewhere below ground or among those working on the surface.

These considerations defeated any proposal, however elegant its design, which suggested a national response to the issue of wage strategy.[12] The solution to the problem of manpower provision, in terms of the quality and quantity which were believed necessary to enhance productivity, forced the Board to endorse fluid pay relativities and increases in differentials, both geographically and between classes of workers. The tendencies toward uniformity which seemed natural in an administratively centralized nationalized industry which was undergoing rapid technological development contradicted the NCB's firm commitment, despite lip service to the contrary, that anomalies be retained. Paradoxically, the Board considered the complex web of differentials which gave the industry's wage structure the appearance of irrationality to be the one certain element in a rational wage strategy.

A Reversal of Bargaining Positions

While the goal which both sides acknowledged to be the core of a fully rationalized wage structure remained distant, namely, a uniform national daywage for face workers, the two parties negotiated. First, in 1955, they agreed to a national uniform daywage for workers underground but not for workers at the face, who were traditionally paid by locally negotiated day rates. Ten years of fruitless negotiations followed. Finally, in 1965, in the one aberrant point of development in the process of rationalization leading to the NPLA, the NUM and NCB agreed on a national daywage structure for Remotely Operated Longwall Faces (ROLFs). Reflecting the excessive optimism of the white-hot technological revolution of the day, the agreement proved far more advanced than the technology, which has consistently proved unworkable. The ROLF agreement, nevertheless, provided the initial break in negotiations which led to the signing of the NPLA the following year, nearly two decades after the initial negotiations had begun, and years after the comprehensive introduction of power loading equipment signaled the permanent technological transformation of the industry.

When the negotiations began, the NUM pressed for uniformity, despite ambivalence from an executive which was committed in principle to wholesale rationalization but knew only too well that existing differentials divided the membership. In the underground world of mining, argued the Union, with the incessant and uncharted interventions of geological factors and the planned inequities of uneven technological innovation, only a national daywage could ensure a fixed proportion between effort and remuneration throughout the industry. But the Board, under the stress of regionally distinct manpower needs and cost structures stood firm on the policy advantages of differentials which would be manipulated as labor markets and changing demand structures might require. During the years of deadlock, the NCB fixed wage policy on the assumption that the financial incentives of a payment-by-results structure were necessary to induce adequate performance under the full range of difficult and demoralizing conditions which might, at any time, develop underground. But by 1965, the bargaining postures had all but reversed.

The ROLF agreement accomplished, the Board was bent on achieving a daywage structure for face workers. With the application of power loading techniques to 85.6 percent of all production, output had become more dependent on machine running time and proper organization of production than on the intentions and the physical exertions of the colliers.[13] Not only was piecework, therefore, cheated of its rational basis, but a transition to a firmly controlled daywage was thought to provide a better check on the all-important ratio of Earnings to Output per Manshift (EMS/OMS).

Technological innovation and wage drift in piece-rate price lists were closely linked, and the two factors mutually reinforced the Board's eventual support for daywage and its convert's passion for the goal of a fully rationalized wage structure. Frequent minor improvements in technology had generated increases in productivity. In turn, the pitmen demanded, and usually received, upward revisions in piecework agreements, for which they expended no additional effort. The further question of control entered the Board's new rationale. In the past, as staff members acknowledged, improved performance could only be won at the expense of management prerogatives. Often, management did not attempt to introduce higher task norms alongside incremental technical improvements in mining methods for fear of causing disputes which would make the exercise futile. Hence, one of the Board's central goals in promoting a national daywage structure for face workers was to increase control, not only over earnings, but over the determination of task, team composition, and the process of production and turnover of the face.[14]

Management would be given full responsibility for ensuring maximum machine utilization, which would essentially define its role. Colliery-level NCB staff would no longer be involved in constant renegotiation of price lists and frequent disputes about piece rates. Pressure on management to revise price lists to meet changes in operating conditions or to correct discrepancies among teams would be substantially reduced. Disputes and stoppages would be few, and management would be freed from constant bargaining and bickering to concentrate on planning strategies for obtaining improved performance. Best of all, management would have the flexibility to plan and implement these productive strategies in a less controversial context. Where in the past every change in technique, every assignment to a team or to a position on the coal face, involved a wages issue, a national daywage structure would, in principle, reduce the political significance of production decisions. The introduction of new face equipment or new technologies would introduce no wages issues. Workers could be relocated more spontaneously and with less potential for dispute. Manpower planning at the local level could proceed flexibly in response to changing imperatives of production. At the regional and national levels, a daywage agreement which limited wage drift for the highly paid face workers would make it easier for the NCB to staff the other jobs underground, which would now be paid on the same basis as face work and subject to carefully planned, rather than arbitrary and uncontrolled, differentials.[15]

A daywage agreement which required nothing more than full cooperation with management "with the object of achieving the best possible utilization of power loading machines" in return for a guaranteed wage at the end of the week, replaced the age-old pattern of continual local bargaining over price lists and compensation for anomalous conditions at the face. National replaced local bargaining, as known standard wages rationalized an industry straining under incessant wages drift. The National Board for Prices and Incomes, convinced of the virtue of the daywage, was officially urged by the National Prices and Incomes Board to rationalize its wages structure,[16] viewing it as the central instrument for rationalizing production and centrally administering the industry.

The Board's Concerns

Convinced of the manifest advantages of firmer control, both of EMS and of the face operation, the Board was nonetheless aware of disadvantages which necessarily attached to a national daywage agreement.[17] Above all, the Board feared the effects of a lack of financial incentive on the performance of any given shift. Second, they were concerned that problems both in the short and long run would likely arise over manning. With wages predetermined, during the settling-in period of the agreement on any given face, conflicts in industrial relations might focus on the number of colliers to be included in the face team. Men would naturally want to increase the size of the team, thereby reducing the stint (which would have no effect whatever on wages). Thus, in the initial period expanded work teams might result, which would bloat the EMS and commensurately reduce OMS and general productive efficiency. Moreover, pitmen used to finding that extraordinary effort resulted in very high wages (e.g., rippers) might consistently endeavor to get additional members onto the team, without fulfilling any greater rate of advance.

The subsequent history of the transition from a piecework to a daywage structure in the British coal industry would confirm these initial fears. In addition, the agreement would have consequences which caught management unawares, for it is not too much to say that the NPLA transformed work relations, intensified local industrial conflict, reduced productivity in the industry, and provided the basis for national political unity which would defeat a government.

A FAILED WEBERIAN BUREAUCRACY

It is obvious from this account of management strategy in the evolution of wages policy leading to the NPLA, that the NCB did everything right—but the policy came out wrong. Not only did the NCB operate as a perfect Jenkinsite public enterprise, imposing centralized structures to advance governmental control of the economy and reduce earnings inequalities, but the NCB conformed also to our theoretical expectations of how a bureaucracy is best supposed to operate. Few have disagreed with Weber's general propositions about the proper characteristics of modern bureaucracy: officials operate within strict areas of competence and responsibility and according to fixed rules; there is a clear elaboration of office hierarchy with appropriate supervision of lower offices; administration is based upon written documents (files); management presupposes specialized training, and its formal responsibilities demand the full capacities of the official.[18] In all these respects, the Board proved itself the exemplary modern bureaucracy. Moreover, as Weber would require, the NCB directed its efforts toward the achievement of a clearly conceived goal, namely, the implementation of a centralized, planned, and coordinated wage structure which would promote maximum production by a labor force which could be maintained at an appropriate level of skill and at the right size, and be paid no more than would be necessary to avoid labor unrest. Thus administrative operations fulfilled the two conditions of the Weberian model. The NCB met both the *structure criterion* (it was based on hierarchy, jurisdictions of responsibility, and fixed rules) and the *logic criterion* (it proceeded by purposive action to further definite goals). But the watershed NPLA policy failed decisively. Most important, it failed, as I will demonstrate, for reasons that were not in the main contingent, such as poor technology, weak market positions, and increasing geological exhaustion. Thus, the failure in practice was also a failure in Weberian theory.

Accordingly, the consequences of this critical NCB policy initiative must be considered from two sides. First, I will attempt to show the connection between the destabilizing consequences of the NPLA and the centralized bureaucratic management structure of the NCB, located as it is within the administrative apparatus of the contemporary state and conforming as it does to the letter and the spirit of the Weberian bureaucracy. In so doing, I will discuss the implications and limits of Weberian theory. Second, I will explain the effects of NCB wages policy on the internal political economy—the labor process, the work relations, the economic performance—of this troubled but resilient industry. While the latter considerations, which are discussed in Chapter Two, govern an understanding of the particular effects of the evolution of wages structure on the industry, the former—on which I will concentrate for the remainder of this chapter—shed light on general problems of centralized, bureaucratic management by state agencies under capitalism.

Why did the "perfect" Weberian bureaucracy fail to meet successfully the challenge of its most critical policy initiative? In answering this question, I will offer a set of general propositions about the contradictions of centralized bureaucratic management which the case of NCB wages policy illustrates, and which may have broader application to an understanding of the limited extent of the state's capacities to resolve the intractable problems of contemporary capitalism.

The Ambigious Heritage of Weberian Theory

Contemporary interpretations of organizations, including the state bureaucracies which are the agency of government policy, have all been influenced in some measure by Weber's *Economy and Society*. This common point of departure has generally, although I think avoidably, resulted in studies which have not effectively illuminated the special pattern of the bureaucratic phenomenon today, a pattern which reflects the structural position of bureaucracies within states that are influencing social processes in new and profound ways. While a growing set of economists, political scientists, and sociologists have recognized and sought to explain this "state intervention," bureaucratic theory has, on the contrary, ignored the phenomenon and remained aloof from the seemingly endless debate over "the relative autonomy" of the state. Those who focus on the study of bureaucracies have neglected the consequences of a bureaucracy's structural position within the apparatus of the state. This position of the bureaucracy as agency of state policy initiative increasingly demands explanation as the tentacles of state administration grip much deeper than Weber envisioned. As the range of activities undertaken by state agencies grows, and the character of policy becomes ever more varied, the Weberian heritage of concern with the inner rationality of administration declines in explanatory power.

The Weberian theory of the evolution and internal dynamic of bureaucracy, whether in the public or the private sphere, has focused on the importance of rational administration. "Weber's basic model of bureaucratic development," summarizes Erik Wright in an unusually clear evaluation of Weber's (and Lenin's) theories of bureaucracy, "centers on the need for rational, predictable administration for capitalist enterprises to be able to make efficient calculations in their production decisions. The central variable which underlies the explanation is the need for *rationality*."[19] The purposive rationality (the *logic*) by which the bureaucracy seeks to realize its aims mirrors its internally rational *structure*, and this two-sided rationality fits the needs of (is functional for) capitalist development.

Although this emphasis, as I will show below, is not altogether fair to Weber, the power of his explanation of the internal rationality of the bureaucratic organization has led many to adopt arguments which focus on the *logic of institutions* rather than on the connection between bureaucracies and the objects of their institutional activity, namely, the classes, elites, and client groups which are influenced by state policy. There has been, of course, significant variation in these formulations. Bureaucracy may be fundamentally rational, despite the nonrational character of people or their limited capacity to adapt to organizational imperatives (Simon, March and Simon, Barnard),[20] or bureaucracy may incorporate elements of irrationality. Accordingly, it may be viewed as inefficient for certain tasks (Blau and Scott, Stinchcombe) and "may directly inhibit intelligent, technically effective action" (Crozier, Merton).[21] Bureaucracy may display an invariant institutional logic (Michels) or a contradictory logic embedded within a broader pattern or capitalist development (Habermas).[22] Whatever the specific formulation, emphasis on the internal features of the bureaucracy as an organization has led to a "predominance of quantitative research studies which can take into account tangible aspects of organizational structures—size, job titles, levels of supervision, spans of control, and the like—much more easily than the less quantifiable elements of the environment."[23] Similar emphasis has resulted in numerous studies which speculate about the aims, motives, and patterns of behavior of bureaucrats as an autonomous social "class" (Downs, Galbraith, Niskanen).[24]

Internalist or logic of institution interpretations of the bureaucratic phenomenon do not, in my view, express the richness and subtlety of Weber's own account. Unfortunately, these modern applications have successfully distorted the orientation of Weberian analysis. Instead of exploring a second-generation neo-Weberianism which adapts the insights of modern social scientific inquiry and Marxist state theory—and which accommodates the historical evolution of bureaucratic structures within capitalist development—these authors have reoriented and revised Weber in a way that makes his insights less applicable than ever to an understanding of the problems of centralized, bureaucratic management today.

Bureaucratization and Capitalist Development

Weber posits a relationship between growing bureaucratization and capitalism; state agencies mirror the hierarchical rule-bound structure and the purposive logic that govern the business operations of the capitalist firm. Accordingly, he argues in *Economy and Society* that "the 'progress' toward the bureaucratic state, adjudicating and administering according to rationally established law and regulation, is nowadays very closely related to the modern capitalist development."[25] But one can search Weber's writings in vain, seeking a satisfactory explanation of the precise character of that relation between the growing bureaucratic centralization of the state and modern capitalism.

Weber cannot specify the structural relationship between bureaucratization and capitalist development for two reasons. First, in his historical account of patterns of bureaucratization in diverse societies he does not isolate the degree to which certain bureaucratic processes may be specific to capitalism, or influenced by capitalist development, per se. Weber seems to give equal weight to the "impact of cultural, economic, and technological forces" on the growth of bureaucracy, even when these forces are wholly independent of capitalist development. At times, his argument smacks of technological determinism, as for example when he explains the bureaucratization of Egypt (the "oldest country of bureaucratic state administration") as following from the "technical necessity of a public regulation of the water economy." More generally, Weber credits the "increasing complexity of civilization," and especially the creation of standing armies and "essentially technical factors" linked to mass communication (the growth of public roads and waterways, railroads, the telegraph), as being the fundamental forces which have led to centralized, bureaucratic administration.[26] Thus, the particular connection between bureaucratization and capitalism is left clouded within an admirably complex but insufficiently precise account of societal evolution.

Second, in Weber's analysis of existing Western society, the specific connection between capitalism and bureaucracy is not structurally explicated. Rather, Weber suggests that bureaucratism in government and in private capitalist administration have a common basis, are functionally interrelated, and are homologous. This says quite a lot, but not enough to provide a method for analysis of patterns of activity by state agencies today. Weber argues:

> [T]he "separation" of the worker from the material means of production, destruction, administration, academic research, and finance in general is the common basis of the modern state, in its political, cultural and military sphere, and of the private capitalist economy. In both cases the disposition over these means is in the hands of that power whom the *bureaucratic apparatus* (of judges, officials, officers, supervisors, clerks and non-commissioned officers) directly obeys or to whom it is available in case of need. This apparatus is nowadays equally typical of all those organizations; its existence and function are inseparably cause and effect of this concentration of the means of operation—in fact, the apparatus is its very form.[27]

Bureaucracy is the common basis of organization in the state and in capitalist industry. The internal organizational structures of the two, rooted in instrumental rationality, are comparable, and the form of the apparatus is equally functional for public agency and private bureaucracy. It is clear that state agencies which operate according to this two-sided rationality contribute functionally to capitalist interests and that the well-oiled capitalist machine provides a model for the rationalization of administrative bureaucracy.

This assumption of harmonious evolutionary codevelopment of private and public institutional forms obscures the issue of whether there is a real causal connection between the organizational form and the class basis of state power. It cannot take the place of a well worked-out theory of the complex evolution of state-society relations under modern capitalism. In the absence of such a theory, Weber cannot effectively apply his insights about the inner workings of bureaucracies and his empirical observations about trends in bureaucratization to his analysis of the changing patterns of state administration. Accordingly, in his criticism of parliament and government in the Germany of 1917, Weber explains the dangers to democracy—the weakness of parliament in the face of the burgeoning bureaucratic influence over governmental policy—as following from a set of contingent causes, such as the constitutional limits of parliamentary power and the continued influence of Bismarckian politics. As his study of parliament and government in a reconstructed Germany indicates, Weber lacks an account of the structural connection between the crisis-ridden path of capitalist development and the changing structure of activities of state agencies and processes of bureaucratic action.

Weber's inability to specify the connections between *internal* organization processes and *external* developments in political economy and class relations, by no means overshadows his contribution to an understanding of the state and the problems of centralized bureaucratic management. But it does suggest an area of fruitful research, namely, a consideration of the connections between bureaucratic processes within the state and the changing contours of capitalist development; patterns in class relations and mediate expressions of class power (e.g., social democratic or communist parties, trade unions); crises of accumulation, etc. Scholars in the Weberian tradition have, however, preferred to pursue organizational studies which focus on the internal processes, as if these were absolutely—and not "relatively"—autonomous with respect to class forces and the exigencies of capitalist development. Recently, some have begun to look at the "externalities," but conventional academics influenced by Weber have so far demonstrated little interest in going beyond weak abstract formulations about the "organizational environment."[28] The connections between bureaucratization and contemporary capitalist development, which were not sufficiently or unambiguously specified by Weber, remain far more vague in these neo-Weberian studies. As a result, crucial ground has been ceded to Marxists.

One final observation about Weber is essential for the

unfolding of this study. It is perhaps obvious that Weber wrote about bureaucracy mainly from the perspective of those dominant in it, from the side of the bureaucratic administration, not the administered.[29] Accordingly, he stressed the power that accrues to bureaucrats by virtue of expertise, information, and access, and a central preoccupation for Weber was the problem of how "bureaucratic power" can be checked. Worried about this, he looked to the countervailing powers of parliament and capitalist elites. Weber neglects the possibility, however (which proves critical in the study at hand), that the relationship between bureaucracy and the subjects of bureaucratic decisions involves, as do all power relations, a relationship of domination and chronic struggle, which itself serves as a crucial check on bureaucratic initiative. Thus, there ensues a "dialectic of control," a fluid struggle for control between administration and administered. Such struggle invariably attends the implementation of bureaucratic policy, and conditions in a significant way the exercise of centralized administration. I will argue that the unraveling of the NPLA follows a significant pattern and exposes a basic contradiction of centralized bureaucratic management under capitalism.

CONTRADICTIONS OF CENTRALIZED BUREAUCRATIC MANAGEMENT

Some integration of state theory with theories of bureaucracy that can be applied to discrete observations about processes of capitalist development and the concrete activities of state bureaucracies seems necessary. For a start, one can jettison simplistic conceptions about the institutional logic versus the organizational environment and seek to specify the connections between the "internal" and the "external"—what Nicos Poulantzas called the "whole series of contradictions between the specific category of state apparatus and the capitalist formation."[30]

Without going far enough in explaining or historically

locating these contradictions, in *Political Power and Social Classes* Poulantzas makes an important contribution by specifically raising the problem of the connection between bureaucratization and the state in terms of contradictions "located in the relations between the functioning of the bureaucracy and the *social classes*" within a capitalist mode of production.[31] The contradictions Poulantzas posits are located within the "capitalist political ideology"—for example, the contradiction between the principles of legitimacy of political democracy (parliamentary representation as an expression of popular sovereignty) and the forms assumed in the functioning of state bureaucracies (hierarchies with specific powers delegated from a unitary central power).[32] Poulantzas' strength here lies in his effort to clarify the character of the connection between the "external" dynamics of social class relations, the economic exigencies of capitalist accumulation/valorization, etc., and the "internal" processes of bureaucratic administration. It remains to specify the "whole series of contradictions" which define the processes of centralized bureaucratic management within the broader patterns of state policy formation and implementation in postwar Europe. Two contradictions in particular shed light on the failed management strategies of the NCB, an exemplary rational bureaucracy which became unwittingly trapped within a grander design of structural mishap.

Proposition One: Centrifugal Undertow

Contradiction betwen the centralizing strategy of the state bureaucracy and the centrifugal undertow of uneven regional development. The result: administrative unraveling and the failure of policies directed at centralization and national uniformity.

Long considered an anachronism left behind during the era of nation-building and one marked by growing irrelevance in the era of alleged post-industrial society, regionalism (alongside "peripheral" nationalism) has emerged in recent years as a leading problem of state management in European polities. States have attempted to promote centralized administration of economic development and to remedy regional imbalances through a wide range of measures including: "carrot and stick" programs of loans and grants to enterprises and employment premiums in combination with industry location controls (Britain); positive incentives to industry, particularly mixed enterprises, and expansion of development planning through the *metropoles d'équilibre* (France); loans and subsidies to local authorities for investment in industrial infrastructure within a context of increased cooperative planning of resource allocation between the Federal and Laender governments (Germany); and steering controls and the integration of regional into national plans (Italy).[33] Nevertheless, despite both specific initiatives from the center to rectify regional imbalance and the introduction of more general economic policy measures to enhance centralized administration through the nationalization of basic industries, despite the evolution of indicative and more coercive planning, the elaboration of prices and incomes policies, and "strings attached" subsidies to major failing producers—despite all these and comparable centralizing practices, uneven regional development persistently exerts tendencies toward deconsolidation from below.

Disparate labor markets force decentralized manpower policies; uneven patterns of investment and the heritage of outmoded patterns of industrial development generate regionally distinctive claims on the social welfare expenditure of the state; unbalanced growth and decline in the standards of living encourage regionally differentiated patterns in the power of particular classes and elites to influence national policy initiatives through industrial or union action, political parties, voting behavior, etc. These tendencies are pronounced in Britain, where labor and Labour strength are concentrated within "peripheral areas" (particularly South Wales, East Central Scotland and Strathclyde, the industrial northeast, and to a lesser extent in

Merseyside and southwest Lancashire), all of which suffer from exaggerated unemployment, underinvestment, and the decline of their traditional industrial base represented by coal, cotton and textiles, shipbuilding, iron and steel, and the automobile industry.[34]

As a consequence, a centrifugal undertow of uneven regional development significantly challenges the tendencies toward centralization and concentration which are typically considered fundamental both to capitalism in the era of monopoly capital and to the development of administrative bureaucratic management in this postwar period of intensified and deepening state intervention. This contradiction between the centralizing strategy of a national bureaucracy and the tendencies for deconsolidation which result from uneven regional development may be expressed politically, as they were dramatically in May 1979, in the decline of a national consensus around issues of welfare policy and economic planning. The contradiction leads to skewed regional patterns in national voting, and increased demands for regional devolution through enterprise boards, planning networks, growth center strategies, etc. More important for this study, the contradiction between national, centralized administration and regional tendencies toward deconsolidation may come to light in the administrative unraveling and failure of policies aimed at centralization and national uniformity.[35] As I will demonstrate, particular regionalist problems—traditions in work relations and industrial conflict which were generated by the uneven and distinctive regional development of the coal industry in Durham and in Nottingham—scuttled the NPLA wages structure, which had been painstakingly negotiated and cautiously introduced by the "perfect" bureaucracy of the NCB.

Proposition Two:
Crisis of Administrative Integration

Contradiction between the instrumental rationality of policies administered through state bureaucracies and the systems of meaning which client groups attach to the policies. The result: *a crisis of administrative integration*, when interpretations of policy outputs by the intended recipients fall outside the purposive design of state policy initiatives, and groups which are the object of policy remain insulated from the effects and segregated from the processes of centralized administration.

In his criticism of existing trends in the administration of the German state, Weber argued:

> Our officialdom has been brilliant wherever it had to prove its sense of duty, its impartiality and mastery of organizational problems in the face of the official, clearly formulated tasks of a specialized nature. . . . [But] . . . bureaucracy failed *completely* whenever it was expected to deal with political problems. . . . [T]he heads of the bureaucracy must continuously solve political problems—problems of *Machtpolitik* as well as *Kulturpolitik*. Parliament's first task is the supervision of these policy-makers. However, not ony the tasks assigned to the top ranks of the bureaucracy but also every single technicality of the lower administrative levels may become politically important and its solution may depend on political criteria.[36]

Weber stresses, according to Wright, that the "control of the administrative apex of the bureaucracy thus leads to politically irresponsible and ineffective direction of bureaucratic activity."[37] Despite assumptions elsewhere that bureaucratization is the more-or-less inevitable consequence of growing societal complexity and "[i]ncreasing public ownership in the economic sphere," in his account of immediate German problems Weber implies that an emboldened parliament could solve the problem of the tendency for excessive bureaucratic determination of policy, simply by being more directive.[38] For Weber the fundamental issue remains clear: governmental policies which are administered with insufficient parliamentary direction fail because bureaucrats do not have the training for, and bureaucracies are not structurally designed for, the consideration of political alongside technical or economic criteria.

Starting from a critique of Weber's basic assumption that the rational bureaucracy is the most efficient (an assumption which Weber clearly amended in his criticism of German democracy), Claus Offe has attempted to demonstrate that no method of state administration can be "adequate for solving the specific problem of the capitalist state," which he characterizes as the "establish[ment] of a balance between its *required functions*, which result from a certain state of the accumulation process, and its dynamics on the one side and its *internal structure* on the other side."[39] Offe argues that the "three 'logics' of policy production" which are available to the capitalist state, based in turn on bureaucratic rules, purposive action, and consensus formation, necessarily undermine its operation once burgeoning demands from the economic sphere impel the state decisively into market-replacing (productive) activities.[40] For Offe, each logic of policy production encounters a particular dynamic of failure: bureaucratic policy production cannot escape its dependence upon fixed hierarchical rules and therefore cannot respond flexibly to externally determined policy objectives; policy production governed by purposive action fails for a lack of clear-cut, uncontroversial, and operational goals transmitted from the environment; the consensus mode of policy production fails because it generates conflict by inviting "more demands and interests to articulate themselves than can be *satisfied*" by the capitalist state, bound as it is by considerations of accumulation.[41]

While more attuned to the specific limits of the bureaucratic mode of operation set by the connection between the capitalist state and the accumulation process, Offe's argument nevertheless resonates closely with Weber's own. Both Weber and Offe suppose that modern state bureaucracies are increasingly called on to make decisions with externally (i.e., socially, economically, and politically) imposed objectives and with snowballing consequences—and this function they cannot perform. They are hamstrung by a bureaucracy which operates by invariant rules and procedures and within overly narrow and strict jurisdictional areas of responsibility which limit the flexibility and, in a word, the rationality of administrative responses to externally formulated demands.

Clearly Weber and Offe understand the internal workings of bureaucracies within states well, and they have captured important truths about the limitations of rule-bound bureaucracies in promoting aims which are beyond their jurisdictional competence. When British Rail considers the elimination of an "unprofitable" service, by what rules—and from what rational stance—can they evaluate the complex consequences of the decision for the pursuit of leisure activities, investment in local industry, employment, settlement patterns, tourism, etc.?

But Weber and Offe skew the problem, assuming wrongly that because of the logic of policy production state bureaucracies cannot successfully execute policies with political ramifications which involve inputs from the environment. Offe, moreover, exaggerates the difference between "allocative" and "productive" measures with regard to the logic of policy formulation.

I see no reason to assume that policy initiatives which Offe places firmly in the allocative mode—taxation, Keynesian economic policy, government demand for commodities produced under conditions of private accumulation—can remain miraculously insulated from diverse environmental pressures. Can a bureaucracy which is bound by fixed hierarchical rules successfully administer macroeconomic policy—and can the policy be calculated according to goals transmitted from the environment which are more clear-cut and less controversial than those governing directly productive activities? More important for the case at hand, I want to argue that decisions which govern the productive mode of activities of the contemporary state do not ineluctably follow a dynamic of failure, and when they do fail it is not necessarily because of the internal logic of policy production.

For a wide range of decisions in both the allocative and productive mode of state intervention, there is no separation of political considerations (which, according to Weber, ought to be made by a higher authority like Parliament) from technical/economic decisions within the purview and competence of the state bureaucrats. Nor, as Offe argues, are those in the policy process too constrained by hierarchical rules or too befuddled by ambiguous and controversial goals transmitted from the environment to initiate appropriate policy measures. The determination of wages policy by NCB officials, to turn again to my main concern, turned on a complex judgment about efficiency, which included consideration of technical, political, and economic issues: the best wages policy would promote technological innovation because it would depoliticize small changes in job description, team selection, and deployment (since wages issues would not be involved); it would reduce the constant bickering over spot bargains and allow for greater but less controversial supervisory control; it would reduce wages drift while it improved productivity. The NCB was structured like a rational bureaucracy and conducted its business toward the instrumental achievement of specified ends. Nevertheless, its approach was superior to that of the higher authority set up by the executive to review NCB decisions, namely, the National Board for Prices and Incomes (NBPI). As a matter of fact, the NBPI had very little in the way of an independent directive role, since it relied on the presentations of the NCB in reaching its conclusions, and advised the NCB to make the very move—toward a daywage structure—which the Board had painstakingly plotted for a decade.

Two lessons emerge from this picture which may have wider application. First, those who presuppose a ready separability between the technical and the political or social elements in policies and insist that bureaucrats are structurally incapable of responding to externally imposed goals may oversimplify and distort the day-to-day administrative processes of state agencies. By indirection, they may, at the same time, overestimate the potential for efficient and effective decision-making by the nonbureaucratic apparatuses of the state. Second, those who suggest that the failure of state policies follows from the logic of policy production place too much emphasis on the internal structure of agencies and are too little concerned with the structured response of client groups.

The failure of the NPLA was not a failure in the logic of policy production, but rather a failure located in the dialectic of control which attends centralized bureaucratic administration. In this case the dialectic of control was doubly conditioned as the crisis of administrative integration was reinforced by the chronic struggles between workers and management which are part of the labor process itself under capitalism.[42] Thus, the affected groups of miners responded in diverse ways to the imposition of a national wage structure, depending on their distinctive regional traditions and attitudes toward productivity and management control, and on the local habits and customs which governed their work relations with each other. As workers and as the objects of centralized state administration, the colliers resisted management prerogatives and efforts by NCB personnel to exercise bureaucratic control over coordination of work tasks, the assignment of position on the coal face, and the selection of work teams. That is, they resisted in ways which reflected local custom and practice and their predisposition toward workers' control, more than they expressed strictly instrumental conduct toward the achievement of higher wage levels.

The miners were not prepared to "instrumentalize" their work relations and their relations with management, insofar as their action was oriented by rules which were chosen and reproduced in relation to a system of meaning, ideas, and values which remained at odds with the simple instrumental rationality of wages policy. While miners might be concerned with productivity and output as a means to achieving higher wages, this was not their sole, invariant concern—and it did not, at a stroke, remove traditional habits and collective values. The failure of policy, accordingly, reflects a crisis of administrative integration, as the logic of policy production encountered both the miners' conscious opposition to particular goals and their inchoate resistance to the one-dimensionality of behavior governed by instrumental logic. The practices of state policy implementation increasingly generate a contradiction between external, objective rules of bureaucratic administration and the internal rules of organization—and systems of meanings—of client groups which are not easily integrated into the rationality of bureaucratic administration.

THE COAL INDUSTRY AND PROBLEMS OF STATE POLICY IMPLEMENTATION

Seen in the light of these propositions, both the NCB's initial decision to introduce a national daywage agreement and the ultimate failure of the agreement become part of a larger story of the contradictory paths and politically problematic processes of the contemporary state under capitalism. Plagued since the First World War by poor productivity and uncertain market position, the British coal industry, since the interwar period, has been subject to capitalist disinvestment, stop-go patterns of government programs of reorganization and amalgamation, uncertain manpower supply, and even inferior geological prospects compared to its continental and American competitors. By the close of World War II, nationalization of the coal industry, with appropriate compensation for owners and management departing in the national interest, was a matter of broad consensus.

Efforts by the state to facilitate reconstruction of the economy by ensuring the cheap and stable provision of essential energy supplies, to provide for a modicum of centralized coordination and management, and yet to preserve the general principles of a capitalist Britain was, to be sure, undertaken as a compromise in response to the pressure of a triumphant working class demanding action from its Labour Government. But moderate nationalization was undertaken with the definite acquiescence of contemporary business interests and the grudging endorsement of their parliamentary representatives. In 1946 Winston Churchill, for example, endorsed the Coal Industry Nationalization Bill, noting that some major state commitment, through systematic reorganization or outright nationalization, provided the only hope for reconstruction of the industry and for provision of the large amount of capital necessary for technological innovation. Thus, state ownership and state management of basic industries represented a process of capitalist rationalization, triggered by specific class forces and immediate crises in the economic sphere.

But the practices of policy implementation by state agencies follow a crisis-ridden path, in part, as the propositions above suggest, due to the contradictions of centralized bureaucratic management. These contradictions reflect the complex connections between the internal structure of state bureaucracies and the external economic and class forces which are the object of management policy: centralization vs. the centrifugal undertow of uneven regional development; the instrumental rationality of state policy measures vs. the systems of meaning attributed by the affected parties to the actions conditioned by bureaucratic intervention.

As I will show directly, these contradictions underlie the dramatic effects of changes in NCB wages policy on the patterns of industrial conflict, work relations, and performance in the British coal industry in the immediate post-NPLA period and up to the present day.

CHAPTER TWO

THE POLITICS OF PRODUCTIVITY

With the introduction of the NPLA, the Board turned its active attention to ensuring the best results during the settling-in period. Throughout the summer and early fall of 1966, the NCB staff worked to secure the advantages of control it hoped to achieve from the agreement. The wages staff considered, but never implemented, proposals that men who were restricting effort be paid at a fall-back rate below the national power loading rate.[1] Management discussed the problem of challenging customary practices such as cavilling or the election of team members by seniority or by waiting lists or by other procedures which limited management prerogative—as guaranteed in the agreement—over selection of the team and manning of the work operations.[2] Members of the Industrial Relations Department consulted with divisional NCB staff over the thorny problems caused by the application of the agreement to new faces. While craftsmen welcomed their inclusion on the face teams (which resulted in substantial pay increases), extension of the agreement only aggravated the discontent of rippers, who lost their traditional differential over face workers.[3] Universally, divisional NCB officials registered concern over reduction of effort, particularly among rippers.[4] Nevertheless, in a series of memoranda and briefings for Board committees, the NCB expressed general satisfaction with the operation of the agreement. Leading members of the Industrial Relations Department stressed that the incidence of industrial unrest had been far below the general expectation, and recommended only minor areas for renegotiation of the NPLA agreement (concerning mechanisms for clarifying the relationship of craftsmen to power loading teams and securing more efficient use of their labor).[5] The NCB was confident that the initial work under the NPLA was progressing according to plan.

THE PROJECT

History has proven their initial judgments far too optimistic. From the start, the NPLA wage structure departed from the management design for its operation, despite its ostensible wisdom. By looking at the effects of the transition in wage structures—from piecework to the daywage structure of the NPLA—on industrial conflict, work relations, and productive performance in a set of Durham and Nottingham collieries, I intend to explain the systematic unraveling of the NCB's best rationalizing strategy. For this, the introduction of regional comparisons is essential.

Durham, just south of the Tyne River, bordering Newcastle, is geologically disadvantaged, and unique in maintaining traditional underground workers' control despite specific prohibition of such control under the NPLA. Nottingham, the commercial center of the East Midlands, with coal seams of a quality the Durham miner can only imagine, possesses a productive capacity which is among the highest in Britain. But the work traditions diverge even more widely than the relative height of the coal seams or the comparative levels of production. Historically, Nottingham developed under a hierarchical subcontracting system of labor relations and a cooperative approach to unionism which continues to mark today's rank-and-file miner, and to distinguish him from his northern counterpart in both work relations and in attitudes toward production and toward management.

The Durham and Nottingham coalfields reflect the distinctive pattern of uneven regional development which results in the failure of centralizing policies (Proposition One). In the one outstanding point of similarity, each coalfield is represented by decidedly moderate union leadership. The similarity in the political perspectives of area unions, however, quickly loses significance in the face of dramatically different rank-and-file traditions. The miners in each region have inherited attitudes toward their labor and habits in work-group relations which effect a sharp divide in the systems of meaning which they attach to NCB initiatives (Proposition Two). Accordingly, a comparison of these two regions contains the potential for a more general understanding of the effects of the transition in wage structures on the inner workings of the industry. At the same time, the comparison of Durham and Nottingham should afford a preliminary estimate of the applicability and explanatory interest of my propositions concerning the contradictions of bureaucratic management under capitalism.

Research Activities and Methods of Investigation

Between the summers of 1974 and 1976 I spent a total of sixteen months studying the operational effects of successive wage structures on the patterns of underground industrial and work relations and on productivity in the Durham and Nottingham coalfields. In each area I made working contact with NUM officials and the NCB area industrial relations officer, and through their combined counsel selected—on the basis of labor organization, traditions of militancy, technological and geological conditions of labor, and the presence of alternative wage structures—a set of five collieries in each area for empirical study. I selected a set of collieries that allowed me to control for wage structure and to consider both polar opposites and typical cases, for each region, of labor organization, militancy, and technical and geological conditions of labor. In this way I approached a comprehensive regional understanding of each coalfield through the detailed study of a set of representative collieries. In each area, the field research was focused on these collieries and proceeded according to an integrated design which included four central elements.

First, as initial preparation, I studied NUM area minutes, and, where they were extant and available for review by nonmembers, analyzed NUM branch minutes of the collieries in question to determine the foci of industrial conflict at each of the selected sites and ascertain the details of union reaction to NCB strategy in the introduction of successive wage structures. The particulars were of real concern here. Had the branch ever moved that a productivity agreement be considered in lieu of a national daywage structure? What were the typical differentials between task groups under piece rates? How fixed were they? Which group dominated branch decisions? More generally, I was concerned with the meaning particular work groups attributed to given wage structures. In addition, I tried to assess both union and rank-and-file perception of the productive effect of successive wage structures, and the differential attitudes of rank-and-file miners performing different tasks to particular wage structures. Also, I learned what I could from minute books about the changing patterns of industrial relations.

Second, with NCB approval I went on underground visits to the selected collieries. This process was in many ways the critical juncture in my field research. Underground visits were essential to my gaining detailed knowledge of the technical conditions of work and the actual organization of labor at a particular coal face. Equally important, they served as an occasion for my meeting many of the officials and miners whom I would subsequently rely on for evidence.

Third, I pursued a series of regular and detailed interviews with management personnel and union officials at both the area and colliery levels and with rank-and-file miners at the selected collieries. My purpose was to piece together, from multiple accounts which could be checked one against the other for accuracy (and reviewed in the context of documentary evidence), a detailed and precise record of the evolution of wage policy in the area and the history of wage structure implementation in the selected collieries. Interviews provided a descriptive account of the effect of wage structures on industrial and productive relations which would be more detailed than any to be found in existing written sources. At the same time, the web of interpretation and subjective inference of the actors in the drama, which informed their presentation of the "bare facts," became in itself an invaluable source of data in my reconstruction of the case studies. The interviews played a critical multiple role in the investigation: to provide the record, per se, of the historical evolution of wage structures in local detail; to suggest, through the subjects' emphasis, repetition, and in some cases avoidance, what the critical issues might be; and to catalogue the subjective interpretations, strategies, and perceptions of participants in the process of wage structure implementation.

Finally, I collected data on productivity and output maintained by NCB area headquarters and by individual collieries, to the extent that they were available. My data include both area time series and weekly or monthly figures for particular task groups at specific coal faces for the period before and after a moment of transition in wage structures. Given the range of geological variables which condition performance and which are constantly in flux (height of seams, their gradient, the friability of the coal, etc.) and the different performances of alternative face teams independent of wage structure, detailed local data are required in order to draw any reasonable inferences about output and productivity under successive wage structures. Unfortunately, the NCB does not maintain records of such precision at either the national or area level, and collieries operate under no imperative to preserve such data. Consequently, this part of the research design proved the most difficult to accomplish. I am convinced that I located all the data that exist, at times surprising NCB officials with what I had found. Data of some sort, although rarely ideal in category or completeness, were located for all but two of the ten selected collieries.

On the basis of this field research I will specify for a set of collieries in Durham and Nottingham: first, the forms, incidence, and intensity of industrial conflict which originates at the coal face under given wage structures; second, the relations among workers conditioned by successive wage structures; and finally, the patterns of productivity which follow from particular work relations and tendencies for industrial conflict at the coal face. The data provided in the colliery anthropologies will support the hypothesis that the Agreement was defeated because the contradictions of centralized bureaucratic management found lively expression in the inner political economy of the British coal industry. Regionally diverse traditions in the work relations among miners, in industrial relations, and in attitudes and habits which condition the performance of labor, undermined the centralizing design of the NPLA and challenged the administrative rationality of the NPLA's principle of national uniformity under a universal time-based wage.

The NCB's Problems in Theory and Practice

By imposing a nationally uniform daywage structure on a regionally distinctive industry—and one whose workmen are particularly disinclined to accept any intrusion upon customary practices—the NCB unwittingly encouraged a whole new world of conflict down the pit. Naturally enough, the management had viewed the rationalization of wage structures as a problem of industrial management. The best wage structure was the one which would result in the highest and most consistent performance throughout the industry. Relying as they were on a mainstream understanding of industrial relations, the NCB could hardly avoid misreading the full political significance of wage structures and underestimating the consequences of the imposition of a single national design upon divergent regional practices. As a result, they could not foresee the fundamental changes in the terrain of political conflict and in the evolution of work relations at the coal face, and badly misjudged the outcomes.

The Blind Spot in Industrial Relations Theory

Ostensibly, the form of payment, e.g., piece-rate payment by results or time-based daywage, is most significant for its effect on the level of payment in relation to the actual performance of work tasks by the laborer (in British coalmining this is referred to as the OMS/EMS ratio). Accordingly, each wage structure conditions the customary performance of work tasks through the institutionalization of a set of work-related rules. For example, worker effort and pacing, as one might expect, are quite different under payment by results as against time-based structures. Performance is also affected by rules which specify the way in which workers are selected for tasks and positioned on the coal face, the way particular work tasks are divided and responsibilities assigned and recombined, the unit by which the wage is determined (individual or group), the character of cooperation across shifts, etc.

But how binding are these rules and how definite are these tendencies? How are these rules formulated—and how is their observation secured (or avoided)? My answers to these questions will signal a departure from the conventional industrial relations application—or better, applications—of the concept of "rules," and will indicate the direction for a new approach to the study of workplace relations.

Whatever the terminological and theoretical disagreements which divide industrial relations theorists, there is at least superficial agreement on both sides of the Atlantic that the "rules approach"[6] is the most insightful. But the consensus ends there, and the division surfaces very nearly at the level of national cultures. The Americans, following John Dunlop, concentrate on the political-economic forces which condition rule formulation within an industrial relations system, and the British, influenced by the Oxford school (but with growing independence), focus more directly on the institutionalized process of rule-making through collective bargaining.

With the British at their most orthodox, the attention to rule formulation was both narrow and ideologically charged. In an article which came to represent the best and the worst of the Oxford school in the period of its ascendency, Alan Fox and Allan Flanders argued that any influence on job regulation which comes from outside the framework of formal collective bargaining automatically promotes a condition of normlessness which they likened to Durkheim's anomie.[7] According to Fox and Flanders, the increasingly independent power of industrial work groups informally to regulate their own work behavior was fundamentally responsible for the "chaotic pay differentials" and "uncontrolled movements of earnings and labour costs" which were said to plague British industry and industrial relations.[8] Alarmed at this apparent "breakdown of normative order," Oxford theorists blamed the prevalence of custom and practice.[9]

There was a grave weakness in the Oxford approach, which is of more than incidental concern here, since Oxford theorists inspired not only the Donovan Commission, but also the National Board for Prices and Incomes—and, indeed, NCB wages policy. The failure of the NCB to recognize the potential effects of the NPLA on practices at the coal face correlates precisely with the theoretical blind spot of the industrial relations theory they applied. Managing an industry where piece-rate bargaining strengthened the informal processes of job regulation, the Board engineered a transition to a uniform national daywage agreement which ultimately proved far more troublesome.

Oxford theorists decried the power of informal agreements which, they thought, reflected a breakdown of negotiated authority and generated extensive wage drift.[10] But ideological enthusiasm by Oxford theorists for formal bilateral agreements which would facilitate strict and more or less unilateral control of the workplace made a balanced consideration of the critical informal processes of industrial and work relations unlikely.[11] They seemed to view norms which were set independently of institutions of collective bargaining as somehow improper, and not simply informal. Their solution, embodied in the report of the Donovan Commission, was a classic "if you can't beat them, join them" formulation. (And if you join them, maybe you can get them to behave themselves.) If, as seemed to be the consistent pattern, agreements must surface in practice at every level of industrial relations down to "spontaneous" arrangements between stewards—or even individual

workers—and foremen, then at least the agreements should
be formalized. In this way, reasoned the Commission, decentralized agreements could potentially be employed by
management for the enforcement of job regulations when
the shopfloor balance of power was favorable, and not only
as instruments in a one-sided guerrilla struggle waged by
shop stewards and rank-and-file agitators.[12]

Whatever the merits of this perspective in theory, little
change in workplace relations occurred in the aftermath of
the Commission's report. Authors of a comprehensive study
based on survey research of the 1966-72 period stressed
that management was coming to accept and facilitate the
work of stewards. Bargaining, they argued, was if anything
becoming more localized and fragmented, moving from the
workplace to the shopfloor. "[O]f the Donovan Commission's enthusiasm for the formalization of factory-wide
agreements, there was," concluded Wilders and Parker,
"remarkably little evidence."[13] Concretely, the study leads
to the unavoidable conclusion that informal bargaining is
probably a permanent fixture of industrial relations in Britain.

Industrial relations theory, accordingly, should turn its
attention to the formulation and growing influence of rules
which comprise the informal processes of work regulation.
At the same time, industrial relations theorists ought to
consider more closely the concrete evolution of workplace
relations as the immediate source of "informal practices
which extend worker control" or at a minimum set the
context for factory-level industrial relations.[14] The notion
of "rules" may have to change to reflect the particular characteristics of the new object of study, namely, the fluid
relations which evolve within and among work groups during the labor process.

Rules on the Shopfloor: The Key to a New Approach

In mainstream industrial relations theory, the concept
"rules" has been applied loosely "as a generic description
for various instruments of regulation including, among

others, legislation, collective agreements, managerial decisions and social conventions."[15] This definition was appropriate for Dunlop and for Flanders, given their focus
on industrial relations systems and formal agreements, where
rules are either protected by shared values or by explicit
mechanisms of enforcement.[16] But can rules which condition informal shopfloor practices be considered, simply,
as "instruments of regulation" in the understanding above,
and added to the list? I think, on the contrary, that rules
which emerge out of shopfloor relations are of a different
generic character. Without a new understanding of rules,
much of what actually goes on on the shopfloor among
workers and between workers and management cannot be
appreciated.

The expectation that the concept of "rules" needs to be
reconsidered has not, however, been common. Despite
growing concern in the period since Donovan with informal rules, with the control of work relations, and with the
complex processes of custom and practice, efforts to amend
the concept of rules and the understanding of workplace
relations have been uncertain and incomplete.[17] Stressing,
rightly, that "customary rules are fluid in nature and variable in localities," William Brown attempts to specify the
particular character of an informal rule based on custom
and practice as a "transactional rule of job regulation that
arises from informal processes." But Brown flounders when
he insists that "[r]ules of job regulation possess *managerial*
legitimacy."[18] One cannot ignore the importance of rules
of job regulation—like "the back of the book" in piecework factories as Brown describes—*before* they achieve
management authorization or during periods when the
"managerial legitimacy" may be withdrawn. And what about
rules which govern workplace relations *among workers*—
like the traditional seniority principle in the steel industry—
which have been left to worker prerogative?

Additional research must be undertaken to illuminate
these hazy areas of evolved customary practices within
work groups identified by Brown, Hobsbawm, Eldridge,

Phelps and Hopkins, Clegg, Hill, Terry, and others. But it seems certain that rules developed within the workers' sphere—informal and fluid, strategic and customary—condition performance and industrial relations in a wide range of industries, including steel, dock working, shipbuilding, printing, engineering, and manufacturing.[19] The relevance of such rules to an understanding of the effects of the NPLA on the coal industry cannot be overestimated.

Workplace Rules in Mining

In mining, a central focus of industrial relations negotiations and a recurrent source of tension and conflict is the problem of "manning," the assignment of workers on a coal face in a particular number or ratio to a task. The assignment of men on the coal face through some mechanism of worker authority—in the North by a traditional lottery system called "cavilling"—is legitimized by management in some collieries, turned a blind eye to in others, and has actually been reintroduced by management in some collieries operating under NPLA (where it is formally prohibited) to promote industrial peace. Whether it appears in the local contract or not, worker authority over manning is passed on from generation to generation of colliers, its origin and formal status long forgotten, and indeed, irrelevant to its operation. The function of cavilling or similar agreements over manning may be identical in two collieries, although in the first it may be "custom and practice" and in the second a formal result of collective bargaining. What is important is that it remains a procedure for the allocation of men on the coal face (their number, task assignment, and location) which has a clear influence on worker performance, and on work and industrial relations. Cavilling tends to promote attitudes toward fellow workers and toward production norms—a noncompetitive cooperation with a complex division of labor—which are generally absent in regions where no such lottery system has prevailed. Finally, it leads to new rules which govern, for example, the division of labor across shift groups.

Whether rules are formal or informal is irrelevant to their practical effect upon work.[20] The actual performance of tasks associated with coalmining—at a certain pace, with acceptance of some task norm, according to a definite organization of labor and procedure for the assignment of task—is influenced sharply by rules embedded in a wage structure. The rules, as conditioned in their evolution by concrete resources such as technology and geology, bring into existence constantly changing patterns of work performance. In this way, rules influence both relations among working pitmen and relations between the miners and the management.

GENERATIVE RULES, WAGE STRUCTURES, AND WAGE SYSTEMS

An effort to explain developments in the systems of production in Durham and Nottingham collieries, therefore, requires a reconsideration of the concept of work rules. My understanding of work rules, wage structures, and systems of production will have much in common with theories of structure which have recently evolved in sociology and anthropology, and will, I hope, resonate with an intuitive sense of the way "rules" of everyday life condition social action.

Miners who labor under a given wage structure perform according to rules for the assignment of position on the coal face, division of labor in the primary work group, etc. The character of the laboring acts is defined by these rules (and the attendant resources), and the rules are preserved, consolidated, and transmitted routinely by the miners' participation in the labor process. Alternatively, the pitmen participate in the process of transformation of the structure of labor: for example, when they introduce "amendments" to the everyday work rules for assignment of position on the coal face by insisting upon the reintroduction of cavilling. Similarly, one might say, following Anthony Giddens, that "a spoken sentence is both generated by syntactical rules and yet by virtue of this serves to participate in the reproduction of the rules."[21] In both instances, rules, whether they concern work performance or the creation of speech, condition the reproduction of social life. The rules, however, are not inviolable, nor are the living subjects simply the passive "bearers" of structures enforced by these rules.

Rules which govern the reproduction of social life, and yet are reproduced themselves in the performance of structured action, are not, of course, limited to the fields of language and labor. One may speak of the cultural rules which govern relations in the family. Without using this specific terminology, Max Horkheimer discusses the "historically conditioned and not originally 'natural' linking of sexuality and tenderness . . . [which became] a characteristic human trait at a given period and can be generated ever anew by suitable cultural habits while conditioning these in turn."[22] Horkheimer offers important confirmation that "social life may," as Giddens argues, "be treated as a set of reproduced practices."[23] By their transmission, rule-governed habits condition the discrete activities, and hence the subsequent patterns, of social action.

Accordingly, the reproduction of social life may be considered in part habitual. But at the same time, the transmission and reproduction of concrete social practices may include distinct elements of intentionality, as a human subject wrestles to "shed" a burdensome structure or actively pursue a strategy by manipulating rules of social conduct in an instrumental way. But the line between the intentional strategy which transforms a structure and the habitual behavior which denies a structure its constraining force cannot be drawn precisely. A recent reviewer of the work of Pierre Bourdieu considered his efforts in *Outline of a Theory of Practice* to explain the central problem of the reproduction of "unseen" structures:

His account . . . of kinship systems in the Algerian peasant communities in which he did his early fieldwork is exemplary. "Rules" governing cross-cousin marriage, Bourdieu observed, were binding only in the eyes of anthropologist observers. Where marriage partners were often related both paternally and maternally, a family's choice of kinship term by which to designate a match was a matter less of rule than of micropolitical strategy.[24]

It is not too farfetched to consider the similarity between work rules and kinship or syntactical rules, and to recognize that industrial habits, like cultural habits, may be understood as reproduced practices. Like Bourdieu's Algerian peasants, Durham colliers view the rules for distribution of work positions as binding only in the eyes of (management) observers, and consider the actual distribution of places at the coal face to be part of a micropolitical strategy. But where does habit end and conscious strategy begin in the reproduction of structured social action? Only northern pitmen, after all, and not their Nottingham counterparts, have been conditioned by work conventions to defend the traditional self-regulating practices. The reintroduction of cavilling, which is anachronistic under a day-wage structure, conforms to time-honored habits of work and shift-group solidarity at the same time that it triggers specific strategic responses to management efforts to control the coordination of production. Thus the attempt to force management to accept the rules of cavilling serves as an example of the structured social action which is at once strategic and habitual. Most important, it exemplifies the complex process by which laboring practices were reproduced in the northern coalfields of Britain when the NPLA intruded upon traditional arrangements, and suggests at the same time the features common to labor and other forms of structured social action.

Syntactic rules, kinship rules, rules which govern relations among family members, the rules which comprise a

wage structure—all such rules condition behavior and govern the patterned reproduction of social life, and all are
subject to strategic (and also habitual or only partly com-
prehending) alteration by active subjects. Borrowing Giddens' terminology, I will attempt to explain the empirical
anthropology of underground work relations through an
approach which views work rules, whether formal or informal, as *generative rules*.[25] By this I mean, at the simplest
level, that these rules bring into existence new patterns of
work performance. These new patterns are, in turn, altered
by strategic or habitual responses—to changes in geological
conditions, to the imposition of new national agreements,
to management incursion against custom and practice, and
so on. New rules are developed and promulgated in this
way. They affect subsequent task performance and condition relations among workers and between the miners
and front line management.

The idea that rules related to the structure of work are
generative may also be understood in a second way, which
presupposes a Marxist view of labor as a form of complex
social interaction (as opposed to the neoclassical view of
labor as a mere "factor of production"). From this perspective, rules which are embedded in wage structures are
generative not only because they bring into existence specific patterns of work performance, but also because they
express and extend definite social relations. The structure
of class relations in capitalist society may in a general way
be implicit in the social act of production, as expressed, for
example, in the division of labor between the miner and
the manager and in the appropriation of the extracted coal
(and its value) by management. But an allegation that class
relations underlie the give and take of industrial "business
as usual" is not the same as an explication of the precise
mechanism by which relations among workers and between workers and managers evolve. What is at issue is
not what workers are thinking or intending, i.e., their consciousness, but what they are actually doing. How do they
coordinate their work tasks? What guides their response

to management initiatives? I am concerned with their laboring activities and with observable relations which are fluid but which, at the same time, conform to a pattern whose general characteristics may be anticipated.

Rules which determine the organization of labor, division of tasks, norms for cooperation between team and shift groups, and so on, directly influence the relationships formed among workers and the attitude of workers toward their labor. In short, these rules condition the pattern of productivity. Generative rules also determine the character of industrial relations conflict, whether opposition is focused on the number of workers to be employed for a given task (typical of a daywage structure) or on rates and payment for anomalies (more typical of a payment-by-results scheme).

In this way, *generative rules* become the main determinant of the patterns of productivity, work relations, and industrial relations at the coal face. Wage *structures* are understood to include a set of generative rules (under given resources) which govern the whole range of activities and relationships which are produced and reproduced in the labor process. Insofar as the rules are generative, I assume that they are also transitive. By this I mean that the guides or principles of action may be transmitted from one wage structure to another. A collier habituated to extremely cooperative relationships with his coworkers—for example, under a wage structure which provides for colliers to work the same location and equally divide the week's wages based on joint output—will continue to work cooperatively. He will "give a dig" to a work mate who is falling behind, even when wages are set by an individual piece-rate basis. Alternatively, norms which have become habitual under one wage structure may be inconsistent with the rules which comprise subsequent wage structures. Rippers, for example, who have become used to receiving wages in excess of those earned by hewers under independently negotiated piece-rate contracts, may slack off when they are included in the face team and lose their traditional differential with the introduction of the NPLA.

This complex interaction of succeeding wage structures—for example, the grafting of an NPLA daywage agreement upon local piece-rate structures—may be said to generate a *wage system*. The complementarity or, alternatively, the irreconcilability of generative rules which comprise successive wage structures determines important characteristics of the wage system. In conjunction with geological and technological resources, this interaction sets the fundamental pattern of productivity, work relations, and industrial relations at the coal face and produces the characteristic patterns of the underground anthropologies.

THE COLLIERY ANTHROPOLOGIES

With its primary empirical focus on the evolution of systems of production in selected Durham and Nottingham collieries, the study is grounded in observation of the production process and in detailed interviews with coalminers and managers. Three basic assumptions about the complex—partly patterned and partly uncharted—evolution of work and industrial relations influenced my interpretation of the data which I uncovered in the field, and allow me to frame the following anthropologies.

The Importance of the Wage Structure

First, I assume that the form of payment directly influences the miner's performance of his task. Each wage structure incorporates a particular set of rules which condition the customary performance of work. As I have said, worker effort and pacing, as one might expect, are likely to be quite different under payment by results as against time-based structures. Other rules which influence performance are more complex and subtle. They concern manning and the organization of work, the relations within and among work groups, the division of labor and responsibility across shifts, the degree of independence of individual earnings from group performance, and so on. Given these complexities, the structural tendencies of a system of pay may not always be revealed straightforwardly in the observation of a production process. But it seems reasonable to suppose that the rules embedded within a wage structure will substantially influence worker performance.

The Politics of Productivity: Power Relations and Laboring Relations

Second, I assume that the influence of wage structures on worker performance is expressed through two related but nonetheless distinct dimensions which together constitute *the politics of productivity*. There is, on the one hand, a dimension which involves the way in which the rules within a wage structure condition the frequency, intensity, and forms of expression of worker opposition to specific management initiatives. As John Goldthorpe argues, since the employment contract remains "incomplete" in that it does not specify the precise tasks a worker is expected to perform, "managerial authority [must] be supplemented by the managerial exercise of power."[26] This power is generally exercised through the manipulation of resources—notably the wage, but also, for example, through the assignment of positions on the face (which may be more or less favorable) and by the provision of materials and equipment needed for consistent productivity (the last, an exercise of power particularly under piece-rate structures). As Goldthorpe suggests, management exercises power through manipulation of resources in an effort to enhance its "*de facto* capacity to secure the compliance of workers" with both the explicit and the unspecified requirements of the job.[27] My study focuses on this issue of de facto compliance—the likelihood that management commands will be obeyed and the character and consequences of worker rejection of commands.[28]

Conflict following from management efforts to coordi-

nate production, I want to argue, may or may not involve
a challenge to the legitimacy of management's authority to
plan the enterprise. The bases of acceptance or refusal of
management commands are more diverse. Acceptance may
involve a perceived duty of compliance or may be simply
the result of a worker's estimate of material advantage or
the direct consequence of a manager's persuasive appeal.
Similarly, mere rejection of a particular managerial command need not imply that a worker has rejected anything
more than that command. He may still be perfectly well
acculturated to the principle of wage labor. Nor can one
know that he acts from fully conscious and rational motivation rather than from custom or habit. Indeed, regionally
specific customs and habits are critical to the evolution of
distinctive patterns of worker-management conflict of the
sort I have in mind. Rank-and-file practices governing the
selection of the work team and the positioning of men on
the coal face, to take a common example from the Durham
coalfield, challenge explicit management prerogatives. They
contest specific commands whether or not, for the workers
involved, these practices constitute a rejection of the legitimate authority of the NCB or represent support for a principle of collective as against hierarchical coordination. I am
concerned in this study with the concrete issues of control
and refusal, not with the underlying problems of workers'
belief in the legitimacy of management authority—with the
observable interaction between given workers and managers, not with the evolution of the consciousness of Labor
vs. Capital.[29]

As management exercises power—in the sense of capacity to influence conduct by intention of harm or
reward[30]—in its efforts to secure the compliance of workers
with its design for production, miners may meet power
with power by attempting to reassert their control over the
performance of works tasks or over the organization of
production. At the same time, colliers may turn the tables,
attempting to pressure management into accepting particular work practices by communicating their intention to

"harm or reward" management by manipulating productivity. I refer to this particular pattern of interaction between managers and workers which directly expresses "command-obedience relations"[31] as *power relations*. As will become clear in the colliery studies, power relations may be expressed through a wide range of activities undertaken by the laborers—anything from the addition of an extra man to a work group (thereby reducing the requisite effort of each miner in the group) to the more extreme measure of a spontaneous work stoppage.

There is also, on the other hand, a second dimension within the politics of productivity which concerns the way in which a wage structure conditions and habituates the worker to a certain way of performing in the labor process. This dimension I will refer to as *laboring relations*. Here I am concerned with the direct relations among workers, which may or may not involve power relations, and with the tendency for wage structures to alter the habits of worker association in the very process of production. This may occur in ways which neither influence productivity directly nor express worker opposition to management initiatives. But the consequences for productivity, and potentially for industrial conflict, are nevertheless critical. Laboring relations evolve through practices which are conditioned by rules embedded in particular wage structures and, in the strongest cases, such as cavilling, by a common and collectively articulated design. Work relations, I argue, never follow simply from the "adjustment" of persons who coordinate activities through individual strategies which are designed to maximize diverse self-interests. Therefore, because these relations are linked to collectively based rules and to common, if not always wholly conscious, designs, laboring relations are decidedly political. It is here, in the evolution of laboring relations, that the systems of meaning which come to influence worker response to management initiative develop.

Laboring relations can never be reduced to the kind of pattern symbolized by the economists' model of exchange relations within the processes of market coordination, nor can such a "mutual adjustment" model explain the patterns of work relations which develop at the coal face.[32] In this dimension of the politics of productivity I include different patterns of cooperation among workers, the character and effectiveness of divisions of labor, the composition of task groups, assignment of positions on the coal face, etc.

The division between *power relations* and *laboring relations*, although not in all cases exclusive or strictly observable, allows for important analytical distinctions. The two dimensions are political in complementary ways—laboring relations because they involve coordination through the influence of common rules and purposes and power relations because they involve explicit confrontation over the exercise of command through management prerogatives. At the same time, as we will see, both dimensions necessarily influence productivity. Accordingly, these two dimensions taken together in their fluid interaction constitute *the politics of productivity*, which is the empirical focus of my study.

The Fluid Character of Laboring Relations

Third, I assume that the best way to understand these power relations and laboring relations is to recognize that the miners are the active subjects and not merely the passive objects of these wage structures. Generative rules which concern laboring relations govern specific work practices but, equally significant, they also express the concrete and fluid evolution of specific relations among workers. True, the application of these generative rules which govern the politics of productivity presupposes a minimal consent to the basic rules of the capitalist wage labor "game." Nevertheless, workers' engagement in (capitalist) production is indistinguishable from their participation in the evolution of laboring relations which are reproduced through generative rules which they in part transmit. Accordingly, when workers are inserted into the labor process, they express a mediate social existence—they are neither individuals nor members of a class, and neither the immediate nor the secular outcome of struggles for control between management and labor is foreordained. Thus, the dialectic of control which follows from the imposition of administrative norms on the objects of policy is inscribed in the labor process itself and becomes a source of endemic struggle.

From this perspective, my study departs from some of the more significant recent studies of the workplace which share a Marxist approach. In *Manufacturing Consent*, Michael Burawoy assumes that workers in a machine shop are "inserted into the labor process as individuals who directly dictate the speed, feed, depth, etc., of their machines."[33] As machine operators they must compete for favorable treatment by auxiliary workers and foremen to ensure the possibility of achieving incentive pay under individual piece-rate wage structures. In Burawoy's study workers respond to management initiatives as individuals, and workplace relations are dominated by personalized strategies which operationalize consent to the hierarchical arrangements of capitalism by reproducing a "culture of making out."[34] Richard Edwards, by contrast, in his account of the evolution of twentieth-century workplace relations in the United States, views the labor process as "an arena of class conflict," and sees the growing process of bureaucratization of the firm's control over the workforce increasing the potential for "revolutionary consequences by linking workplace struggle with class conflict in society at large."[35] Revolutionary potential grows because the state is increasingly implicated, through the National Labor Relations Board and myriad administrative agencies, in formulating and reviewing the rules of bureaucratic control.

The problem is that each author charts only one side in the process of workplace control. For Burawoy, management controls workers as individuals, who are reduced to playing a series of games in an effort to achieve levels of production which will attract incentive pay; for Edwards, management can never control workers, whatever its apparent victories, since workers as a class follow the certain telos of struggle and each new technique of control generates a rising level and new strategy of class struggle. In my view, one cannot assume either that workers submit tamely as individuals or that they struggle on an ascending trajectory, consciously as a class. Rather, the labor process, like the process of bureaucratic administration, involves continual, contingent, fluid episodes in the dialectic of control. Workers, I will argue, typically engage in production as members of a work group which internally reproduces, however partially and in however unconscious a manner, definite class relations as well as immediate strategies for resistance to management rules for the regulation of work.[36]

Perhaps the most striking feature of what is conventionally called "industrial relations" at the colliery level is the range of outcomes—forms of conflict and norms of productivity—which may be observed under the very same collectively bargained agreements. A group of colliers working on a coal face in Nottingham will respond to a union policy which limits overtime work to safety operations by coordinating their work during regular shift time to make sure that a bi-directional coal cutter is left in an unsafe position at the end of the regular shift time. The cutter therefore must, for safety reasons, be returned to its starting position during overtime. This activity has the "incidental" side effect that an extra band of coal is cut, and the pitmen compensated accordingly.[37] In Durham, the same policy is strictly observed, not only in letter but in spirit. The colliers are likely to stop coal cutting well before a shift is completed (rather than risk the need for any overtime coaling work) in order to ensure that the machine is left in a safe position; the overtime ban on directly productive work is observed fully.

Dozens of similar examples could be supplied and, indeed, the anthropologies of selected collieries in Nottingham and Durham are designed to document the diversity of power and laboring relations which occur at the coal face, and to illustrate the miners' varied and creative

responses to the implementation of successive wage structures. I hope to show that tendencies toward a particular
pattern of production which are associated with a given
wage structure condition the range of available responses,
but do not set unbreakable limits. Since the actual observable variations conform to no simple predictive logic, one
cannot infer the actual patterns of productivity from general knowledge about a wage structure. For this reason,
throughout the empirical anthropologies I will assume that
the miners engaged in laboring processes are never trapped
into structured patterns of responses which are predetermined by the collectively bargained agreement. Rather, I
assume that the miners themselves generate these fluid
structures of power relations and laboring relations in the
processes of working, as their behavior is conditioned by
formal and informal agreements, by preexisting habits and
customs of working, and by the resources and conditions
under which they work.

Power Relations and Laboring Relations

These concepts provide the framework for my presentation of underground anthropologies in the ten selected
collieries. Insofar as generative rules guide the actual performance of work tasks and directly influence their coordination, it stands to reason that these rules influence productivity. What is more interesting and complex is the way
these same rules also define the politics of productivity. A
piece-rate wage structure incorporates a structural tendency for the focus of conflict to be localized at the individual
coal face and to concern issues of individual or group payment for anomalies; a daywage, on the contrary, tends to
generate conflict over the number of workers to be assigned
to a task, over the task norm, and over expectations as to
the intensity and duration of actual labor time during the
specified shift time. As the colliery studies will demonstrate, generative rules in large measure fashion the power
relations of production.

But perhaps the more interesting effect of these generative rules is on the laboring relations among the men. The colliery studies reveal a fascinating pattern of displaced response to wage structures. In many cases the miners' reaction is initially expressed as an alteration in the laboring relations among themselves, which may only indirectly influence power relations or affect productivity.

Thus a transition in the wage structure from a daywage to a spot-bargained productivity agreement may directly affect the rules governing intragroup cooperation long before it raises issues to be collectively bargained, e.g., a claim for the upgrading of a worker's job category to a higher wage level. In this way, generative rules embedded within particular wage structures may be seen to influence not only productivity and power relations between management and men, but what I have called laboring relations.

The drama began to unfold as soon as the NPLA challenged the patchwork quilt of existing—and regionally distinctive—underground practices. In Chapter Three, I explore a third context for understanding the evolution of systems of production in the post-NPLA period by taking account of traditions of work which inspired the miners' response to NCB initiatives in the Durham and Nottingham coalfields.

CHAPTER THREE

TOWARD AN EXPLANATION

In the colliery anthropologies which follow, I will discuss changes which I observed in power and laboring relations in a set of ten collieries and demonstrate distinctive regional patterns in the politics of productivity under piece-rate and under time-based daywage structures. In so doing, I will illustrate the processes by which a well planned and executed effort by the competent, highly motivated management of a state-run industry came undone, and how all efforts to impose a centralized structure on a reluctant and fragmented industry were defeated. These colliery studies reveal a broad and complex evolution in national wages policy, centered on a single dramatic innovation, the introduction of the National Power Loading Agreement in the years between 1966 and 1971. Some explanation of this approach is necessary since, for one thing, the colliery anthropologies isolate a British phenomenon within two English counties, Durham and Nottingham. Moreover, I presuppose throughout the study that county or regional distinctions are essential despite—or ironically because of—the existence of a firm national policy within a centralized, nationalized industry. These are strong assumptions which should not be left unexamined. In this chapter, I outline the pre-NPLA history of modern wage structures in the British coal industry to provide a sense of the common starting point from which regional departures must be evaluated. My main intention, therefore, is to clarify the connection between regional matters—high and low productivity, diverse labor markets, wage differentials—and the general articulation of national policy.

The history of national wages policy is essential for two additional reasons. First, a sketch of the evolution of wage structures provides a context in which to understand the historic importance of the NPLA. At the same time, it locates the issues between management and labor which made implementation of a national daywage agreement for face workers so controversial and the operation of the agreement conflict-ridden. Second, a historical and national perspective on the development of wage structures will serve as an important corrective to the predominantly structural and regional approach of this study. This counterbalance is necessary since, in fundamental ways, the underground experience and work culture are British, not regional. In even more basic ways, the work situation recognizes no culture beyond the underground environs. There are universal facts about underground labor on the coal face which influence performance regardless of wage structures, and which therefore subvert a pure political economy approach. Physical geography and social psychology determine an important part of the story of productivity. A collier must enter the cage and go down the pit, and not simply punch a card and enter a factory, before he can experience the effects of any wage system. This simple fact holds enormous significance.

Physical and emotional realities vitiate any purely structural, and in this case regional, analysis of the relationship between wages and productive performance. Instinctual factors and associated beliefs which are difficult to specify and impossible to measure, nonetheless influence the habits of working in a powerful way. These "raw attitudes" which underlie the essential patterns of conflictual and cooperative relations underground are then accommodated, channeled, and recast by structures of custom and practice which are associated with distinct regions and specific to given wage structures.

Universal features of underground work—the danger and memory of dangers, the dark, the wetness and heat, the cramped space—influence the politics of productivity before the structure of the wage enters the problem. Features such as the form and level of payment, assignment of position on the coal face, the division of labor, etc., generate differences in laboring and power relations, and in patterns of productivity within the colliery and at the regional level. But physical-geological and psychological factors affect all who labor in this way. Consequently, these factors promote a unity in miners' responses to wage structures throughout the coalfields. However inchoate and imprecisely perceived, and however imperfectly articulated during the course of collective bargaining, these factors nevertheless lie beneath the overt bargains which are struck between NCB and NUM negotiators. In this way, these universalizing attitudinal factors influence the evolution of wage structures in the industry to the extent that they condition performance and orient both long-term NCB strategy and the immediate NUM response to that strategy.

These subjective factors which influence the course of annual NCB-NUM negotiations are ever-present, submerged in the pace and pain of the labor. The history of wages policy in the British coal industry reflects a complex effort to humanize and rationalize this process, an attempt to make up in technological capacity and effective labor organization what all parties would be delighted to sacrifice in raw intensity. Toward this end, the NUM and NCB have worked jointly to introduce wage structures which, against the great weight of tradition, reconcile effort and remuneration. At the same time, through technological innovation, they have tried to limit the effects of the natural forces of geology and space—and the danger and discomfort that go with underground working—on the political and productive attitudes of the working collier. Therefore, the evolution of wage structures has involved a twofold struggle: the NCB bargains with the NUM over the determination of performance norms, wages, and conditions of labor; management and labor, potentially united on this issue, apply new technologies to combat the imperious underground forces. Technological innovation makes possible a rationalization of forms of payment, then new wage structures alter the focus of conflict both nationally and between miners and managers at the coal face. In this chapter, I will review the historical legacy of wage regulation and wage structures which both informed NCB strategy as the Board reflected on the centralizing mechanisms it might employ to plan and administer the industry, and conditioned the expectations of miners and managers once the NPLA was introduced. I will then turn to a discussion of the regional patterns in laboring and power relations which, in the end, crucially eroded the NCB's rationalizing strategy.

STRATEGIES OF WAGE REGULATION

Looking at the British coal industry, one gets the impression that collective bargaining as a strategy of wage regulation is a decidedly modern, even a transitory, phenomenon. In the period before nationalization, the industry attempted a whole range of approaches to wage regulation, some of which involved traces of bargaining, but all of which focused on automatic or externally determined wage regulation at the district or regional level.

During the eighteenth and much of the nineteenth centuries, both the determination of wage levels and the regulation and control of labor were straightforward. Indeed, in some regions, wage regulation was by custom coercive.[1] While in the Midlands and parts of North and South Wales free colliers were frequently paid according to a modern piece-rate collective contract, in Scotland and in the North of England, methods of pay and job regulations were decidedly less commercial.

In Scotland, until the Emancipation Bill of 1774, lifelong servitude was not uncommon, and the status of the pitman was officially described by Parliament as one of slavery.[2] Indeed, Adam Smith lectured on the applicability of the word "slave" to these Scottish collier-serfs, arguing that their privileges—they could not be sold, they could "enjoy the privileges of marriage and religion"—exceeded those of true slaves.[3] One gets the impression that Smith thought the distinction between slave and collier subtle.[4] Whatever the formal applicability of the term "slave" to Scottish colliers, there is no doubt that wage regulation involved severe limitations on the freedom of the laborers. Like slaves, moreover, they were granted inferior legal and social status. Colliers were excluded from the Scottish Habeas Corpus Act of 1701, and in Fifeshire pitmen were not allowed to be buried in cemetery plots alongside free citizens.

In the North of England, until the early 1870s coalowners enforced wage and hiring regulations against miners similar to those which were traditionally applied to agricultural laborers.[5] The collier signed an annual bond which set his pay and determined his precise laboring responsibilities for an entire year. Typically, a set of severe conditions enforced the rather one-sided bargain. First, the owners could deduct a substantial charge (for example, one shilling or approximately two-thirds the wage paid for a score of tubs filled by a hewer) for each day of unexcused absence from work. Second, a miner who attempted to break the bond and leave his employ during the course of an annual contract forfeited all claims to back wages (which were usually paid on a fortnightly basis). Worse, he became subject to legal sanctions including fines and imprisonment.[6]

In February 1872 the first deputation of the Durham Miners' Association (DMA), which had been formed in 1869, met representatives of the coalowners in Newcastle. At the top of the agenda, they requested the termination of the yearly bond. Recognizing both the incipient power of the DMA and the advantage of more frequent negotiations of wage rates during a period of falling output and declining prices, by the end of the month the owners had agreed to a fundamental alteration in the wage structure.[7] A fortnightly negotiation of wage rates replaced the signing of an annual bond. But a new mechanism for the regulation of wages, independent of bargaining, was to replace the annual bond and limit the effectiveness of the DMA.

Following the first countywide strike in May 1874, the owners initiated a "General Arbitration" as a means of settling disputed wage rates. A local MP, acting as umpire, awarded a broad reduction in wages of 9 percent; a second arbitration in February 1876 resulted in a 7 percent decline for underground workers and 4 percent for surface workers; and, in September 1876, a further reduction of 6 percent was ordered.[8] With output and prices—the principal criteria cited in awards—falling after 1873, arbitration consistently resulted in reduced wage awards. Although miners' confidence in arbitration was, therefore, extremely low in the Northeast and throughout Britain, weak unionism and unfavorable trade conditions limited their capacity not simply to bargain effectively, but to insist that wage regulation be in fact determined by bargaining, rather than by arbitration or some automatic regulating mechanism.

Systems of Automatic Wage Regulation

By the 1870s, majority opinion on both sides of the industry, for very different reasons, found common ground in support of the sliding scale, which replaced arbitration as the predominant system of nonbargained wage regulation. A proportion of the miner's wage (a percentage addition to basis rates) was linked automatically to the selling price of some standard quality of coal, determined either at the pithead or at some port of export.[9] Against the backdrop of successive reductions in wages by arbitration umpires, pitmen were prepared to accept a system of wage regulation which was ostensibly based on an objective standard of prosperity and adversity in the industry which, it was assumed, might condition the coalowners' capacity and willingness to pay. At the same time, during a recession, the owners benefited from a scale which allowed them to reduce wages in response to falling prices. With the wage bill accounting for approximately 70 percent of the total cost of production, sliding scales "conferred upon the owners the considerable benefit of an early and downwards revision of the major component of their costs of production."[10]

After a decade of sliding scale adjustments, however, the miners' opposition to automatic regulation based directly on the price of coal led to the development of a new and more sophisticated form of automatic wage regulation. As a measure of capacity to pay, sliding scales were inadequate, since, with the adjustment mechanism based solely on prices, other critical factors—costs of production, volume of trade, and indeed, profit—were entirely overlooked in the setting of wage rates. During the period of the sliding scale agreements, miners suffered substantial fluctuations in wage rates and were frequently subject to temporary layoffs. Faced with conditions such as these, which would have been impossible even under the semifeudal obligations of the annual bond, miners responded by restricting output in an effort to support prices and thereby raise or at least stabilize wage levels.[11] During the same period, with sliding scales negotiated on a district-by-district basis, regional owners' associations reduced prices. This short-run competitive strategy did little to promote trade and nothing to stabilize either profits or wages.

By the 1880s, in response to mounting opposition from the miners and particularly due to the opposition of pitmen in the inland coalfields now organized as the Miners' Federation of Great Britain (MFGB), sliding scale agreements were superseded by district conciliation boards. Whether wage rates during this period were determined by conciliation boards or by sliding scales, however, the coalowners "continued to take selling prices as the principal criteria for wage-rate adjustments."[12]

District Wage Ascertainments

During and immediately after the First World War, wage rates were set nationally by direct state involvement through a variety of administrative boards, a pattern which was to be repeated after World War II. The settlement which concluded the national strike of 1921, however, revived automatic wage regulation according to a new set of criteria which were applied until 1944. The district wage ascertainments represented an attempt to remedy the deficiencies of the sliding scales, which were based exclusively on the selling price of coal. Wages were to be fixed as a proportion—in the agreement of July 1921 the figure was only 17 percent—of the net proceeds of the industry, defined as all revenues less all nonwage costs.[13] The "disposable" revenues were divided between profits and wages in a proportion which varied among wage districts.

The system of district wage ascertainments was thus in principle a profit-sharing scheme, although complex mechanisms augmented the initial reference to net proceeds alone. District minima were set and long-range procedures were added so that owners might recoup the excess wages paid in years when the minima exceeded the "ascertained" wages based on the fixed proportional distribution of net proceeds. Moreover, from 1936 to 1944 miners and government tribunals forced a series of five national flat rate additions, which augmented the ascertained district wage rates.[14] Taken together, district minima and flat rate additions of a total of 7s. 2d. per shift constituted a substantial part, typically one-third or more, of the miners' earnings.[15]

The Board Accepts the Principle of Collective Bargaining

The NCB learned a simple lesson from the history of attempts at systems of automatic regulation in the period before nationalization. Automatic systems did not effectively regulate wages, and willingness or capacity to pay did not go very far toward determining wage levels. In an internal document circulated in July 1951, a senior member of the wages division argued that whatever their intrinsic merits, and even when they were accepted by both parties, automatic systems did not preclude the advancement of claims for higher wages or for better working conditions over and above those granted automatically.[16] These mechanisms had not prevented major stoppages when market conditions forced down proceeds and profits. The Board, he admitted, was unlikely to resist encroachments upon fixed norms of pay when private coalowners had been unable to do so. He explained that no automatic system was secure from initial claims above the fixed rates nor from industrial action in pursuit of additional claims, and no system of wage regulation could be enforced against an NUM desire to withdraw from an agreement.

The NCB retrospective attack on regulating mechanisms of all kinds was comprehensive and complete. No scheme which linked payments to a single index such as selling prices, proceeds, or even Output per Manshift (OMS) was likely to be satisfactory. The problems were, indeed, more severe for a public than for a private firm. When linked to questions of the national or public interest, capacity and willingness to pay were particularly difficult to determine for a nationalized industry. Such a determination involved considerations beyond commercial or industrial criteria and introduced factors outside the Board's statutory discretion. The official referred to above concluded with a warning, which seems particularly ominous today in the post-NPLA period of productivity agreements. Any scheme which linked payments to productivity alone, he reasoned, was even more dangerous than schemes of automatic wage regulation according to the single factors of price and proceeds as had been previously attempted.

NCB reasoning justified what NUM power demanded, namely, a system of wage determination and regulation based on collective bargaining. It would be national, comprehensive, and designed to rationalize the incoherent pattern of wage structures which had been bequeathed to the industry by the departing private owners. This confluence of interest and shared design underlies the subsequent evolution of wage structures which would, a decade and a half later, culminate in the pathbreaking National Power Loading Agreement.

SYSTEMS OF PAY

On Vesting Day, along with 1,400 collieries the NCB inherited a disorganized, indeed an incoherent, wage structure. The basis on which wages were calculated varied regionally and from pit to pit. Earnings depended not only on the type of work performed or on the efforts of pitmen, but on geological conditions, on the efficiency of coal-getting and transporting operations, on the power and character of custom and practice, on sub rosa agreements, and on the balance of local bargaining power.

Although prior to nationalization the wage structure of the coal industry developed locally and along fundamentally unpredictable avenues, each wage rate was compounded from two main elements—a basis rate fixed at each colliery for a particular job, and a percentage addition. The basis rate varied according to the grade of the job, and might be augmented by additional compensation for conditions such as water on the face or faulting—referred to as "anomalies"—which adversely affected the rate at which a task could be performed. The percentage addition was set at the district level, and consequently differed among regions. Its level was determined by the prosperity and relative market position of particular districts, and fluctuated as collective bargaining power within and among areas shifted. In addition, firms might offer separate bonuses and local additions.

Two systems of pay set the pattern of wage structures which dominated the industry from the termination of bonding in the North of England in 1872 until the introduction of the NPLA in 1966: time work and piecework. Each of these methods of payment involved serious difficulties in the fixing of standards of work and generated constant inequities in wage levels. No fixed ratio of effort to remuneration could be set, with the result that the ratio varied widely among collieries and operations at the coal face. Thus the common-sense axiom, "equal pay for equal work," was continually violated as task and pay norms remained constantly in flux.[17] Both NCB efforts to rationalize the wage system, and NUM efforts to achieve wage structures which set earnings levels free from determination by effort or output, stem from dissatisfaction with the uncertainties of these traditional systems of pay.

Time Work

In the period from 1947 to 1955, for the industry at large, the majority of workers (57-60 percent) were time workers, paid a fixed wage per shift.[18] The rates varied according to the work performed, but the pay for these men was generally substantially below that of pieceworkers. Shift rates for time workers on identical or comparable jobs, moreover, were not coordinated even within a single region. Consequently, wide pay differentials for equal work persisted among mineworkers who labored in neighboring collieries.

Although these time workers are properly called "day-wagemen," the character of their work distinguishes the traditional daywage structure from the NPLA structure, which transformed the face worker from a pieceworker into a new daywageman. Traditional daywagemen, on the contrary, were very seldom face workers. They neither set the pace of production nor were they engaged directly in the processes of coaling, but rather they performed subsidiary tasks elsewhere below ground. The pace at which pieceworkers at the coal face performed the coaling operation determined the effort required of the traditional daywagemen.

For this reason, the NCB, in a study of the systems of remuneration in the industry in August 1951, dismissed as ill-informed the frequent criticism that 60 percent of colliery employees lacked appropriate incentives.[19] The author of this study argued that the nature of the work of the traditional daywagemen obviated the need for any wage structure which included piece-rate incentives. Payment by results was necessary for workers who were directly involved in the process of production, he continued. But the traditional daywagemen, while necessary to the production, were not directly engaged in the extraction of coal.

Hence, their efforts were not closely reflected in fluctuations in output, and a change to payment by results for these men was not indicated.

In fact, argued this industrial relations official, the converse was more true, since fluctuations in production influenced the efforts required of the traditional daywagemen. The pace of production at the coal face, for example, affects the work required of men working on haulage of materials and the removal or packing of stone. But the problem of determining how effort should be rewarded is a trickly one.

A pumpsman, for example, is absolutely essential to maintaining conditions which allow for continued extraction of coal and the smooth turning over of the face operations.[20] He is paid a dayrate for the job which is, presumably, set at an appropriate level in comparison to other nonface underground jobs. But how, concretely, does the Coal Board measure his output or gauge his effort? It is no more difficult to work a pump which delivers 10,000 gallons per hour than to work a pump which delivers 1,000 gallons. Although the NCB could rate the horsepower or the output of the pump, such a procedure would entail an evaluation of the "effort" or efficiency of the machine rather than of the worker. There simply is no appropriate way to fix a piece-rate wage or to determine an incentive element for nonface work as part of a complex basis-rate-plus-bonus wage structure.

The case of the pumpsman illustrates the broader difficulties which the Board faced in any attempt to relate the wages of traditional daywagemen to a piece-rate formula. First, argued the writer of the 1951 report, it was difficult to measure individual performance in terms of real work output. Second, it was equally hard to construct a wage system which would justly reward a daywageman's contribution to production and at the same time serve as a practical incentive to improved performance. The NCB concluded that the difficulty of putting traditional daywage jobs onto a piecework basis did not justify the trouble involved, given the meager increase in production that might be expected. The farther the job from the point of production, the greater was the difficulty and the smaller the advantage in constructing a piecework or complex basis-rate-plus-incentive scheme.

Piecework

Most mineworkers at the face, upon whom coal production depends directly, were, until 1966, paid according to the results of their work. The distinction between men employed at the coal face who were paid by results and those performing supporting tasks elsewhere underground and on the surface who were paid a daily wage was never absolute, to be sure. But the sharp division readily appears in a statistical summary of pieceworkers as a percentage of all workers by location of work. In 1951, according to NCB figures, approximately 83 percent of all men employed elsewhere underground (not at the face) were paid a time-based daywage. Above ground nearly all (98.5 percent) were on daywage (see Table 3.1).

TABLE 3.1. Pieceworkers as Percentage of All Workers by Location of Work (1951)

	Face	Elsewhere Below Ground	Surface
Pieceworkers at location as percentage of all pieceworkers	83.3	15.9	0.8
Pieceworkers at location as percentage of all workers at location	80.8	16.7	1.5

SOURCE: NCB, Memorandum on Systems of Remuneration in the Coal Mining Industry, August 1951.

The determination of piecework wages includes two distinct elements which at least in principle are separable: productivity and the rate to be paid for each unit which is produced. The assessment of productivity—tubs of coal loaded or tonnage or yardage filled off for a collier, number of arches set for a ripper, etc.—involves the choice of appropriate units of measurement, evaluation of quantity, and some agreement by bargain or convention about quality. Inevitably, disputes over quality shade over into disagreements about the "fair price" to be paid for each unit of production.

The very choice of units to be measured is problematic and is influenced by considerations such as working conditions, anomalous conditions encountered, technological and organizational factors in the method of mining, previous custom and practice, and the local balance of bargaining power. Colliers filling coal, for example, were traditionally paid either a tonnage or a yardage rate. In either case, the value was conventionally considered as if it were a measure of cubic content. If the mineworker was paid a tonnage rate, then weight determined the cubic content; if he was paid a yardage rate, then linear units along the face determined the cubic content. The remaining two dimensions, width corresponding to the depth of the cut and height corresponding to the thickness of the seam, were taken as constants in the figuring of the unit piece rates.

Although yardage rates are simpler to measure on conveyor faces, they allow payments for coal which is thrown over the conveyor into the waste area and never reaches the surface. There is the added problem of pay for the filling of stone and dirt along with the coal. Tonnage rates tended to meet a specified extraction ratio of coal to waste materials. But in this case, management's request for quality in the product resonated too closely with the traditional capitalist practices of dishonest and vindictive short-weighting, so the men were likely to make the cure more crippling to productivity than the disease.

Beyond the technical choices involved in the selection of

units used to assess productivity, the piece-rate structure involves deeper complexities and ambiguities. Historically, it has never been clear exactly what features identified a piecework wage structure. Usage in collieries varied, although in general the term "piecework" tended to include three classes of laborers: men who were paid a bonus addition to a basis daywage rate; men who were paid by results according to price lists which specified piece rates for every separate task which might be encountered in the performance of the overall job (hewing and filling off, timbering, shoring up the floor, etc.); and men who were paid by a comprehensive ("all in") price list for the composite set of tasks. In the third variation, which was predominant during the period of piece rates under nationalization, all the ancillary jobs were taken into consideration and were expressed in the tonnage or yardage rate. But the most striking complexities of piecework mining lie deeper, in the fixing of a notional wage which, in practice, transforms the meaning of piecework.

Properly speaking, true piecework disappeared long ago with the introduction of cyclical mining. As the NCB recognized in its early discussions of revisions in the piece-rate structures, payment by results in the coal industry violated the central premise of piece rates.[21] In true piecework, personal effort and capacity set the practical limit on potential earnings within a broad theoretical limit determined by machine capacity and the organization of production. No limit may be set on the work which is available during a given shift. Looked at from this perspective, payment by results in the British coal industry did not hold out the possibility of genuine piecework, since the cyclical method of production and the safeguards added by management to ensure cyclical continuity robbed the worker of his ability substantially to alter his "normal" production. Although the limit varied, longwall cyclical mining as practiced in British mines imposed severe restrictions on the available work, hence on productivity and wage levels.

Typically, management fixed a standard task (a stint).

The standard task—for example, the filling off of ten yards of coal along the face—expressed a customary assumption or bargained specification about a collier's normal effort. But, more critically, it involved a safe estimate about a task which could be completed during the specified shift time with no exceptional expenditure of effort and with ample allowance for a typical assortment of interruptions in machine running time and the intrusion of anomalous conditions. The NCB strategy promoted the selection of a safe, feasible task which could be completed, potentially, by all the workers on the face. This choice of a safe norm reflected management's highest imperative, cyclical continuity—a smooth transition from filling off the coal to breaking down and resetting the roof supports and repositioning the conveyors. Continuity in turning over the face, the Board reasoned, results in higher productivity in the long run than hit-or-miss "commando results" which enhance the raw OMS figures but have the added consequence of more frequent discontinuities in production. This strategy, however, indicates the ephemeral character of the piece-rate structure as it has been practiced in the British coal industry.

Once the worker completed his stint, no additional remunerative work was available. Therefore, for reasons entirely outside his control, a filler could not perform, say, one-and-a-half times his normal shift task even though he might have both the desire and the ability to do so. He might help a fellow collier having difficulty filling off his stint, but he was seldom paid for this additional work. More likely, he performed ancillary tasks or attempted to leave work before the shift was completed ("early loosing"), a practice which has consistently been opposed by the NCB and has thus become the subject of clandestine agreements at the local level. Alternatively, the collier restricted his effort and regulated his output throughout the shift as a defense against either a reduction in the rate of pay for each unit of production or a reduction in the number of colliers required to work the face (which would have the added consequence of expanding the stint norm).

In cyclical longwall mining, tasks were organized to allot specific jobs to a class of workers on a particular shift, and within that class to divide laboring responsibilities to ensure that the cycle was not disrupted and production lost. Since it is difficult to gauge average intensity of effort, and impossible to predict the occurrence of anomalous conditions with precision, the NCB assigned a stint which was less than it could be, perhaps 75 percent of an optimal target. The setting of the stint and not the effort of the worker, therefore, fundamentally circumscribed the potential earnings of the "pieceworker." Payment by results became, in practice, measured daywork.[22] Indeed, in privately circulated documents, members of the NCB industrial relations staff acknowledged that especially in cyclical longwall systems of mining, mechanization of face operations transformed ostensible payment-by-results wage structures into the equivalent of daywage.[23]

Accordingly, once a decisive technological threshold was reached, the move to a national daywage agreement for faceworkers, which would allow management to accept a time-based wage in return for manifest advantages of control and centralized coordination of production, could not be far behind. Throughout the second decade of nationalization the NCB continued to eliminate, wherever possible, all manual operations along the face. The performance of complex multi-task machines replaced the traditional collier's initiative as the fundamental regulator of productivity. First, the getting and haulage operations were modernized through the use of machines which undercut and loaded the coal onto conveyors in a single operation. Concomitant advances in methods of support—from individual hand-placed props, to hydraulic metal roof supports, to a fully mechanical "push-me-pull-you" which pushed the supports forward and then pulled the conveyor into position to advance the face instantly—made possible the general technological progress toward power loading which galvanized the Board's will to proceed toward a new wage structure. Machine running time was, year by year, replacing worker effort as the determinant of the pace of production. Wages drift through anarchic procedures of spot bargaining was increasingly incompatible with the technological character of the industry, destructive of EMS/OMS efficiency, and at odds with the centralizing mandate of the management of a state-owned industry.

The Importance of Regional Traditions

The Board pressed for and won agreement on the NPLA. But the difficulties and uncertainties of centralized bureaucratic administration only then began in earnest, rather than ended there. With the introduction of the NPLA, and hence the superimposition of national upon regional agreements, actual underground practices evolved in a complex response to the rules of job regulation, which in some ways reinforced and in some ways contradicted local expectations and habits. As I have suggested, the character of pre-NPLA regional traditions critically influenced the evolution of systems of production under the daywage agreement. Despite the broad similarities in the forms of agreements which existed before, based as they were on time work or piecework, these regional traditions are markedly different in Durham and Nottingham. Indeed, their dissimilarities largely determined the selection of these regions for comparison.

The most significant traditions in Durham involve lottery selection of positions on the coal face (cavilling) and the relationship between pitmen sharing a paynote in bord and pillar working (the marra relation). In Nottingham, the most lasting and influential traditions emerged from a system of hierarchical subcontracting in the nineteenth century (the butty system), which generated more individuated and competitive work relations. Each regional heritage determined in crucial ways the responses of working miners to the NPLA. Thus, these traditions set in motion the con-

tradictions of centralized bureaucratic management out-
lined above. They concretely articulate the *centrifugal undertow of uneven regional development* as they pull the industry
away from the direction of the centralized wages policy
sought by management. At the same time, these regional
traditions explicitly determine the meanings working miners attach to a uniform daywage imposed from above,
meanings which undermine the new wages policy in different ways in different regions, and in this way express
what I have called a *crisis of administrative integration*.

DURHAM: THE CAVILLING / MARRA SYSTEM

The importance of local variations in methods of working
coal has long been noted, but has seldom received systematic attention. In the half century since H. F. Bulman and
R.A.S. Redmayne published the first serious account of the
organization and operation of coal mining in Britain, little
progress has been made in revealing the roots of regional
distinctions in the industry. The observations of these two
influential mining engineers remain the most authoritative
point of reference for reconsidering the early development
of regionally specific traditions. Bulman and Redmayne
wrote in 1925:

> Considering the close proximity of the coalfields of
> Great Britain, it is remarkable that so much variation
> should exist in the arrangements of labour and systems
> of working. Each district—especially the older dis-
> tricts, as Northumberland and Durham, and Stafford-
> shire and South Wales—has developed its particular
> system under the stress of local conditions and re-
> quirements, and in the main independently of others.[24]

Unfortunately, there has never been any ready agreement or precise specification of the "local conditions and
requirements" which have led to particular regional systems of mining. The peculiarities of the Durham coalfield
have been explained in rather diverse ways, and the ex-

planations may be grouped for convenience into three "schools" of interpretation:

(a) *Geological-technological determinism*: the physical character of the northern coal seams, in combination with the primitive technology available during the "take-off" period in the growth of the Durham coalfield, led to the predominance of a single place as against a longwall system of mining, from which traditions of worker self-regulation naturally developed.[25]

(b) *Economic functionalism*: the uncertain market position of the industry in the North, dependent directly upon the export demand for coal which suffered a serious decline in the interwar period, set severe constraints on the industry and generated oppositional forms of industrial organization which were neither required nor appropriate elsewhere.[26]

(c) *Regional political culture* (with a pro-Durham and an anti-Durham variant): the political attitudes and consciousness of the Geordie miners, who are alternatively described as militantly egalitarian or "bloody-minded," reflecting regional isolation and an unusual development of working-class culture, led to the maintenance of anachronistic anti-hierarchical laboring traditions.[27]

None of these explanations seems wholly satisfactory, and there is no sign of current research into the development of the distinctive northern methods of working, either from the technical view of the mining engineer or from the broader perspective of the sociology of work organization, which is likely to provide a more comprehensive account in the near future. But there is little disagreement over the actual structural features of the traditional systems of working in the northeast region. In Durham, the generative rules which characterize the traditional "arrangements of labour and methods of working" are based on the historical practices associated with the *marra relation* and with *cavilling*. These generative rules originated in the unique method of *bord and pillar* working.

Bord and Pillar

Starting from the most concrete observation, one may say that the distinguishing feature of traditional mining in Durham (and Northumberland) is the physical organization of the mining operation into an interlacing system of *single place* workings. This system, called bord and pillar (or room and pillar) mining, although it has many and intricate variations, may be visualized simply as the excavation of the red squares (the bords, or rooms) and the leaving behind of the black (the pillars) in an underground checkerboard pattern of coal seams. Single place working such as bord and pillar is the most primitive organization of mining, developed on a large scale in the coalfields of northern England in the seventeenth and eighteenth centuries. Highly mechanized, exceptionally productive bord and pillar mining dominates the American coal industry.[28] But, with few exceptions, some variation of *longwall* mining—distinguished from single place methods by the length of the coal seam worked, typically some 100-200 yards—is the only method of working coal in Britain, outside the North of England. Comparative figures for bord and pillar and longwall mining for a typical week in 1974 reveal the sharp regional variation in the occurrence of bord and pillar working (see Table 3.2).

NCB engineers and industrial relations officials in the northeast admit a preference for longwall mining under conditions which are equally appropriate to longwall or single place working. They contend, however, that the particular geological conditions of the northeast require that some mines be worked by the bord and pillar method. In support, they offer evidence that OMS may be enhanced, under certain conditions, by single place working which, generally, facilitates continuity between shifts and requires relatively fewer datal, i.e., nonface, underground workers. Although bord and pillar mining, therefore, allows a higher proportion of workers to be directly engaged in winning the coal, longwall facilitates the extraction of a higher pro-

Table 3.2. A Comparison of Methods of Working
for a Sample Week in March 1974

Area	Mechanized Room and Pillar as a Percentage of Total Face Output
Northumberland	42.8
North Durham	1.5
South Durham	7.4
South Wales	4.2
North Yorkshire	1.2
All other areas	0

Source: NCB, Statistics Department [1974].

portion of coal, as compared to what must be left underground (60 to 70 percent as against 30 to 45 percent).[29]
Longwall's very efficiency in the proportion of coal extracted, however, rules out its application in locations where
strata above the coal are weak or where the threat of sub-
sidence, for example in populous areas or near motorways,
must take precedence over narrow considerations of productivity.

Were it not for the extraordinary local concentration of
bord and pillar mining in the northeast, which defies any
simple technical explanation, one could be satisfied that
geological conditions at a particular colliery shaded the decision in favor of one or the other method of mining. Indeed, the alternative claims for the two methods remain
in close balance. The greater proportion of coal which can
be extracted under the longwall method facilitates global
output (production); the more favorable ratio of face workers to nonface workers indicates higher potential OMS
(productivity) under bord and pillar. Although the imperatives for higher productivity as distinct from greater total
output under some conditions favor single place working,
on balance longwall mining would seem to have a definite
edge even in the North. The massive capital requirements
for modern machine mining, coupled with the shrinking

availability of high quality seams, tend to make the apparent advantage of longwall in its potential for global output the paramount consideration. Moreover, under existing levels of technological innovation in Britain, a fuller introduction of multi-task mechanization—of the cutting or hewing, roof support, and transport operations—seems more likely with longwall mining.

Recognizing the narrowness of the technical claims in support of bord and pillar, its "old-fashioned" nature, and the total absence of single place working in Britain outside England's northern counties, Durham NCB officials are defensive in their support of the continued practice of bord and pillar mining. Clearly, its use is limited and declining. But outside the northeast, the continued existence of any single place workings is dismissed as anachronistic, and ridiculed as an example of management submission to the illogic of convention, Geordie cultural intransigence, and the special power in the North of traditions which enhance worker militancy. An observer from the highly mechanized longwall system of the East Midlands dismisses all the technical arguments without a second thought. He argues, in fact, that there was no "physical impediment to the introduction of longwall into parts of the northeast, as elsewhere, in the nineteenth century."[30] But bord and pillar mining, whatever its merits from the point of view of mining engineering, left its unmistakable mark on the generative rules for laboring relations and power relations in Durham in the form of the marra relationship.

The Marra Relationship

A single place working tradition with primitive mechanization sets constraints on the coordination and division of labor which accompany the laboring effort. The *hewers* pick at the coal in a bord or room which is roughly eighteen to thirty feet across. At most, two men work together, hewing the coal—nowadays with pneumatic picks called "windies." These same men then support the roof with timber, and shovel the coal by hand into tubs, which are removed "outbye"—away from the coal face to await removal above ground—by *putters*. Each room is a "small, self-contained coal producing unit, in relation to which all face work operations are carried out independently."[31] Traditionally, hewers who work at the same place, whether together during a given shift or on different shifts, share the same paynote. They are said to comprise a marra (or marrow) group.

Under piecework, the wage is therefore determined by the output of the marra group, which is self-selected, responsible for the whole set of tasks required of the composite collier in the hewing and timbering operations, and typically made up of men of a comparable standard of work performance. Within the marra group, "the total task was shared: it was a contrast to the 'every man for himself' principle that ruled elsewhere; men worked to each other's speed and shared particularly hard tasks."[32] Although the marra relationship dominated the laboring relations among Durham miners, there were, of course, individuals who may have found such generative principles uncongenial. A former miner at Easington recalls in this light his unusual decision to stay on putting, removed from the marra relationship.

> [The gaffer] said to me, "Jack, you're in turn with hewing." Now there's some men want hewing. But I did not want hewing, because when you were hewing, there was six of you. There was two at first, two on night shifts. It meant that you could go in and get a good shift. Other men got a bad shift and night men could go down and get a bad shift. Well, that pulled you down. When you were putting, you were putting for yourself. If you putt a tub, you got that tub, nobody else had anything to do with it . . . that's why I liked it. . . . [H]e let me stop at putting until I was quite a good age, getting on till forty-two. Because I was working for myself you see, and I know what I could do and I thought I'd be better off like. . . . it all depended on what cavils you got. . . . [33]

Particularly for hewers, the relationship between marras was exceedingly close, even if they worked on different shifts: they depended on each other for their paynote and their safety; the closeness of the bond between marras, even carried above ground to influence the social structure of the pit village, comes through uniformly in interviews with miners, and is expressed in numerous songs, stories, and biographical accounts of the underground life. "Pit talk"—the unique underground lexicon of miners—in its own way reveals the fundamental character of the relationship. In Durham collieries to this day, the basic greeting exchanged when encountering a work mate along the face is simply "hoi marra" or the shorter "ho ma" ("how are you, friend/marra").[34]

However complex the mining operations may have become since the marra relationship first developed under primitive technological conditions, the traditions which developed under single place working linger today to influence the attitudes and performance of the Durham miner. Generative rules for the performance of work tasks and for power and laboring relations remain linked to the practices of bord and pillar working, and the marra relationship remains at the core of the traditional work conventions in County Durham.

With the introduction of longwall methods of working, the marra relationship broadened in both number and definition. No longer limited to a maximum of six hewers (two men on each of three shifts), the marra group or primary work team might now include all face workers, as many as two or three dozen men on each of three shifts, hewing, pulling, and doing caunchwork. The principles of self-selection and composite sharing of tasks remained. Most important, the marra group took on new importance in the day-to-day development of the power relations which emerged between management and men. The marra group became the unit around which opposition to management initiative naturally coalesced.

It was a general rule that if any member of the team had a dispute then the whole team came out. It is hard to imagine a situation where a worker found himself alone in dispute without it involving all of his marras; it is a very rare thing in a pit to have a class of worker on a face come out on strike without the other classes on the face joining them.[35]

Long after the bord and pillar system which generated it had receded to marginal existence in the anomalous pit nearing closure, the marra relationship continued to condition the laboring relations and the power relations of Durham miners. It generates rules for worker self-selection of work team and assignment of task, and cooperative regulation of output. It has fundamentally conditioned the political culture of the underground life. A recent comprehensive study of mining in northwest Durham confirms the continued effect of the marra relationship on what I have called laboring and political relations at the coal face.

The existence of marrow groups has given the Durham face-worker great experience in handling relations in the small group. It has also given rise to the widespread belief that only small groups can work successfully—because in large groups the range of individual differences would be too great for a common paynote to be equitably shared; either trouble would arise inside the group, or the group would restrict its output to that of the slowest member, while using its collective strength to bargain for a higher price—when trouble would arise with management.[36]

A tradition of cavilling—a casting of lots to select work positions on the coal face—complements the marra relationship in the unique configuration of laboring relations in the northern coalfields.

Cavilling

From the twelfth century on, the word "kevel" or "kevil" referred to a lot which was cast to determine a share, regardless of the object of the lottery. Sir Walter Scott uses the word this way in "Fause Foodrage" from the *Minstrelsy of the Scottish Border* written in 1803:

> And they cast kevils them amang
> And kevils them between
> And they cast kevils them amang
> Wha suld gal kill the King.
>
> • • •
>
> Then they cast kevils them amang
> Which suld gal seek the Queen
> And the kevil fell upon Wise William
> And he sent his wife for him.[37]

Generally, by the nineteenth century however, the term seems to have passed out of wider use, retaining only a standard meaning, with a somewhat altered spelling, in the coal industry of the northeast. G. C. Greenwell's *Glossary of Terms Used in the Coal Trade of Northumberland and Durham*, published originally in 1888, confirms this modern usage.

> Cavils.—Lots. A periodical allotment of working places to the hewers and putters of a colliery, usually made quarterly, each person having assigned to him by lot that place in which he is to work during the ensuing quarter.[39]

The lots may be cast in a variety of ways (from a rotating drum or a simple cap), at various intervals and for different units of underground space (a single face, a district of contiguous coal faces, or an entire colliery). Putters and hewers may be cavilled together or separately, or one group cavilled, with the others assigned positions by another principle, e.g., by continuation of previous position regulated loosely by seniority or simply through management prerogative.

Despite some diversity in the specific application, cavilling—which was practiced only in the coalfields of Durham and Northumberland—had a clear and unified purpose. The lottery system augmented the rules of the marra relationship to extend self-regulation, beyond the selection of the team and assignment of labor, to include procedurally fair distribution of work places. Cavilling, like the marra relationship, developed under bord and pillar working, and remains

> . . . highly adaptive to single place working, since there are a large number of places and wide differences between them, which directly affects earnings. In practice, cavilling does not always ensure equal sharing of the good and the bad. What cavilling does ensure is a randomness of allocation that provides a safeguard against victimization.[39]

The randomness of allocation is particularly critical under piece-rate wage structure and potentially unfavorable geological conditions. Under these conditions assignment of position is everything. It determines wages, the difficulty of work, and its danger—who will work with water underfoot, and who will be shoveling across his chest, lying on his back in an eleven-inch seam.

While cavilling is a rank-and-file procedure which has an ambiguous relationship to the official union and is often carried on directly between management and men, Durham area union officials have historically recognized, in no uncertain terms, the importance of cavilling as an explicit protection from management. A Durham Miners' Association circular from August 1882 acknowledges the importance of cavils for the survival of the union against management victimization: "Let the cavillings remain. Even with them, we have an amount of favouritism amongst overmen. Without them, our leading men might call for heaven's aid."[40] The importance of cavilling as a weapon in power relations between management and men is also indirectly supported by the vehemence of complaints concerning cavilling and the frequency of requests for the sus-

pension of cavilling rules brought to conciliation committees by colliery managers in the late nineteenth century.[41]

Most important, both the procedures of cavilling and the
rules of the marra relationship remained significant. With
the introduction of the National Power Loading Agreement, management won the right to assess manpower requirements and to distribute tasks and personnel at each
face. Having lost by contract the right to cavil for position,
determine task groups, and establish routines for access to
particular face tasks, the miners were now required to "fully
cooperate with Management with the object of achieving
the best possible utilisation of power loading machines
throughout the full time of each shift."[42] In practice, however, Durham has witnessed a movement for the tacit reintroduction of traditional mechanisms for worker self-regulation. Even where cavilling, per se, is not followed, the
attitudes of Durham miners toward each other and toward
production have been strongly marked by the cavilling and
the marra traditions. Accordingly, the systems of meaning
which Durham miners attach to management initiatives
under the NPLA, and their resistance to the contractual
rules of the national agreement, stand in stark contrast to
the understanding of the NPLA and the response to it
evidenced by Nottingham colliers, who have been conditioned by the more competitive and highly disciplined butty
system.

Nottingham: The Butty System

Alan Griffin, who is both a historian and the industrial
relations officer for the Nottingham area of the NCB, argues
in his authoritative study of the Nottingham Miners' Union:

> Nottingham has been favored by good geological con-
> ditions. There are many workable seams of coal within
> a few hundred yards of the surface in most parts of
> the county. Most of these seams are of good quality
> coal; are reasonably free from faults, and are fairly

easily worked. . . . However, geological conditions alone do not account for Nottinghamshire's leading position. Yorkshire, whose geological conditions are probably better than Nottingham's, has a lower output per man shift. It may be that the "Butty" system, which operated in Nottinghamshire but not in Yorkshire, has resulted in a higher tempo of work in the former county.[43]

What is valid in comparing Nottingham and Yorkshire seems even more striking when comparing Nottingham and Durham. Although in the latter comparison geology is doubtless a strong factor in Nottingham's favor, it seems certain that the "tempo of work," and the whole set of what I have called laboring and power relations, conform to very different patterns in the two regions, and that the fundamental difference between the butty and the cavilling/marra systems lies at the heart of the contemporary distinctions.

The butty system, a hierarchical system of sub-contracting by large-scale capitalists, prevailed in North Wales and the Midlands, including Nottingham, in the first half of the nineteenth century. Indeed, during this period of capitalist development in England, "subcontracting was a central element in the rise of large scale industry in virtually every type of manufacturing" and even in farming.[44] So the butty system in Nottingham takes its place beside the gang system used in agriculture in Cambridgeshire, Lincolnshire, and Norfolk; the hiring of assistants by spinners in the textile industry; and a similar hierarchical arrangement in tin and copper mining in Cornwall.

In the butty system—more precisely, the "big butty" system, in contrast to the "little butty" (or butty/chargeman) system which would develop in the second half of the nineteenth century and remain in effect in parts of Nottingham until nationalization—the owner hired a subcontractor who was responsible for the work of an entire thirty- to fifty-man colliery operation.[45] He sank the shaft, maintained all major items of fixed capital—winding gear, pumps, ventilation equipment—and controlled access to the market for the extracted coal. The butty, for his part, "would contract with the capitalists to deliver mined coal at a stated price, and would be wholly responsible for finding and organizing labor to do the work."[46] The butty maintained responsibility over recruitment, provided the working capital for ropes, candles, props, etc., and paid wages directly out of his own capital (often a system of barter, paying men in "tommy shop tickets" to be used at his own retail shops or inns). The butty remunerated the owner on the basis of a pure tonnage agreement, typically handing over no more than half the retail selling price of the coal. He essentially ran and managed the pit, acting as agent for an owner who would seldom interfere.

By the middle of the century, the size and technological sophistication of mining installations had increased dramatically. The capital outlay had become too great—as much as £50,000—to entrust to the butty, to whom even an explosion which destroyed the entire stock of fixed capital might mean only an interruption in income, and not a personal loss. The owner now typically employed a salaried manager, perhaps a mining engineer, who was directly responsible to him. The "little butty" was responsible only for the organization of production, no longer for running the mine. He was still paid a tonnage rate on extracted coal and still employed other men, now usually paid a daywage. In a typical late nineteenth-century Nottingham colliery two butties might work in pairs, with three to four men working under them. Ultimately, with the development of the concealed coalfield around Mansfield in northern Nottingham in the second quarter of the twentieth century, the increased size of the operations—perhaps 2,000 men in a colliery as against the 200 of the mid-nineteenth century—led to a revival of the butty system. At this point the butty had tens or hundreds working under him, and might in turn hire assistants, called chargemen, who would receive the butty's "take" from the manager or owner and divide piece-rate earnings among the hired men.

The effect of the butty system on the generation of colliers who worked during the post-1918 era of high unemployment in the coalfields, revealed both in documentary material and in interviews with older or retired Nottingham miners, was direct and harsh.[47] The contrast with Durham—concerning the selection of the work team, attitudes to cooperation among the workers, norms of laboring effort, attitudes toward productivity, and determination of coal face positions—is very marked.

In the interwar period in Nottingham, there was underemployment at every colliery. Owners would take on more colliers than were required, i.e., enough to work "full out"on the rare occasions when maximum production was needed, only to lay them off most of the time. The miners without regular places, called "market men," would not know whether there would be work on a given day until they arrived at the colliery gates. The butties selected the men who would get work, organized the teams, and determined the position on the coal face. Each hewer had a particular length of coal (typically about ten yards, called a "stint") which he was required to "fill off." The incentives for extreme, competitive effort were powerful. The butty (or the chargeman) had at his command, as people in the industry put it: the stick—complete discipline; the carrot—piece-rate pay administered for individual production through the chargemen; and the extra threat—dismissal or relegation back to "the market." In this way, the butty system generated rules governing relations among workers which are entirely different from the basically collective, egalitarian relations of Durham miners. A former Nottingham miner recalls:

> The chargeman measured stints out . . . the men were led by the chargeman. He was in charge of production. A man who didn't pull his weight was pushed out of the contract. He had the squeeze put on him. If [he was] behind on a stint, had that "Monday morning feeling," other men would come and help him, "dig

him off." If [it] occurred regularly, eventually [we] put the squeeze on him. You don't want the man on the team. . . . If he had a bad stint regularly, [the charge-men] cut his yardage down [then] fetched in a "market man."[48]

There was no cavilling and no marra relationship and, what is most important, miners in Nottingham do not in any way feel the absence of these traditions. However severe the victimization or inequality of potential pay, they give no thought to having a lottery to determine positions on the coal face; however their labor may be divided, they have little impulse to regulate production collectively or coordinate themselves in work groups to forestall management initiative. They have no tradition of sharing pay-notes as do miners who work under or are influenced by rules for work relations generated under, the cavilling/marra system.

Accordingly, Nottingham miners and Durham miners attach entirely different meanings to the national agreement, and to the specific contractual rules for job regulation under the NPLA. The Nottingham and Durham colliery studies will show the decisive importance of these very nearly opposite regional traditions for the laboring relations and power relations which have developed under the NPLA.

THE NPLA's UNEXPECTED CONSEQUENCES

Uneven regional development has resulted not only in the different productive capacities of the Durham and Nottingham coalfields, but also in the specific evolution of generative rules for laboring relations which condition the differential regional responses to the NPLA. Thus, the effort by the NCB to force national uniformity upon diverse regional "industries" encountered both the contradictions of centralized bureaucratic management which were introduced in Chapter One, above. The centrifugal undertow of uneven development was reflected in distinct productive capacities, levels of technological innovation, and diverse organizations of work which threatened the centralizing strategy inherent in a uniform national daywage for face workers. The threat was made good, as will become clear in the colliery studies, because the systems of meaning which groups of miners in Durham and in Nottingham attached to management intrusions upon customary work group practices made the terms of the deal—simple cooperation in exchange for a guaranteed (and reasonably high) weekly wage—less than acceptable to the British collier.

The NPLA effected a fundamental change in the power relations in the industry which at the most basic level upset the traditional basis of the politics of productivity and triggered regionally distinctive responses to the new national wage agreement. In general, the primary locus of labor-management conflict shifted from issues of pay—the level of the piece rate, the nature of the spot bargain for anomalous conditions, etc.—to issues of control over the pace and organization of production at the coal face. This struggle for control was expressed typically in two ways, which reflect the miners' reactions to specific features of the NPLA: (a) intransigence directed at supervisory personnel (in response to the increasing number of underground officials who were assigned to supervise labor, invoke discipline, and exert control over the pace and manning of productive activities); and (b) direct conflict over manning (in response to the introduction of method, or time-motion, study to determine manpower requirements underground). These fundamental changes in the locus of conflict were, I suggest, uniform nationally because they are linked directly to the structural features of the daywage agreement.

The NPLA effected dramatic responses in power relations in two additional ways which were regionally distinct. In Durham, the struggle for control was expressed, in addition to the ways noted above, as pressure for the reintroduction or continued tacit acceptance of traditional mechanisms for worker self-regulation (in response to the contractual transfer of full authority to management for the selection of work teams and the assignment of task and position). In Nottingham, where there existed no comparable traditions of self-regulation, miners sought to exert control, and to gain material advantages, by limiting particular management prerogatives and not by resisting management authority over the coordination of the production process. They exchanged full cooperation with management efforts to control production for assurances of overtime working and the upward grading of men so that they might be paid in excess of officials rates (in response to the contractual loss of financial rewards for high productivity). Nottingham miners also sought to ensure by their "good behavior" that local management would support any national initiative to return the industry to some payment-by-results wage formula. In this way, the meanings which Nottingham and Durham miners attributed to the NPLA were conditioned by their experience with the butty system and the cavilling/marra system, respectively. Nottingham miners, conditioned to permit competitive high productivity in exchange for high wages, interpreted the NPLA as an impediment to increased earnings, caring little about the formalization of management prerogative over coordination of production. Durham miners, on the contrary, who saw few opportunities for high piece-rate earnings traditionally and therefore did not miss them as much, understood the NPLA to be a fundamental attack upon traditional work group practices which ensured independent job control, protected the working pitmen from management intrusion, and made possible the relatively uncontested continuation of "worker prerogative."

The effect of the NPLA on *laboring relations*, however, was more varied from the start. The way in which relations among miners changed under the implementation of the agreement depended on the influence of previous wage structures on the miner's customary performance of work and attitude toward his labor, and on the norms which conditioned his relations with fellow workers. As the former were regionally distinct, so too were the latter. In general, the character of laboring relations under the NPLA—whether there was extensive cooperation among task groups, whether there developed a cooperative or competitive attitude toward work among members of a primary work group—reflected the pre-NPLA habits and traditions of laboring relations.

Finally, the effect of the NPLA on *productivity* also remained regionally distinct and locally varied. Accordingly, any general conclusion about the national effect of the NPLA on productivity should be viewed as an average of substantially different regional and local outcomes. Local patterns of productivity under the NPLA were determined by a combination of new power and laboring relations as well as by geological and technological resources. New conflicts over control of the organization of production might be expressed, through the evolution of new relations among workers, in decreased working effort and increased opposition to management initiatives. The result, in that case, would be falling productivity. Alternatively, a different regional heritage of laboring relations might lead to cooperative power relations and new forms of coordination among work groups which might facilitate higher productivity. In general, I will try to show that when the habits and traditions of pre-NPLA laboring relations were irreconcilable with the requirements of production under the new wage structure, then power relations became more conflictual and productivity tended to decline. Conversely, where old and new laboring relations remained complementary, power conflict was subdued and productivity tended to remain stable or to increase. Thus, I argue that regionally distinct patterns of laboring relations hold the key to subsequent patterns of productivity and industrial conflict at the coal face.

In short, the NPLA generated nationally two new forms of conflict between miners and management—over the increase of underground supervisory personnel and over the issue of manning. The intensity, form, and incidence of conflict and the general character of the power relations which evolved were conditioned, however, by the meaning which groups of miners attributed to management initiatives and rules of job regulation under the NPLA—and these were determined by the regionally distinctive pre-NPLA habits and traditions of working. These emergent power relations in turn influenced productivity. So, while the national agreement uniformly redirected management-labor conflict from issues of pay to issues of control over the organization of production, its actual effects on productivity remained decisively linked to patterns of uneven development in Durham and Nottingham. In this way, the failure of a discrete set of NCB policy initiatives may be traced back to fundamental contradictions in state bureaucratic management which plague the transmission and implementation of policy and set in motion the dialectic of control which accompanies bureaucratic administration: centralization vs. the decentralizing pressures of uneven regional development; the instrumental rationality of policies vs. the diverse meanings attributed to the policies by affected parties.

Power Relations and Laboring Relations: Formal Summary

One further elaboration is necessary before the introduction of the colliery anthropologies. To simplify the analysis of systems of production in the selected collieries, some formal representation of the historical traditions of working in Durham and Nottingham may prove helpful. In the colliery studies below, I will follow a set of conventions in explaining the changing patterns of productivity and power and laboring relations.

I will characterize as *Wage Structure I* that set of rules conditioned by technological and geological resources which, in the initial period, governs the workers' performance of the work task; this set of rules in turn influences the character of relations and the mode, incidence, and intensity of industrial disputes. These rules will be considered the last term in a progression of rules generated prior to the implementation of the NPLA and are therefore based upon regional traditions and agreements. These initial wage structures are of two forms, either (a) payment-by-results structures in the *regional* variations, as influenced by area agreements, considered as generic approximations: the cavilling/marra structure in Durham and the butty/chargeman structure in Nottingham; or (b) piece-rate or "clandestine" productivity structures in the local *colliery* variations. The inclusion of a local empirical description of an initial wage structure will be necessary for cases in which the selected colliery departs radically from the generic regional formulation or in which an intervening wage structure draws special attention to the period between the dominance of the regional structure and the post-NPLA wage structure. In cases where an area agreement reinforces the generative rules of the generic formulation, as in the case of the Nottingham Power Loading Agreement, the initial wage structure will indicate the hybrid character of *Wage Structure I*.

All the colliery studies rely on the assumption that there is a close connection between the generative rules of *Wage Structure I* and the patterns of productivity and power and laboring relations which develop under subsequent wage structures. *Wage Structure II* will be taken to be the rules (in conjunction with resources) which follow in practice from the contractual expectations of the NPLA or from selectively introduced productivity agreements in the "pockets of resistance" to the national agreements. Contractual expectations become generative rules only by their observation and transmission in the concrete performance of labor. I assume that the rules of different initial wage structures generate discrete work practices which can be accommodated to a greater or lesser degree under the rules of *Wage Structure II*. The miners have no choice but to resolve the conflicting pressures exerted by the more or less contrary rules generated by successive wage structures. The resolution may include elements of micro-political strategy or of habit in combinations which will, in terms of the particular mix of elements which condition the resulting conduct, remain opaque to the observer (and may be only dimly perceived by the participant). Whatever the combination of elements or the degree of strategic deliberation, the system of production which emerges from the interplay of work rules which are generated under successive wage structures (and resource conditions) reflects the transitory resolution achieved by a particular work group.

In cases where successive wage structures generate irreconcilable work rules, conflict is likely to occur among colliers, or more likely among work groups, whose interests lie in the support and reproduction of alternative patterns of organization. At the same time, I assume that the generation of a pattern of inconsistent rules need not lead to conflict. The central point is that with any transition in wage structures, there is a superimposition of generative rules, and therefore either an overlapping or intersection of rules which favor one or another interest. Thus a complex wage system reflects the structural possibility of conflict, which may be expressed either as a competition for domination of rules favorable to different work groups or as a general struggle against the management imposition of a new set of rules. The transition in wage structures directly affects both the performance of work tasks (which in turn influences productivity) and the character of industrial relations. Consideration of the relation between successive generative rules for the performance of work tasks is essential to understanding the way in which the transition in wage structures produces a new systematic pattern of production.

The cavilling/marra structure generates rules for worker self-selection of task groups and determination of position on the coal face. The butty/chargeman structure institutionalizes full management prerogative over the constitution of the work and assignment of task to the group. The Durham wage structure produces and reproduces by its

generative rules a tendency for noncompetitive self-regulated output; the Nottingham structure encourages determined (and often competitive) high productivity. The NPLA
structure institutionalizes, at last formally, full management prerogative over task group selection and assignment
of position on the coal face. This time-based daywage structure generates rules for task norm and intensity of worker
performance which tend toward limited effort and relative
indifference to productivity and output.

Clearly, the NPLA structure will interact differently with
each initial regional wage structure as the respective generative rules prove more or less compatible and workers,
whose particular interests require the continuation of alternative patterns of productive activity, resolve their differences. A new pattern of laboring relations conditions
the specific loci and intensity of industrial struggle and
determines both the general and the particular patterns of
productivity. In practice, the colliery studies suggest diverse and very specific pre- and post-NPLA patterns of
productivity, laboring relations, and power relations. The
patterns are sufficiently subtle in variation that pit by pit
profiles are illuminating while, at the same time, distinct
regional patterns may be seen to emerge.

The disjunction between particular generative rules
channels the division between miners and managers, which
one may assume to be inherent in the capitalist organization of the industry, into particular patterns of observable
conflict. The location and degree of conflict and the extent
to which structural incompatibility between generative rules
is explicitly played out can only be revealed at the empirical
level. At this point, it is necessary, therefore, to consider
in some detail the systems of production which developed
under successive wage structures in the two regional sets
of selected collieries.[49]

CHAPTER FOUR

DURHAM COLLIERY STUDIES

Introduction

George Harvey, the "Wardley Lenin" and leading rank-and-file activist in the interwar years, wrote about the leadership of the Durham Miners' Association (DMA): "The religion of the area official is compromise."[1] Dave Douglass, a contemporary pitman-agitator in Harvey's mold, who also worked at Wardley Colliery as a young man, expands on Harvey's theme.

> When the Durham Miners' Association was founded in 1869, the county was divided into three districts and an agent appointed to each of them. . . . the number increased as the union prospered. . . . [T]heir full-time officials soon developed a particular character. Almost invariably they were drawn from the ranks of the moderate, self-educated, temperate miners. Once elected, they thought their role was to inflict upon the members their own moderation and lead rather than serve. As early as 1870 they ruled that "any colliery which struck in an unconstitutional manner should be denied union aid." The members found that they were being policed by the men to whom they were paying wages. The officials became more and more pre-occupied with arbitration and conciliation as a cure for all ills, and more and more impatient of local action which ran up against it.[2]

The impatience and exasperation of moderate union leadership are still evident today and so is the tradition of unusually militant, resourceful rank-and-file activity on the coal face which I have characterized as the cavilling/marra tradition. These two factors—union moderation vs. independent rank-and-file agitation—combined with a third, the general decline of the industry in the northeast, are the central influences upon the politics of productivity in the coal mines of County Durham. The three factors come together dramatically in the recent period of colliery closings which, unless the industry is to be completely lost to the region, will be remembered as the most humbling to Britain's oldest coalfield.

The historical decline of coal in Durham has been both lengthy and severe. In 1750, for example, the term "Jarrow Colliery" referred to a set of 38 pits which were coordinated into a single enterprise. In 1773, a square mile area of Gateshead, just south of the river Tyne, contained 20 collieries.[3] In 1975, by contrast, there remained but 22 collieries working throughout the county, less than one-sixth of the 135 pits inherited by the NCB from capitalist owners in 1947.

Growing in importance with the burgeoning demand for coal in the eighteenth century, the Durham and Northumberland coalfield dominated both the London and the export market as long as its geographical advantage in exploiting seaborne trade gave it a near monopoly within the industry. Natural barriers against the expansion of inland coalmining enabled northern coalowners to expand their enterprises, while instituting strict output and price controls to make the most of their commanding position.

With the introduction of the railway in the mid-nineteenth century, other coalmining areas began to challenge Durham's supremacy. Between 1850 and 1880, inland coal, particularly from the Midlands, began to dominate the London market. The removal of duties, however, on coal export in 1850 allowed the northern foreign trade to expand during this period, which more than offset the decline in domestic sales. A pattern of reliance on export markets, and restrictive manipulations by owners to ensure profitability, was thus set by the second half of the nineteenth century. Production and employment in the Durham coalfield expanded steadily between 1880 and 1913, but World

War I brought a definitive end to coalmining prosperity in the region.[4]

As demand for coal declined with the close of World War I and export markets for northern coal failed, "it became 'cheaper' for combines to write off collieries rather than to reinvest in the fixed capital necessary to bolster productivity."[5] A capitalist strategy which once again focused on restriction of output in response to failing market conditions led in the interwar period to the worst incidence of closures in the history of the northeast. In Durham, in eleven months from 1925 to 1926, 42 pits were closed by the private coalowners.

By contrast, the immediate postwar period saw relatively few closures, the first decade of nationalization being a period marked by high investment and the introduction of major modernization schemes in an effort to meet renewed demand. Expansion of output and relatively stable manpower requirements in the northeast meant that closure in nearly all cases followed only from genuine exhaustion of workable reserves. In Durham, the entire decade of 1947-57 witnessed only 15 closures and a loss in manpower of nine thousand (from 109,721 to 100,881). Later, as many collieries and nearly as many men would be lost to the industry in a single year (1968).

The first postwar slump in 1957 indicated a major change in the fortunes of the industry, and led in 1958 to the beginning of a pit closure program which was principally market oriented. It was also drastic. Between 4 January 1958 and 2 February 1968, 120 collieries were closed in the northeast. Manpower in Durham fell from 97,924 in 1958 to 44,160 a decade later. The extent of the decline, when measured from the period of Durham's dominance within the industry, may easily be seen in employment figures. The number of men working in Durham collieries dropped from a peak of 165,807 in 1913 to 109,721 when the industry was nationalized. In 1975, the industry employed 26,072 men.[6] A series of concentrated coastal pits replaced the age-old pattern of village collieries scattered throughout the county.

In a way that is hard to gauge, and yet unmistakable, the historical weight of the region's decline burdens today's miners, and influences the meanings they attach to management initiatives. The history of decline and colliery closure helps reveal a central theme of the Durham coalfield: the remarkable moderation of the DMA.

In 1969, having just witnessed 15 closures the previous year—the worst figure since 1926—the DMA general secretary wrote to his members, as part of the foreword to a pamphlet which commemorated the first hundred years of the union:

> The record of our Union in the sphere of industrial relations is second to none, and a shining example to the members of some of the other great Unions in this country. If the workers in all industries showed the same fair-minded attitude towards the acceptance of change and undertook the same degree of joint responsibility for the efficient running of their particular industry, the Nation would be in a much healthier economic position today. . . .

> It is true that we have been subject during the last few years to a manpower reduction which has caused the closure of many pits, the uprooting of families and the necessity for many men to travel long distances to their work. Our paid-up membership, at one time 128,000 has dwindled to a mere 28,000 or so.

> But the Durham coalfield is by no means finished. Assuming a continuing demand for our product, there will be work for many years to come. Some of the pits which have closed were losing heavily and were a positive threat to the viability of the coalfield; the programme of closures has resulted in the industry achieving the transition from a losing coalfield to a profitable one. 1968 was marked by a high rate of closures but

in the 12 months ending in March, 1970, the rate of closures will be down by some 50%. Durham could well emerge as one of the most compact, streamlined and prosperous coalfields in Britain.[7]

Even at the peak of the closure program, the DMA continued to endorse NCB regional policy for the northeast, despite the severe consequences for its membership.

Never having publicly criticized the NCB for its closure policy, a DMA official admitted to me in January 1977, "the area did not fight hard enough against closures."[8] But, asked in the same conversation to describe, from his perspective, what special attitudes marked a Durham miner, he offered the following characterization: "The Durham miner has always been accepted for his loyalty, while they might have been dubbed as always being sort of moderate. They've been moderate, taking into consideration the country. If there had to be a decision supported [on a national basis], he hasn't had any hesitation whatever in carrying the decision out."[9] It is fair to say that the Durham miner has been loyal on national questions, moderate as a member of the DMA, and militant in defense—and in creative modern application—of rank-and-file traditions. In the past, under strong leadership, the DMA has been able in large measure to control the branch activities and to tone down rank-and-file practices. The working miners who comprise the area executive committee traditionally support the moderate policies initiated by the full-time paid officials, the secretary and agents. Sam Watson, the DMA leader until 1963, who served more than a quarter century as agent and whose name marks an epoch in the history of Durham mining, "ruled the roost" and single-handedly set policy.[10] But times have changed. In 1977, a young working miner, a member of the executive committee, told the general secretary, Walter Malt: "You're working for us, mind."[11] An NCB official, noting that Malt could control neither the branch locals nor his own executive, emphasized the potential militance of the northern coalfield: "We have *ten* areas in Northumberland and Durham now."[12] Dismissing the reputation for militancy which is widely attributed to the Yorkshire miners under the leadership of Arthur Scargill (now national NUM president), the NCB official remarked: "Durham is the most militant area. You can take your Scargills. [This area is the most militant because] the area doesn't control the pits."[13]

The five colliery studies which follow will demonstrate the decentralization of NCB-NUM relations in Durham, and the variety of laboring relations and power relations which develop under these conditions. The decline of the region, the generally severe geological and technological constraints, and the lack of direction and leadership from the area NUM contribute to the growth of the systems of production which characterize the Durham collieries. But the effects of wage structures on productivity are determined ultimately by the laboring and power relations which are generated at each coal face—and these distinctive patterns develop from the unique cavilling/marra tradition of the northern coalfield. That all five collieries share the tradition makes the multiplicity of productive and political outcomes in each colliery all the more intriguing.

First, I present Boldon Colliery, a "typical" pit which shows how the cavilling/marra tradition interacts in general with the NPLA. Boldon, for this reason, represents the central Durham dynamic. Second, Sacriston, a pit with extremely adverse geological conditions, demonstrates the potential of productivity agreements, and the flexibility of laboring relations in accommodating innovative management solutions to production problems. Eden, the third colliery examined below, shows the strength of traditional rules for working which emerge under new and innovative systems of production, in this case, rules which tend to limit productivity. Fourth, Rainton Adventure, an old bord and pillar colliery, indicates the complexities of traditional Durham laboring relations and the positive influence they may have on the regulation of work tasks. Finally, Horden, representing the set of large, highly capitalized pits along the eastern coast of the county, demonstrates that even the exceptional Durham pit—one which seems physically more like a Nottingham pit—conforms to Durham's cavilling/ marra traditions.

Together, the underground anthropologies of these five collieries indicate both the range of outcomes within Durham and the common regional effect of laboring relations on performance and on the relations between management and miners which develop under successive wage structures. Most important, these changes reflect the unfolding of the dialectic of control at the coal face, a process which undermines the capacity of the NCB to rationalize production through the imposition of centralized structures. Accordingly, quite apart from the colliery-by-colliery or industry specifics, the evolution of the systems of production in post-NPLA Durham illustrates some of the general problems of centralized bureaucratic management under capitalism.

BOLDON

Summary / Description of Resources

In a region which is remarkable for its variety of geological conditions and systems of production, Boldon comes as near as any pit to being typical of the Durham coalfield. Sunk between 1866 and 1870, it is old and traditional. Nearly 100 percent power loaded, Boldon has passed through the cavilling/marra wage structure and now operates under the NPLA. Thus Boldon reflects the classic pattern of change in County Durham. It was a "family" pit which, with the wave of northeast pit closures a decade ago, has absorbed men from seven surrounding collieries. It is now not quite so isolated, and yet too at home with its traditions to become cosmopolitan.

Union officials who have witnessed the change seem trapped between the old and new. The "big hewer" is gone, they say with regret. They feel the loss of tradition and resent the brash young miners who cannot share their respect for the mythic big hewer, "the hewer who could work as hard as ten ordinary men and perform wondrous feats of strength, and who was blessed with a colossal degree of 'pit sense.' "[14] But there is also relief, for although mechanization erodes traditions and pride in accomplishment it also reduces laboring effort. The older miners exude a paternal affection for the young pitmen who would rather go to the pub than the union meeting, but whom they consider "smarter" (they *are* better educated) and more in tune with the world of modern technologies and new management strategies.

The modern mineworker is less the collier proud of his skill and strength and more, for better or worse, the highly skilled "machine operator." Technical progress and a comparative easing of laboring effort delight the traditional pitman. But a change of attitude—a reduced sense of accomplishment and of the solidarity that grows from adversity—pleases him much less. A union official expressed his ambivalence about the change: "An old miner's eyes would boggle if he came back and saw what's coming off the Panzer [an armored flexible conveyor]. The slugger and the slugger mentality is gone. The best sluggers are those Panzers."[15]

Despite a growing acceptance of new attitudes toward production, Boldon men retain the traditional "them and us" attitude. Union officials express their antipathy toward the colliery management simply and directly. While it may be obvious that there is a formal opposition between management and men, this "old-fashioned" conflictual perspective is not so near the surface in many modern collieries. At the same time, even at Boldon, the explicit manifestation of conflict is hardly what it was. "My grandfather stood where the canteen is today," relates the present NUM Secretary with obvious pride, and the pleasure of an often savored memory. "He threw his cap up. If the cap comes down, he said, we strike." With nationalization, mechanization, and the end of village seclusion, laboring and power relations have changed. But more clearly than in most pits I have observed, traditions linger. The men, particularly the older union leaders, are aware of the changes and preoccupied with their own uncertain place in the evolution of the Durham coalfield. "We are the inbetweens. Not of the old type and yet not of the new."

Within the last few years, Boldon has "undergone dramatic change" in another, more technical sense.[16] (These are the words used by the pit manager.) Until 1975, Boldon had produced coal for the steam market from the Brass Thill seam, predominantly, and from the Harvey seam. Exhaustion of these seams was imminent. The NCB has in consequence developed a bold strategy of entering the Harvey and Yard seams, and moving Boldon entirely into the coking coal market. Because of the rapid closure of many Durham pits which had provided prime coking coal, the NCB could no longer be certain of meeting this demand. Since it cannot put back into production collieries with rich coke deposits which were hastily closed, the Board neglects few opportunities to mine coking coal today where it is accessible from existing installations. While the transfer of markets guarantees Boldon's continued operation, the change has serious implications for the politics of productivity. Miners and management have to face the problem of a "reduced vend," that is, a reduction in the ratio of total to saleable output. Given the strict separation necessary to provide the high quality coking cole, today's saleable output is only 50-55 percent of total output (as against the previous average of 85 percent). Although the price is higher by as much as 40 percent, the imperatives for increased productivity are extremely severe. If production with the new vend were equal to that of the old, the saleable OMS would be reduced sharply. Increasing pressure for productivity generates a new tension in power relations at the colliery.

A second related change suggests the seriousness of the problem. The Harvey seam is substantially thinner than the Brass Thill, ranging from thirty-three to thirty-six inches compared to four feet in height. In earlier periods at Boldon, seams had been even five or six feet thick. The manager admits, "There is a big change from four feet to three feet. It is dramatic. Equipment behaves in a different way. The task of mobility of men [is] very different . . . the conditions cannot produce massive quantities of coal."

This situation of increased pressure and yet diminished geological potential for high productivity defines the contemporary system of production at Boldon. As a union leader observes, "Production is not going up like we want it to. Morale is low."

Wage Structure I

Boldon represents a clear case of a cavilling/marra initial wage structure. Before the introduction of the NPLA in 1966, the majority of the men worked under the traditional piece-rate wage structure. Stonemen, for example, tendered (bid) for a caunch, and worked for a price based on directly negotiated spot bargains. Conflict under this wage structure flared up consistently over the issue of payment for anomalies. A union official recalls, "Used to be on Thursdays when we got the [pay]note, we were all day arguing over anomalies. It was a different kind of man. Nine out of ten times before the NPLA, there was violence [on a Thursday]."

Beginning in 1956, a second set of men, working in the first section of the pit to be mechanized, went onto the District Power Loading Agreement (DPLA), a daywage contract which set the wage level at roughly £3 per shift.[17] In the initial period, when only some faces were mechanized, the management could use the DPLA selectively to recruit and reward men. As long as "hand-got" (nonmechanized) faces continued to be worked under the traditional cavilling/marra structure—which paid on average substantially below the £3 daywage average—the daywage agreement could be used as a "carrot" to promote high productivity and peaceful industrial relations. The "stick" of reduced wages and more arduous working conditions under hand-got piece-rate mining in a neighboring district was always in view. With this set of incentives, the manager could explicitly controvert rules associated with cavilling, undermine the laboring relations typical of the marra relationship, and induce high, competitive productivity. "The results," recalls the present manager, "were very good indeed. This was champion [excellent] because the whole pit [was] not on power loading and the normal [piece-rate] wage was well below."

The traditional cavilling/marra rules for worker self-regulation of the work pace, even when formally supplanted by management manipulation of incentives under the DPLA, continued to condition the workers' performance. When the DPLA rate was higher than the typical piece-rate wage level, the men on power-loaded faces regulated their pace *upward* to ensure their continued selection by management for the daywage agreement. But traditions of self-regulation, which facilitate innovative and unified worker response to management initiative, can cut productivity both ways.

Although the piece rates, in general, were set to ensure success for the novel daywage agreement, effective spot bargaining by the men who remained on piece-rate agreements could make the DPLA backfire. When the men working under the traditional wage structure bargained piece-rate payments up to a level where the DPLA rate dropped below the typical payment-by-results average, men on the DPLA expressed displeasure—and exerted pressure for upward revision of the area daywage rates—by regulating their work pace *downward*. Productivity declined, with hand-got faces actually registering a higher OMS than mechanized faces. The manager recalls that in one seam the DPLA was "a dismal failure . . . [power loading] pay was 62 shillings and [it was] 80 shillings for the [piece rate]. So we got 'duck-eggs' [bad workers] and power loading did not go at all."

Boldon Wage Structure I may be summarized in this way.[18]

1. Identification: cavilling-marra/DPLA structure.
2. Form and level of payment: time-based wage; level set fairly high; wage differentials (compared to men on contract work) determined by spot bargaining and performance of pieceworkers.
3. Generative Rules
   3.1 Assignment of position on coal face: by management prerogative (as DPLA is introduced).
   3.2 Work pace and attitude toward productivity: noncompetitive; effort regulated upward when daywage pay level above piece-rate norm; pace reflecting indifference to productivity when daywage level below piece-rate norm.
   3.3 Division of labor in primary work group: by management prerogative.
   3.4 Relationship among shift and task groups: formal and practical indifference.

Wage Structure II

The contemporary wage structure at Boldon is the NPLA daywage. The manager wistfully recalls the time when he could pick and choose the men for a particular wage structure. Under the NPLA, management retains no prerogative to leave the less able or less cooperative workers on a payment-by-results scheme and reward the better workers with a higher daywage. "As time went on [power loading] ultimately included everyone. No ifs and buts. While [the manager] still chose teams, he had to choose everyone [to be] fitted in somewhere. If [a man] is a bloody duck egg, we still have to find him a place."

Cavilling was immediately suspended with the introduction of the NPLA. When reminded that some Durham collieries, such as Sacriston, still cavilled under the power loading agreement, the manager bluntly observed,

"This is the fault of management." The lodge chairman agrees: "We've always left management to choose [us]. We keep a hands-off attitude. We have a right to say yea or nea, but we never exercise it. [We] don't want to be saddled with it." Although there is little conflict over assignment of position, serious conflict does arise over the number of men needed to work a particular face operation, as will become clear shortly.

Conforming to the typical pattern of a daywage structure, Boldon Wage Structure II may be summarized in this way.

1. Identification: NPLA daywage structure.
2. Form and level of payment: daywage payment at nationally negotiated NPLA rates.
3. Generative Rules
    3.1 Assignment of position on coal face: management prerogative, union involved only as a courtesy.
    3.2 Work pace and attitude toward productivity: self-regulated effort and relative indifference to output.
    3.3 Division of labor in primary work group: by management prerogative.
    3.4 Relationship among shift and task groups: formal and practical indifference.

Systematic Pattern of Production

PRODUCTIVITY

Boldon reflects the national pattern of a generally unfavorable effect on productivity of the National Power Loading Agreement. The Boldon manager says, with some heat:

I will not deny it. I am not satisfied that [the current] method of payment lends itself to efficiency. We have conditions wherein extra effort [would] no doubt produce extra coal. [Under these conditions, it] become[s] valuable to have flexibility. I cannot say, "Look, pull your fingers out, we'll get more coal, you get more money." A lot of men are dying to get cracking. They would undoubtedly give me more coal if [they could] get more money. Who gives a day's work, [when we] give bloody peanuts! As time goes on under NPLA, there are men who say: "I'm gonna get paid no matter what I do."

Union officials deny, of course, that men are slacking, although they quickly grant that productivity is not favorable, and that men do not work as hard with NPLA as under a payment-by-results wage structure.

Clear statistical evidence of a decline in productivity under NPLA does not exist. The switch in market and movement to geologically inferior seams makes reliable comparison impossible. The manager admits, when challenged for evidence to support his assertion that the "NPLA has had a big detrimental effect," that there can be no such evidence. "You won't see it—there is nothing you can put down." Nonetheless, he seems certain of his contention, and is convincing. The manager argues, and the union agrees, that production targets have been lowered, and expectations of productivity continue to be eroded as the span of years under daywage increases.

The clearest available evidence of declining performance is for operations whose conditions remain relatively consistent, despite dramatic changes in face conditions. One such operation is the construction of the roadways underground which lead to new coal faces. Because development work is a support activity which facilitates mining but is not part of the extractive process as such, the physical conditions which influence work efficiency are independent of the changes in Boldon's productive potential, such as the changes in the height of seams and the vend of saleable coal. The manager confirms a downward spiral in worker performance, attributable to the change in wage structure. "Take development drivage: when you create your own conditions, particularly in drifting. At the moment we're looking for ten yards per week from twelve men: there is no doubt in our minds, [that it] would be at least fifteen if wage rates were correct [i.e., if there were a payment-by-results structure]."

POWER RELATIONS

When asked about the kind of conflicts that occur under the NPLA, at first the lodge chairman deflects the question, choosing to emphasize the decline of active unionism at Boldon. "I don't see the young unless they want something. They're not interested in trade unionism. They have outside interests. They go to pictures, to bars." The NPLA has reduced the ongoing importance of the NUM lodge, because it has altered the source of conflict. "When the lodge negotiated wages, on Thursdays there [were] always good numbers at meetings directly before the union men would meet the management," the chairman recalled. Today, by contrast, he estimates that thirty out of a membership of 600-650 typically attend meetings. A decreasing influence on wage rates leads to a declining attendance at meetings. "Other things become bigger issues now, for example [concessionary] coal delivery." But these issues cannot attract the same consistent and militant support of the rank and file.

Removed by the NPLA from direct negotiation over wages, the lodge exerts its greatest effort toward a reduction of the task norm required from the men. As a result, union and management are frequently at odds over manning. In November 1976 a disagreement developed over the number of men required to work a new face. Management suggested sixty-one men, the union sixty-four. The dispute concerned the requirements of a new mechanical system. A machine that cut the coal forward and back along the face was introduced, whereas before Boldon had been worked with unidirectional coal cutters. Was a special team required to pull chocks in (that is, readjust the roof supports) to allow for cutting in the second direction, or were fewer workers needed because the machine passed more slowly along the face than a unidirectional cutter? It seems that the issue of manning, long a point of contention at Boldon, was likely to flare up again and again as new faces were opened.[19] Both sides agreed that this particular dispute would not be settled amicably at the pit level.

Boldon exemplifies the general pattern of conflict under the NPLA: a weakening of the lodge's ability to confront wage issues and increased conflict over manning or subsidiary issues such as the delivery of concessionary coal.

Summary

Reflecting on the transitional character of Boldon and on the uneasy "inbetween" existence of the men of his generation, a union official observed: "In the past the men accepted a crust of bread with a lump of sugar. They never thought of other men getting more bread. They only thought that [at least] they got some sugar." Today the miners seem to make more comparative judgments. The colliery management, for its part, recalls the "good old days" of preferential and selective assignment under the district daywage structure and looks with optimism to a future of productivity agreements. On all sides there is an impatience and dissatisfaction with the present, which is reflected in conflict over manpower policy and joint concern about poor productivity.

Boldon colliery reproduces many themes of the northern coalfields, and its productivity failures represent the "typical" pattern of production of the North. While the independent importance of the cavilling/marra tradition is difficult to assess, it seems clear that the generative rules of Wage Structure I—tendencies for noncompetitive self-regulated output, limited effort, and relative indifference to productivity—are reproduced by the daywage structure of Wage Structure II. Under worsening geological conditions and a level of technological innovation which allows productivity to be regulated in large measure by worker initiative, generative rules for relative indifference to productivity which are superimposed upon a tradition of self-regulated output lead to declining productivity. The management has no resources with which to counter the generative rules of the contemporary wage system, and remains incapable either of reclaiming its initiative or improving the colliery's efficiency.

SACRISTON

Summary / Description of Resources

Sacriston is an old pit in central Durham, drawing coal since the 1880s under extremely adverse conditions. A local colliery, "a family pit of fathers and sons," it conforms to the traditional northern pattern of inland mining in isolated villages.[20] The men say with satisfaction that everybody knows everybody. They all live in Sacriston. There is no need to run buses. Sacriston may have the worst geological conditions of any mine in Britain. But unique laboring and power relations which result from an innovative (and lucrative) wage structure have, in recent years, transformed it into a pit the miners are determined to keep open. Says a union official, "It was a queer pit when we first got here, a bad pit, let's be honest about it. . . . Now you rarely hear men twist [complain] about it, you never hear men twist."

There is much to complain about. One seam, T-13, is eighteen inches high, including four or five inches of water. But that is not the worst. "T-28 is *very* low," remarks a Sacriston miner, "twelve inches and only ten inches coal. We have to take the bottom stone up and the top down. Absolutely diabolical conditions." The hewer must lie in a lopsided position, leaning on one shoulder, half on his back, the coal face on one side, the conveyor belt on the other. He then shovels the coal which he has hewed off the seam, across his chest and lower shoulder onto the belt. He works in this position for perhaps 6½ hours, the remaining 45 minutes of the standard 7¼ hour shift being occupied with the approach through the tunnel to the coal seam—crawling, flat out, propelled by outstretched elbows to the position along the coal face—from the point at pit bottom where the cage ends its descent from the surface. The contract allows for a 20 minute bait (meal) break, but under these conditions the effort to get to a place along the tunnel where one could get into a position to eat comfortably rarely seems worth the effort. Given the meager geological potential of Sacriston, productivity is excellent. From a lodge official:

> We class the hewers here a special breed. No doubt about it. That's how we get the performance we do. No bait breaks. The hewer on the 8:00 shift eats a few sandwiches before he goes on the face. [He] can't even take a bottle out. Eight to three and nothing to eat. Even when [there is] a major breakdown. It's that difficult a task to get up and down. A fifty-yard crawl on your stomach, especially when [the belts have been] filled. He'd rather stay there and putter around with the hand pick even two or three hours until the machine is repaired.

After nearly a century and a half there is not a great deal of coal left at Sacriston. Because the seams are thin, they are very difficult to mechanize, and it would be impossible to justify the necessary capital expenditure. The men hew the coal by hand with pneumatic picks and fill it by shovel onto conveyor belts. There are 278 men on the books, 38 percent of whom are face workers. Between 12 and 18 are on development work, extending tunnels for new faces. Work proceeds on a three-shift circle, although the actual hewing of coal takes place on one shift only, beginning at 8 a.m. This starting time is remarkable and must be considered a major management concession and a sign of the relative power of the hewers within the local union. Traditionally the day shift begins at 6 a.m. This requires the collier to rise at about 4:30 a.m., in time to get to the colliery, change into pit clothes, and get to the pit bottom in time to begin the shift. Sacriston is the only colliery I know where such antisocial hours have been eliminated for any significant group of face workers. The second and third shifts are for pulling (advancing the belts) and doing caunchwork.

Productivity, although high within its potential, is not comparable to that of collieries which are more favored geologically, and hence more highly mechanized. According to the manager, "The seams are thin, very difficult to mechanize. Really, the reason we are still going—we have very high grade coking, number 301 coking coal. The best you can get, pricing £32 per ton, the highest price at which the Coal Board sells coal."[21] More important, Sacriston has a unique system of "spot-bargain" incentive agreements overlaid upon the continuing operation of the classical cavilling/marra system. This overarching factor is readily granted by the manager and by union officials.

The manager:
I don't think that at a colliery like this we could work— get reasonable output—on daywage. I can't imagine men working in 18 inches on daywage. This is an opinion. We would get five or six feet [on hewing], rather than eight to nine feet if there was daywage. If the task dropped like this, the colliery would close. . . . I think I've proven here, a good agreement improves productivity.

A union official:
Ten or twelve years ago, I don't think the men cared whether the pit closed or not. The majority are under fifty-five, a very low age group. They know one of the things in the back of their mind, if the colliery closes, they are going to lose £20 [each week]. The majority of coal hewers they know as well as I do. An 8 a.m. shift.

If the pit were closed, the hewers would lose the unique privilege of a shift beginning at 8 a.m., the men might find themselves working in collieries where there were no

agreements for early riding,[22] and the familiarity and cama-
raderie of a family pit would be lost. This recognition and
the active endorsement of Sacriston's unusual wage agreements keep Sacriston in operation—despite eighteen-inch
seams with four to five inches of water—and returning an
annual profit, estimated in 1976 at £350,000.

Wage Structure I

The traditional wage structure, in practice undisturbed
until 1974, was a straightforward piece-rate payment-by-
results scheme. The level of payment remained entirely
independent of the National Power Loading Agreement,
and varied above or below the existing power loading rate
according to the luck of the cavil, changing geological and
technological conditions, and worker initiative. Assignment of position on the coal face and formation and selection of task groups were strictly by cavilling rules, signed
by both lodge and management officials:

—Each face in any one seam or district to be cavilled
   sunways round.

—Teams to consist of five or less.

—Last cavils on teams of five or less shall be first to
   move, if required from seam or district, unless face
   be shortened, then last cavils on units to come off.

—Should a man's cavil not be available, all vacancies
   to be cavilled for, this applies to all classes of work,
   except where power loading is in operation.

—The Miners' Lodge reserve the right to agree to any
   exchange of work.

—When teams are selected by the work men, the names
   of each team must be submitted to the Secretary of
   the Miners' Lodge seven days before cavils are drawn,
   also to the Undermanager or Overman.[23]

Each team shared the same paynote and maintained joint
responsibility for the work task. They were marras, strictly

and traditionally, and identified themselves as such. There was no incentive for cooperation, however, between teams, whether or not they were performing the same task, for example, hewing.

The manager:
Up until two years ago [the time Wage Structure II was introduced] cavilling was in ones and twos. There were five sets of two for hewing. They didn't pool earnings . . . [they] didn't work as a team.

A union official:
Let's be quite honest. [When the men were cavilled in small sets] some loaded the belt [which breaks the belt, particularly if it has been stopped because of a mechanical failure]. If the coal is good on one side, they would load the belts. If there is a breakdown, they would fill their coal off and not worry whether the belt went or not, once their five foot was cut.

The "diabolical" conditions and uncertain level of remuneration, combined with inflexible and uncompromising management (at that time) led to gradual decline in productivity. Threats of closure were common. The men, management and union agree, worked hard enough to achieve a level of earnings which was acceptable to them, and which became habitual over time. With a classical marra relationship among team members, adverse geological conditions, and the absence of financial incentives for cooperation among nonmarra'd colliers, Wage Structure I generated strong habits of worker self-regulation of production.

Sacriston Wage Structure I may be summarized in this way.

1. Identification: cavilling/marra structure.
2. Form and level of payment: payment by results pooled within marra group which comprises team; level variable, but generally low.
3. Generative Rules

3.1 Assignment of position on coal face: entirely by cavil; management involved only by courtesy.

3.2 Work pace and attitude toward productivity: self-regulated productivity; performance adjusted to achieve habitual pay norm.

3.3 Division of labor in primary work group: self-selected; conditioned by marra relationship.

3.4 Relationship among shift and task groups: co-operation within marra group which comprises only part of a shift or task group; independent relations and little coordination among non-marra'd men (hence little coordination among shift and task groups).

Wage Structure II

In 1974, the straightforward payment-by-results scheme in Sacriston was replaced for hewing by an incentive scheme.

The manager:
We find men can hew eight-nine yards in length for a five-foot advance. We take eight yards. Six yards [75 percent] converted to square yards will pay power loaded rate. We pay eighty-five pence per man shift per square yard above. . . . hewers and pullers average £3.50-£4.00 more than the power loading rate [per shift].

Thus the form of payment is a productivity agreement, stipulating the NPLA as a minimum or fall-back rate combined with additional payment by results. The level is set substantially above the NPLA rate: for hewers and pullers approximately £20 per week over the 1976 NPLA rate of £67.

In the autumn of 1976, a similar incentive scheme was introduced for men working on the development of tunnels.[24] For these development men, the expectation is that rewards will go even higher. (Union officials anticipate £3-£7 more per shift than men doing exactly the same kind of work under very similar geological and technological conditions at the other, larger and more modern installations.) Moreover, for the development agreement, one important distinction from the hewing agreement must be noted. The ostensible justification is gone. Whereas the absence of power loading equipment at the coal face is the formal justification for setting up procedures in Sacriston which are in violation of national agreements, no such explanation can be offered for development work. As a regional Coal Board official noted, with a mixture of pride and anxiety, although "pockets of resistance" to the NPLA exist in other regions, the northeast "is the most guilty"—it is the only place where the very scheme rejected by the NUM in a national pithead ballot in 1971 has been put into effect.[25] The NCB in London has displayed growing concern over this problematic situation, which has led to the self-conscious turning of a blind eye by the regional and national Coal Board officials in express authority. They recognize that because of the strict nature of the national agreements there is no scope for flexibility. Therefore, it is asserted, "if anything is to be done, it has to be unofficial."[26] In this way, local colliery arrangements remain at least within the letter, if not the spirit of the national agreement.

Thus, the contract stipulating a productivity agreement for the development of a particular gate (tunnel) at Sacriston is offered as a "private bargain." Tenders (bids) are invited from marra groups, but with the understanding that the lowest tender is not necessarily invited. Very rarely, in fact, are tenders actually put in; the manager only goes through the motions of inviting a private tender. He will walk around, he will "put a word in their ear," so that the appropriate marra leaders know the going price. The manager attempts—for any job and particularly for a task such as stonework which may last as long as two years—to alternate his acceptance of tenders but reserve the jobs for marra groups with high performance records. Both the appearance of fairness and the formal observation of the NPLA proscription on productivity agreements are critical. For these reasons, the manager goes through the charade of inviting tenders only to "fix" their acceptance, while avoiding any official transaction with the NUM lodge which might include a negotiated incentive guarantee as such. The manager explains this complex custom-and-practice procedure at Sacriston:

> I am not guaranteeing the powerloading rate. The only thing I have to agree to is manning, agree with the lodge, then put out a tender, then it becomes a private bargain. The lodge agrees to the private bargain, then the lodge is not in it. . . . If I get it this way, I will have my way and the men will get some money out of it. I know the men who are putting in for it. They will be prepared to work for it.

The NCB calculates that the men will receive on the average £15 per shift as compared to the NPLA rate of £12.20; the union anticipates a higher average pay. Nevertheless, the NCB will pay less in wages per yard of coal mined than is typical for NPLA pits, the witness to an elegant productivity agreement.

Assignment of position on the coal face and formation and selection of task groups remain strictly by cavil, and solidly within the marra tradition. Names of team captains are placed in a cap, drawn in sequence, and the men positioned "sunwise" (clockwise) on the face in the order of selection.[27] Hewers are cavilled two weeks before each quarter begins; pullers are cavilled for the life of the face. Moreover, the cavilling tradition at Sacriston is unusually nonhierarchical. Under most cavilling procedures, men who regularly comprise face teams are cavilled ahead of the "spare" men, new or extra colliers, who are marra'd separately and only when positions are available. At Sacriston, when a new face starts spare men go on first, the previous "regulars" cavilling for the remaining positions, and the remaining former regulars becoming spare. This procedure functions as an unusual and thus noteworthy extension of the original intention behind any form of cavilling: to apportion jobs through a system that ensures just distribution, and over time, tends toward equitable division of opportunities.

Teams of hewers now consist of ten men, rather than marra groups of two to five men as under Wage Structure I. Thus, on a given face there may well be one marra group composed solely of hewers who share a common paynote. Teams, as before, are selected by the captains in consultation with the men, the lists submitted to management only by courtesy. "Green labour," that is, men or boys who have not worked in the industry before, train for several jobs. Each collier then "more or less selects himself" for a particular task and is selected by his marras for a particular team. As a union official observes, teams self-selected in this way are largely self-governing and slow to shed members.

> Most of the time, the teams stick together year in and year out. All ten have been marras year in and year out. The wages are all pooled and shared out at the end of the week. [A man who is getting old, who cannot pull his stint and is therefore undermining the incentive earnings for his team] will say to the team, "I've had enough." The team would carry him along til he made a decision or they needed an extra man spare with him. The team captain wouldn't say, "Next cavil you're off." We would not put up with him if he was slacking on purpose, but if he was old—no, no— we wouldn't throw him off the team.

The increase in size of the marra group to ten and the introduction of productivity agreements have led to significant coordination among all men working on a given task and among task groups. The management is very flexible and not loathe to introduce unofficial gentlemen's agreements which, supplementing the financial incentives, generate rules which ensure adequate productivity through unusual cooperation between marra and task groups. In a system of production which, to the best of my knowledge

and advice, is unique within the U.K., an agreement for
"early riding" on Friday ensures upward self-regulation of
laboring effort and extensive multi-task coordination
throughout the week.

A union official explains the intricate effect on laboring
and power relations of this hybrid productivity/gentle-
men's agreement wage structure:

> On Friday the stonemen come in at 1:00 [rather than
> 3:00] and [the undermanager] lets them ride earlier and
> all! . . . We can ride when we get the work completed,
> provided that it is agreed by the undermanager, un-
> officially, a gentlemen's agreement. Sometimes he has
> to jump on us, if the standard is not as good. But we
> might get off three hours. I dasn't tell you some of the
> times [how early we ride]! Now [beginning Wednes-
> day] we do as much as we possibly can. Thursday [the
> hewers] may even fill caunches, may even do away
> with bait to get work in order. The stonemen. They
> are only on power loading. Time is their incentive [early
> riding], rather than payment. They even work hand
> in hand with hewers on this. The hewer takes five feet
> six inches or six feet instead of five feet so on Friday
> he only takes three feet. So the caunch is less to do.
> They work hand in hand very cannily.

Rules indicating cooperative effort within and between
task groups are embedded in the new cavilling/marra structure as it is reproduced in conjunction with both financial
and time incentives. The imperative for high productivity
is clear.

> The manager:
> We did a study on haulage. [We were] doing excep-
> tionally well. All faces were spot on. Everything was
> going well . . . [but we were] finding that the shaft
> was not going fast enough. We were getting 89 percent
> of [what was] possible. We were filling faster than
> could be brought to the surface.

A union official:
We wanted to know what could be done.

Another union official:
The men were losing money. If we were on daywage, I don't suppose you would have heard about it. Now the men comment on the big board with weekly productivity, "Hey, we're up there well. . . ." Before [they] couldn't have cared two hoots.

At the same time, despite the imperatives for high productivity, the traditional rules of worker self-regulation remain in effect.

The manager:
[Since the introduction of the new incentive and early riding agreements] productivity has leveled out, but not gone back down. The men reach a level of earnings which is acceptable to them. They get a certain level of money; they are quite happy with it for a certain level of work. And it is not worth it to them to work harder.

Sacriston Wage Structure II may be summarized in this way.

1. Identification: cavilling/marra structure augmented by spot-bargained productivity agreements.
2. Form and level of payment: spot-bargained productivity agreements (effectively, incentive payment by results added to NPLA minimum); level substantially above NPLA rate.
3. Generative Rules
    3.1 Assignment of position on coal face: entirely by cavil; management involved only by courtesy.
    3.2 Work pace and attitude toward productivity: self-regulated productivity, sufficiently high to justify continuation of productivity and gentlemen's agreements.

3.3 Division of labor in primary work group: by cavil and according to marra relationship.

3.4 Relationship among shift and task groups: independent with regard to paynotes; those involved in productivity agreement (e.g., hewers) integrated in performance of composite mining tasks with those subject only to the incentives of gentlemen's agreements covering early riding (e.g., caunchmen).

Systematic Pattern of Production

POWER RELATIONS

Conflicts arise over issues subsidiary to production, notably absenteeism. At 16 percent, the absenteeism is characterized by the manager as "fairly high," but the percentage (which is below the regional average) should be considered low given the unusually difficult physical conditions. What is more remarkable, when questioned closely about the kind of conflicts that emerge nowadays at Sacriston, the union officials speak of nothing but machine breakdowns and insufficiency and irregularity in the supply of materials, particularly for stonework.

> The overman will say: "You loaded the belts." We'll say, "Come on, hey, the belt stood two hours, we think you should abide by the agreement." [It's] very rare [that the overman doesn't give in].[28]

The locus of disagreements, over explicit productive matters in which miners express an ostensible commonality of interest with management reflects the nonconflictual character of the power relations at Sacriston.

PRODUCTIVITY

> The manager:
> Looking back in the records, productivity has gone down a little in the last ten years. If you go back far

enough, they are doing less than was done in the old days, when wages were low. They were doing a higher task. They had to. There was so much pressure. Nowadays the task isn't so high. But the task we get is a good task. Going back prior to nationalization, if we read back into [the history of] negotiations, nationally and locally, people were even taking reductions in wages. They were awarded by umpires. The men actually applied for reduction of wages. Even with high unemployment now, this is nothing compared to then. They lived in fear. "If you don't do the task, ten men are waiting to take your place."

Beyond the manager's own historical estimate, the scant data which are available indicate, as the manager puts it, that the task performed at Sacriston "is a good task." Since geological and technological conditions have remained substantially unaltered during the period of transition in wage structures, changes in OMS are most likely attributable to the introduction of the productivity-linked incentive agreements. Summaries of weekly productivity data provided (and analyzed) by the NCB indicate:

(1) Productivity increased 4 percent for hewers in the sixteen months following the introduction of Wage Structure II, when compared to the six weeks prior to the incentive agreement of 16 November 1974 (from an average of 6.86 tons to 7.11 tons).

(2) Productivity for all face workers increased 36 percent, when comparing OMS for the last two quarters preceding the introduction of the incentive agreements for hewers and pullers to the last two quarters of the following year (from an average of 49.35 for the quarters ending June and September 1974 to an average of 66.95 for the quarters ending June and September 1975). Moreover, the first several weeks of an incentive agreement for development work indicate an increase in performance in the yardage advanced per shift of some 28 percent (see Table 4.1).

While the evidence is too schematic to do any more than hint at the productive effects of Wage Structure II, it sup-

TABLE 4.1. The Effect of Incentive Agreements
on Performance at Sacriston Colliery

	Performance Before Incentive Agreement	Performance After Incentive Agreement	Percentage Change
All face workers	49.35[a]	66.95[b]	+36%
Hewers	6.86[c]	7.11[d]	+ 4%
Development work	.28[e]	.36[f]	+28%

SOURCE: NCB, Sacriston Colliery, Memo from Colliery Manager to Area Headquarters on Incentive Agreements.

[a] Represents overall face OMS April-September, 1974.

[b] Represents overall face OMS April-September, 1975.

[c] Represents OMS tonnage hewed for six weeks prior to introduction of incentive agreement on 15 November 1974.

[d] Represents OMS tonnage hewed for sixteen months subsequent to introduction of incentive agreement for hewers.

[e] Represents advance yds/shift for 8 × 7 return drift for six weeks prior to incentive agreement for development work.

[f] Represents advance yds/shift for 8 × 7 return drift for six weeks subsequent to incentive agreement for development work.

ports the qualitative judgments of miners and NCB officials that the productivity-incentive agreements have increased worker performance. The disparity in outcomes between the increase in hewers' OMS (4 percent) and OMS for all face workers (36 percent), although puzzling, may reflect the remarkable shift in laboring relations under Wage Structure II—the unusual coordination of effort among marra, task, and shift groups—which results in a more efficient "turning over" of the whole cycle of production, rather than simply the more efficient performance of a single independent task such as hewing.

Summary

In Sacriston the rules generated by Wage Structures I and II are more complementary than contradictory. Consequently, for no important group of workers does self-interest lie in the support and reproduction of alternative work rules. What is more critical, Wage Structure II—a productivity agreement augmented by a very attractive gentlemen's agreement—conditions an application of the marra tradition of self-regulation and flexible worker co-ordination which supports high production. Here is a clear case where a transformation of laboring relations is not expressed in conflictual power relations and where traditions of worker self-regulation are applied not to restrict, but to advance productivity. A colliery which has defied the NCB strategy of concentrating production in large coastal installations, old, cramped, undercapitalized Sacriston demonstrates the gains in productivity the NCB hopes to achieve through the wider introduction of incentive agreements. At the same time, Sacriston indicates something critical about the dialectic of control inscribed in the capitalist labor process, namely, the fluidity and openness of the struggle for control and the unexpected, contingent outcomes. In this unusual case, traditions of worker self-regulation, interacting with savvy management efforts at coordination, resulted in relatively high, consistent productivity. The point is not, of course, that Sacriston miners are less "class conscious" than their Boldon comrades, but that management strategy which encouraged the traditional exercise of workers' control over immediate elements in the labor process also allowed management to maintain its general prerogative to coordinate production.

Eden

Summary / Description of Resources

Eden is a small colliery in northwest Durham with only one coal face in operation, and a pit which has, like Sacriston, proceeded from a piece-work to an incentive productivity agreement. The main difference—and what marks Eden for special attention—is its long tradition of "composite" longwall working. As opposed to the typical division of work among three relatively independent and specialized task groups which are separated by shifts—cutting/hewing, filling, and pulling—at Eden the paynote is shared among men in different shift groups. Each work group is intended to perform a variety of tasks, advancing the overall coaling operation at whatever point the previous team left off, and in this way ensuring a continuous multi-shift work cycle. The operation of a composite longwall system at Eden has attracted wide attention, for there had been some hope that the system would be widely applicable and serve as a general stimulant to increased productivity. Rules for working which were generated by the cavilling/marra tradition have resulted in a system of production with complex laboring relations and fundamentally nonconflictual power relations, but with fairly poor productivity prospects.

It is said, always with a simple pride: "Eden is a family pit."[29] All the miners live within four miles of the colliery. Everyone knows everyone else and they meet each other socially. This, by all accounts, makes for a "happier pit."

The manager:
I myself was born and bred in this village, I've come the full circle back. I know most of the men and families and they know me. There are very few deputations with the lodge. I just keep an open door. We try to clear it up there and then.[30]

A union official:
Working at the colliery affects everything. It's also involved in the general life and run of the village. Not only politically but religiously and the whole damn lot. It used to be a whole wild west. . . . [Now] we [have] good relations. We [are] gonna negotiate. We know the pit depends on it. [We] gotta bend a wee bit. This colliery has always done well. Relations among the men are very, very good.

With only one face working (there had been three faces working steadily until 1976), survival of the pit, which has to be counted in months and not too many years, requires high productivity. Production, as always, remains contingent on two factors. First, it requires adequate geological (and technological) conditions. The men are working in a three-foot seam and to a man refer to that as "lovely," a characterization that is only understandable with the added knowledge that the previous seam where the men worked, the Brockwell, averaged fifteen to sixteen inches. Second, continued operation of Eden depends on a high degree of effort and cooperation which can be generated by an appropriate wage structure. Hence the importance of the successive composite agreements. Union officials insist that the pit would have been closed but for the new productivity agreement. At the same time, they are wary about the terms of this agreement becoming widely known even within Durham since, as in Sacriston, the Eden agreement falls outside the nationally negotiated power loading agreement.

Wage Structure I

Composite working, which is intended to eliminate bottlenecks between tasks and facilitate better coordination of the whole range of activities required in coalmining, succeeds to the extent that "all members believe that the level of their personal earnings is kept up by regular completion of the overall task—perceived as an outcome of interdependence rather than of separate achievement."[31] Management relies upon the complementary assumption that the particular composite team working on a given shift will, upon completion of their primary job (e.g., filling) redeploy and perform the tasks which are conventionally left to the subsequent task group (e.g., pulling or stonework). Accordingly, to ensure task continuity between shift groups, the men must be multi-skilled colliers and—what is crucial—they must consider themselves to be such. Consequently, the work group is intended to be self-selected for a full assortment of skills and abilities and ought to be prepared to allocate any new task responsibilities internally. There is no cavilling as such, but there is close coordination; self-selection of team, work deployment, and position on the face; and rotation of task, shift, and face positions within the marra tradition.

The close cooperative relationship among members of each composite work group, formalized through the sharing of a paynote based on composite performance and enhanced by the multi-task orientation of the marra group, would seem to endow composite working with definite productive advantages over conventional longwall mining. In practice, however, composite organization of longwall mining has proved disappointing.[32] Certainly at Eden, there are strong indications that productivity has been eroded by failure to specify the obligation of each group of workmen, which has resulted in a general lack of initiative in "turning over the face." Composite working has failed precisely where it was most expected to succeed, generating serious discontinuities in the production cycle between specific task operations.

Under conventional piece-rate structures, the caunchmen, for example, tended to fill in all the stone required for the face operation to proceed to the next cycle in the production process. Failure to complete this task during the given shift constituted noncompletion of the contracted job. Accordingly, the caunchmen could be docked the wages paid to men on the subsequent shift who were assigned to complete the unfinished task. The management might invoke to the limit its contractual authority and its power to manipulate financial incentives. If, for example, the unfinished stonework, by any reasonable estimate, required one or two extra men for completion of the task during the additional shift, the management would habitually assign three or four men to the task, then subtract the deliberately inflated "extra" wage from the weekly wages of the negligent caunchmen. Under conventional longwall mining, the prospect of a deliberately inflated reduction of wages in cases of unfinished tasks—called "ploting the note"—generally induced the caunchman to complete his task during his shift time.[33] Alternatively, he might work overtime without additional pay to return the face over rather than accept a reduced wage note.

The definition of the face worker as composite "task worker" now takes on practical significance. With no miner (and no single shift group) responsible for any particular task, there is no incentive for any miner to complete a given task. Consequently, more so than under a conventional longwall agreement, composite work contains the possibility of severe discontinuity in the production cycle. "Now the caunch area is one of the real problems," reflected an NCB official on the effects of Eden's composite agreement, "the caunchman can always come up with something to excuse [himself]."[34]

In this way completion of a particular task is not ensured by composite organization. On the contrary, financial incentives for completion of a task are removed. Moreover, should the composite work group complete its primary responsibility, the men seldom redeploy for completion of a different task, despite the agreement's object of facilitating multi-task performance by a single shift of men. Traditional rules, in Durham embedded within the cavilling/marra structure and generated prior to the introduction of composite work, continue to condition worker self-identification as hewer, puller, etc.—never as composite worker.[35] These traditional rules, in express contradiction of the formal requirements of composite work organization, re-emerge to erode task continuity by defeating the multi-task orientation of the composite work group. Production, at first invigorated by the new agreement and artificially inflated by management selection of an unusually hard-working and cooperative team, subsequently returned to the former pattern and level.

An NCB official:
Eden is no different than before. Composite working

is always frowned on by the Area NUM, also the men themselves. They think of themselves as individuals. Cutters had a higher average [wage] than pullers, so cutters are reluctant to go on a composite agreement. In theory composite working frees the manager of demarcation between stonemen, cutters, etc. . . . Generally speaking, the important thing has remained getting the cycle turned over. . . . If [it is] not composite, [the men] still tend to pick up the other man's task, so they can clear out to do their own yardage. It comes down to personality. Theoretically, fillers should do stone work. Doesn't make a bit of difference.

The composite agreement of Wage Structure I in combination with the rules embedded in the cavilling/marra structure, generated a complex set of rules which governed worker attitude toward performance of the work task. Minimally, the sharing of a wage which was based on the composite performance of men working different jobs on the same shift forged a formal relationship of cooperation among miners within the multi-task groups. In this way, the composite agreement helped eliminate the more explicit kinds of opposition which arose under individuated piece-rate agreements.

The former manager:
Under piece rates, I've seen two men pulling a tub in opposite directions. This would not happen with composite.

But the traditional cavilling/marra tendency toward self-regulation of work continued under the composite system. Workers generally preferred to maintain relatively constant wage levels by regulating effort appropriately, rather than achieve higher pay through extraordinary laboring effort. It seems that those less inclined to achieve increased productivity tended to "pull down" the more highly motivated. The NCB official responsible for negotiating agreements at Eden, a former pitman at the colliery, confirms these tendencies.

Trist talks about morale. Morale on composite can equally be found on noncomposite. There is a sense of togetherness anyway. [This is] the failure of Trist: you can't find a piece-work graph that continues to rise. Composite fails if it does not satisfy what each [traditional single task] group expects. Each group has a level of earnings that satisfies that group, though it may be different and unsatisfactory for a different task group. Earnings do not vary. Men don't work harder than they are going to work. And that is known by experience. . . .[36]

Eden Wage Structure I may be summarized in this way.

1. Identification: composite longwall structure.
2. Form and level of payment: by results (piece rate) pooled among members of multi-task (single shift) group; variable level.
3. Generative Rules
   3.1 Assignment of position on coal face: rotational, without the presence of cavilling agreements.
   3.2 Work pace and attitude toward productivity: self-regulated productivity tending toward fixed wage level, with effort adjusted accordingly.
   3.3 Division of labor in primary work group: self-selected within context of multi-skilled composite team; tendency toward a preservation of single-task work tradition.
   3.4 Relationship among shift and task groups: formal interdependence of multi-task groups across shifts; full cooperation within work groups; some coordination among work groups, but relative unconcern for cyclical continuity and overall productivity.

Wage Structure II

In June 1976 men and management negotiated a new agreement which stipulated an incentive scheme for composite working. Like Wage Structure I, the new agreement incorporated self-selected teams which were intended to perform the whole range of coal face operations. But now, to ensure cooperation among shift groups and acceptance in practice of the multi-task character of the work groups, the men would be paid on the basis of performance for a marra group, regardless of shift. It was agreed as follows (to quote directly from the existing contract):

TASK/PAYMENT

10. The basic task per manshift will be 5.00 cu yds for which a payment of 12.20[37] per shift will be made.

11. Cubic yardage in excess of that task will be paid at the rate of 1.15 per manshift.

12. All earnings derived from the cubic yardage in excess of the basic task by the team shall be pooled and divided amongst the manshift or the composite team.[38]

An unusual stipulation in the contract—elimination of payment for anomalous conditions—further influences laboring relations in favor of full coordination among workers within a composite team, and among colliers on different shifts.

14. No allowances will be made for any abnormalities, delays, breakdowns or other circumstances, except that, when teams are prevented through geological conditions or mechanical breakdowns beyond their control, from achieving their basic cubic yards per manshift, then cubic yards corresponding to the shortfall will be included into the calculation.[39]

The NCB does not intend to avoid remuneration for genuine abnormalities and thereby cheat the pitmen of their opportunities for achieving bonus payments under the productivity agreement. Rather, management hopes to generate rules for the performance of work tasks which lead workers to avoid preventable conditions, such as the

overloading of a belt, which may lead to cyclical discontinuities. If the men want to take full advantage of the incentive agreement, they must work cooperatively, coordinate
work effectively among shift groups—since the wage note
now extends across shifts—and deploy men within the
marra groups in genuine recognition of the multi-task potential of the composite longwall system. In the absence of
such coordination the productivity agreement might simply become an agreement for sharing increased wages among
a larger group of men.

A branch official confirms the potential for increased wages
and improved coordination which is inherent in Wage
Structure II.

> The bigger your pull, the more money you get. . . . I
> would say a composite agreement [leads to men] work-
> ing with each other. Even more so since 1976. It stops
> lots of friction with deputies. . . . Relations among the
> men are very, very good.

According to the manager's figures, the men are earning
an average of £17–£18 per shift, which is fully one-third
above the NPLA rate. The colliers consider it, simply, the
"best agreement ever." Eden has the lowest absentee rate
in the area.

Eden Wage Structure II may be summarized in this way.

1. Identification: composite longwall structure with incentive bonus.
2. Form and level of payment: productivity bonus with
daywage minimum; wage shared among shift groups;
level very high (one-third over NPLA rate on average).
3. Generative Rules
   3.1 Assignment of position on coal face: rotational
   but with no cavilling agreement.
   3.2 Work pace and attitude toward productivity: self-
   regulated productivity, with relatively high concern for cyclical continuity to ensure productivity sufficient to achieve bonus.

3.3 Division of labor in primary work group: self-selected within the context of multi-skilled composite team; some rotation of tasks to promote turnover of coal face.

3.4 Relationship among shift and task groups: full cooperation within marra group; fairly extensive coordination among work groups.

Systematic Pattern of Production

PRODUCTIVITY

A high-ranking NCB official gives his assessment of the effect on productivity of composite working at Eden.

Although heartening at first, [the adoption of composite working at Eden] ultimately gave results which did not compare favourably with that of separate work groups, that is, conventional longwall in the Trist terminology. Anything that is an innovation gives a good initial result. Also, it was applied in a selective situation. They picked a part of the pit which was new and hand-picked the men. [So they] got commando results. [There is meant to be] interchangeability of jobs in a composite team, but the team is comprised from distinctive work groups, so workers tend to identify themselves as [being] from [their] original work group.[40]

The official indicated in subsequent interviews that composite working continued to produce little or no positive effects on productivity after the 1976 agreement.

With geological conditions steadily worsening, clear comparisons of productivity under Wage Structure I and Wage Structure II cannot be offered for Eden. Therefore, the subjective interpretations of management and men must remain the only index by which one can evaluate the effects of the change in wage structures. Union officials assert that productivity has increased under Wage Structure II. "There is more put into it," states a branch official. "I would think

OMS went up." Regional NCB officials are less optimistic. Indeed, the wage structure could be succeeding, and declining geological conditions preventing a rise in productivity. But, despite the intention of management to introduce an incentive scheme that would encourage the miners to accept the full implications of composite working, NCB officials insist that patterns of laboring relations which developed under the cavilling/marra tradition continue to make it unlikely that the miner who has always considered himself a hewer, for example, will cheerfully take on composite work responsibilities. With this reluctance, the effectiveness of the new wage structure is seriously jeopardized.

POWER RELATIONS

Given the full composite organization of Wage Structure II, then for no set of workers does their interest lie in the reproduction of generative rules which might be at variance with the dominant pattern of laboring relations. At the same time, traditions of self-selection of team and self-regulation of productivity remain strong. Therefore, in the absence of spot-bargaining over anomalous conditions (which is explicitly precluded by Wage Structure II), the locus of conflict is transferred from matters of pay to issues of control over the organization of production at the coal face. At Eden, disputes are focused on the issue of manning—in particular, the number of colliers needed to comprise a composite work team. As is often the case in manning disputes, the NCB advocates manpower assignment by method study appraisal, while the miners assert the right of self-selection which is consonant with the marra tradition. At Eden, according to both management and union accounts, disputes are infrequent and settled immediately upon the manning of a new face. The testimony from an NCB official confirms both the nature of the conflict and the typical result.

[The men] won't shed the team. They have a sense of how many. . . . if, for example, you have a team of four caunchmen, they won't shed two [which would commensurately increase the individual's share of pooled earnings] even if they only need two for that shift. Method study picked teams . . . the men picked them more efficiently. Try to put in a man less, and the men make sure the face never gets turned over.[41]

Summary

The traditional rules for self-identification as a member of a particular task group—hewer, puller, caunchman, etc.—remain in conflict with the central principle of the composite multi-task shift group. Cyclical discontinuities continue to erode production under the composite system, despite some indications of greater worker effort and co-ordination among tasks. This tendency for cyclical breakdown, when combined with the traditional cavilling/marra habits of self-regulated productivity, substantially negates the theoretical advantages of the composite longwall system.

An NCB official explains the failure of composite working at Eden.

Men don't work harder than they are going to work. And that is known by their own experience. . . . If at Eden you [were to] put piece-rate back, they would produce the same coal, provided the teams were left the way they were. Bring in any situation of pay or a productivity scheme: [you will] not get more coal off the face. Men can only fill so much coal per cycle. [You] can improve output per manshift by changing the number of men or the way of figuring, but [you will] not get more gross output. It is still cyclical because there is not a continuous loader [a machine that would "create" cyclical continuity]. Whether [it is] cyclical or not—the inner man says, "I've done enough."[42]

The pit is in no little jeopardy of closing.

Rainton Adventure

Summary / Description of Resources

Rainton may be the most backward undercapitalized NCB pit in England. A miner out of Orwell's *Road to Wigan Pier* would find nothing in the least unfamiliar here. Rainton is a drift mine typical of another era—cramped, uneven roof along an unpredictable downward incline for a mile and a half, now high enough to stand, now forcing one almost onto one's knees, with wires for pulling the tubs of coal to the surface slick and rapidly moving underfoot. I found it maddening, not knowing when or indeed whether it would be possible to stand upright again; and I found the easy gait of the miners, who were able to traverse the terrain with so little apparent difficulty, somehow troubling. This is an ancient mine, with no cage, no machinery beyond small, pneumatic picks. Indeed, the tubs are still pulled by pit ponies until they connect with a pulley system halfway to the surface.

The coal is mined by the bord and pillar method. As a result, Rainton colliers work more than most miners under the explicit influence of the traditional marra relationships. In addition, a peculiar geological fact influences the rules generated by the bord and pillar method. Coal, which has a cleat (rather like the grain in wood), conforms in its geophysical orientation to global patterns. In Britain, the cleat always runs east and west, and the colliery is planned so that coal can be hewed along an east-west axis. Work then has to be performed either with or against the cleat, the two tasks requiring significantly different measures of effort and strength. Hewing the *bord* (E-W) is easier, the *wall* (N-S) very much more difficult. The management comes to expect so many tubs for a bord, fewer for a wall, an intermediate number for a cross-cut.

It is a central rule of the marra tradition, confirmed time and again with pride and never questioned by miners, that a marra maneuvers himself into the position and paces himself so that he may work the wall (the more difficult) and leave his marra the easier bord to hew. "When we had marras in bord and pillar, the bord was easy. For the wall you had to do nicking, you had to work harder. There was a bond. . . . [you did] not like to leave the hard job for [your] marra."[43]

With workable reserves dwindling, Rainton is in great danger of closing. In 1972, the pit moved from piece-rate agreements to the NPLA. The reserves are getting harder and harder to find and to excavate. OMS has not been maintained in recent years. A union official describes the miners' attitude toward the closure policy at Rainton.

As long as the pit showed profit [they said], we would carry on until every nook is out. Profit (for 1976) was £105,000. We haven't shown that much from April to the present. Before we went on powerloading (day-wage) they must have had a fantastic profit. The face worker had almost a 50 percent increase, just like that. [They] still continued to show profit. So [they] must have had quite a profit before. They didn't tell you then what the profits [were]. . . . Must have been fantastic. . . . Always they say: if we get a bigger rise, we'll have to close it like, but it never happened yet.[44]

Rainton remains an anachronistic pit in methods of working, size (some seventy underground workers), and productivity. The manager remarked in 1974, "Up to thirty hundredweight* output per manshift is a damn good week."[45] (The national average for OMS had already exceeded that figure in 1961.) Nevertheless, Rainton reveals the distinctive Durham pattern of response to the NPLA agreement, which curiously would never have been introduced at this colliery had the cavilling/marra tradition not been so strong.

---

* "Hundredweight" (cwt.) is a standard measure of weight in the coal industry and is the equivalent of 112 lb.

Wage Structure I

Until late April 1972, Rainton worked according to a cavilling/marra wage structure, unusually pure because of the bord and pillar system. Contract rates for tonnage were negotiated by the lodge. Hewers cavilled quarterly and worked in teams of two on a two-shift cycle: 7:15 a.m.-2:30 p.m. and 2:00 p.m.-9:15 p.m., a man beginning the afternoon shift meeting his marra at the close of the day shift. Face work was divided by the traditional rules generated by bord and pillar working—one putter led outbye the tubs filled by every two or three hewers. Inevitably there had to be close coordination between the two task workers, to ensure continuity of production. If an empty tub is not available when the last has been filled, a hewer will not reach his maximum potential tonnage. Two hewers might fight over an available tub; each might work to arrange priority treatment from a putter. "To generalize," recalls a former manager, "[the] putter [worked] harder than the hewer. Hewers [were] not keen on putting. It was considered a harder job, but [the] hewer was more prestigious," for the hewer actually mined the coal and the tradition of the "big hewer" remained strong in Durham. A working miner at Rainton recalls, "A putter could make more than a face worker [hewer]. He always had a better agreement than a hewer." The former manager confirms that the putter earned £5 more than the hewer per week, a sizeable amount of money when average take-home pay as late as 1974 was under £30 per week.

Rainton Wage Structure I may be summarized in this way.

1. Identification: bord and pillar cavilling/marra structure.
2. Form and level of payment: by results (piece rate) pooled by marra group; variable level, tending toward low for hewers, fairly high for putters.
3. Generative Rules

3.1 Assignment of position on coal face: strictly by cavil, self-selection of marra groups.

3.2 Work pace and attitude toward productivity: self-regulated productivity; cyclical continuity ensured by rules of marra relationship.

3.3 Division of labor in primary work group: extensive coordination within marra group.

3.4 Relationship among shift and task groups: formal coordination between task groups (hewers and putters) but some conflict among nonmarra'd hewers working on same shift (particularly if served by same putter); intense self-identification by task (e.g., hewer or putter) remaining.

Wage Structure II

Rainton, working entirely under piece-rate contracts negotiated locally, remained untouched by the sizeable wage increase won by the miners nationally after the 1972 strike. "After the first power loading strike, we got nothing here," recalled a Rainton branch official. The Rainton lodge at first considered negotiating higher piece rates, but recalled that in the past increases in the power loading (NPLA) rate had always exceeded their increases in local piece rates. They decided to negotiate, instead, for a power loading agreement. Union and management agree, "It took quite a fight to go on NPLA." The struggle included a four-day work stoppage, initiated because (as union officials recall with some heat), "the pieceworker here was working for less money than the daywage man [i.e., the man working away from the face, in the tunnel, for example] on the national agreement."

The manager sought a guarantee that output would remain fixed despite the termination of monetary incentives. He asked that the number of tubs filled be counted in such a way that output per hewer could be recorded (although the check on productivity would not influence wages); he asked that there be a six-month trial period with an understanding that falling productivity would either return the colliery to a piece-rate structure or close the pit. These are stringent stipulations under the adverse conditions of geological exhaustion—and when the nationally negotiated agreement includes no quid pro quo to safeguard productivity.

The lodge records suggest both the bare facts and the political drama of the negotiations.

Meeting in Office held on Tuesday 2nd May 1972

The deputation met management and Coal Board officials to discuss power loading wages at our colliery.

A long and hard meeting.

We the officials argued that everything possible would be done by the members to keep the pit open and also that if the management and members worked hand in hand this could be achieved. . . . the delegates asked for a six-month trial period on power loading wages.

Although this was a way of progress, I [the Branch Secretary] asked that we should be given power loading wages from members without any trial period hanging over Pit.

[The chairman] also argued that if we could not get power loading for our members they may as well close the pit.

In the end we achieved our aim and I was pleased with the way our members all stood together for once, and helped prove our point.[46]

From the management side, the argument which had to be won is readily apparent. As one union official points out, "Management thought we were gonna go and lie about, that was the trouble, and not return [the] same output." There is another point of conflict of interest—this among the men—which makes the secretary's statement that the men had "for once" all stood together more than a self-congratulatory addendum.

The form and level of payment of the piece-rate wage structure makes the united struggle for the introduction of NPLA a striking example of the power of work rules generated by the cavilling/marra tradition. As indicated above, under Wage Structure I, the putter consistently earned £5 or more per week than the hewer. Under a power loading agreement, the level of earnings would be uniform and set in such a way that not merely differentials would be lost— putters would suffer an actual decline in weekly pay. A prominent branch official recalls with some emotion:

> The putter sacrificed part of [his] earnings to get power loading for the hewer. They sacrificed, [they were] always making more than the power loading [rate]. The pit had to vote. A full lodge meeting and all putters voted for power loading. For all [it would] lower their wages. The majority was for it. The majority of putters voted for it. Those that didn't—[there was] no dissension, one of them is still working here. Only two voted against.

Estimates of the actual change in typical take-home pay are difficult to make precisely, for piecework earnings vary individually week by week and according to the luck of the cavil. The manager during the period of transition asserts—and there is no basis for doubting him or for anticipating exaggeration—that the movement to daywage effected a rise of £5-6 for the hewers and a loss (not relatively, but an *actual reduction*) of £10 per week for putters. The willingness of the putters to vote in favor of a sizeable reduction in pay (we are talking of take-home pay of not more than £30 per week) strains credibility.

The generative rules of the cavilling/marra tradition must bear most of the explanatory weight. Cavilling developed first and foremost to equalize wage opportunities among marras; the bord and pillar system of production requires unusual coordination among putters and hewers to facilitate high earnings for either; and the marra tradition in bord and pillar working generates rules for altruistic solidarity over matters of production—each marra taking for himself the cleat and leaving the easier bord for his marra to hew. Overburdened or not, there simply is no other explanation, and no doubt whatsoever that a high level of solidarity, and no little strategic planning, were required to convince the NCB to accept the introduction of NPLA at Rainton.

With power loading, assignment of position on the coal face and formation and selection of task groups became management prerogatives. Cavilling as such did break down directly upon acceptance by management of a daywage agreement. However, upon the request of the men, an approximation of cavilling that would equalize work chances under different geological conditions (although, of course, leaving wages unaffected) was reintroduced after approximately six months. As under the prior cavilling agreement, the main and low main seams remained separate and each working position was numbered clockwise round. The men alternated one "hour" every month. The manager explains this curious reintroduction of a cavilling procedure under the NPLA. "If [there had] not been a voluntary cavil, if [I] stuck religiously to 'I'll put you there' [they] might well get back at the manager by lowering output." Marra relations continued, although the miners now received a daywage and in no way shared a common paynote.

Rainton Wage Structure II may be summarized in this way.

1. Identification: National Power Loading Agreement daywage structure.
2. Form and level of payment: time-based daywage payment, completely individuated.
3. Generative Rules
   3.1 Assignment of position on coal face: formally by management prerogative; in practice assignment of position by rotational variant of cavilling.

3.2 Work pace and attitude toward productivity: self-regulated productivity.

3.3 Division of labor in primary work group: continued traditional divisions between hewers and putters.

3.4 Relationship among shift and task groups: task groups formally and practically interdependent (although independent with regard to pay levels); extensive cooperation between task groups (e.g. hewers and putters no longer fight over a tub).

Systematic Pattern of Production

PRODUCTIVITY

The clerk at Rainton, the man who records and assesses production figures, states simply and directly the effect on productivity of changing wage structures and geological conditions: "Production has dropped—100 and odd ton per week in the last two years. Two years ago it was 600 [tons/week]. Now we are struggling for 500. Now we have to ga'an looking for it, the reserves are low." Separating the effect of changing wage structures from that of exhaustion of coal reserves is today a practical impossibility. Weekly data for production at Rainton indicate that the average weekly output (excluding the periods of the national strikes in 1972 and 1974) varied very little during the period of transition from Wage Structure I to Wage Structure II. Indeed the average weekly output increased very slightly: from 568 tons/week for the period 7 May 1971–28 April 1972 to 577 tons/week for the period 5 May 1972–27 April 1973; then a slight decline to 571 tons/week for the period from 4 May 1973–26 April 1974 (see Table 4.2).

The subjective accounts differ, largely according to interest, but generally support the indications of the data that production has not been significantly affected by the introduction of the NPLA. The former manager complains

TABLE 4.2. The Effect of the NPLA on Production
at Rainton Colliery

	Total Production	Average Weekly Production
7 May 1971- 28 April 1972 (Pre-NPLA)	19,890 (35 weeks)	568
5 May 1972- 27 April 1973 (NPLA)	26,537 (46 weeks)	577
4 May 1973- 26 April 1974 (NPLA)	17,123 (30 weeks)	571

SOURCE: NCB, Rainton Colliery, Weekly Productivity Data.

NOTE: All figures for production are expressed in saleable tons and represent the sum of output in the Low Main and Main seams. Totals for weeks in which fewer than five days were worked are omitted. The periods of the national strikes, 8 January–27 February 1972 and 8 February–15 March 1974, are not included; nor is the period of the overtime ban from 12 November–8 February 1972. All dates in the table represent the last day of the week whose productivity is measured. (Tabulation begins for week ending 7 May 1971.)

of reduced productivity, but locates the decline well past the introduction of the NPLA as such. "There has been a reduction of one tub or half a tub per shift since the last [1974] strike. We are losing 7½ to 8 percent up to 10 percent since the last strike. Men realize they can work a little less hard." What is unusual, colliers from neighboring pits seem to concur with the manager's judgment. A union official at Sacriston used Rainton as a counterexample to support the advantages of their productivity agreement:

Rainton [is] now on power loading. We know—the lads are not filling as many tubs. [They have] a task to do and that's it. If [they do] not get the task done [there is] no reduction in wages. It's just a question for the manager: "What have you got to say about it. . . ."[47]

The men at Rainton assert that the custom and practice of marra working—for example, taking the cleat and leaving the bord—continue, so that the pace of work and productivity remain fundamentally unchanged.

Output didn't change at all. People still go in and do a day's work. . . . [the] men [are] *that* used to coming in, working and geting out. [We are] used to working . . . [and that is] carried on. . . . [NPLA or piece rate] makes no difference to anybody. It means we are more happy now at the end of the week. [We] had to knock ten tubs to get minimum. Now [we] know what [we will] have at the weekend.

None of the people interviewed is unbiased or uniquely reliable. The Sacriston men were promoting the virtues of their existing productivity agreement; the former Rainton manager, for his own reasons, chose mildly to decry the attitudes of the miners and in that way promote his vision of a future productivity agreement; and the Rainton men were speaking to their own character as hardworking miners and, perhaps, fighting old battles to show they would not "take advantage" of a daywage agreement. The representations are not so very contradictory. It is likely that productivity has declined in recent years. One can infer from the weekly output data that the change in wage structure was not, at least initially, a strong contributing cause. As the years pass, however, exhaustion of reserves augments the rules generated by Wage Structure II to produce a steady tendency toward a loss in output per manshift.

POWER RELATIONS

As elsewhere, the transition from piece rate to daywage has signaled a shift in the orientation of the power relations at the colliery and a decline in the initiative of the local lodge. The former manager at Rainton expresses this in an unusually direct manner. "The power of the local is broken when they no longer determine tonnage rates." The union leadership admits—and express the fact as an important

measure of growing lack of interest and union weakness—
that of the hundred men on the books, a lodge meeting
attracts usually fourteen to twenty. It seems clear that the
prospects of closure will frame the power relations in the
colliery in the coming period. But for the time being serious
conflict is not visible.

Did the transition to power loading generally affect the
character of labor-management relations at Rainton?

There is not so much disagreement as there used to
be, not as many disputes since power loading. [Dis-
agreements are about] what [a man] does and what
he doesn't. Most of the squabbles are worked out at
the fortnightly consultative meeting. A man out without sick notes and like that; [the manager] starts slap-
ping fines. I'm against it. . . .

On a day-to-day basis, absenteeism is the major source
of conflict at Rainton. The current manager, unwittingly
exaggerating, explains that with regard to absenteeism,
Rainton is "the worst of all thirty-four pits in the northeast
area. Naturally people are asking what I'm gonna do." The
miners are allowed eight "rest days" for which they must
apply ten days in advance. Only prior approval for a rest
day or a doctor's note ensures pay for absence. The manager has a lot of discretion over the acceptance of requests
for rest days on shorter notice, and over disciplinary measures—including downgrading or even dismissal—in chronic
cases or for particularly unacceptable patterns of absenteeism. Sometimes, on a Monday, absenteeism in putting
reaches 40 percent, and overall underground absence will
be as high as 29 percent. One day when I visited Rainton,
a man had just been dismissed for excessive unexcused
absences over a long period of time. While I was inter-
viewing the manager, he received a strongly worded note
from the young miner's father. Somewhat shaken, the
manager explained, apologetically, "[This is the] only man
given notice. [It's] very, very rare. [The] idea . . . is to get
them to come to work by any means possible." Conflict at

Rainton, an old and moribund pit, is subdued. It is expressed more by grumbling than struggling.

Summary

Rainton is a harsh anachronism for the colliers and a minor footnote to production for the northeast region. This colliery, however, reflects broader patterns of productivity and power and laboring relations in County Durham. The manager remarks: "Old County Durham, old fashioned idea . . . bord and pillar. Putters, when they were on piecework, putt as many tubs as they could and used to fill a few. Now they are not filling any tubs." This simple statement captures the dynamic of productivity under the new daywage agreement in the context of rules, customs, and practice generated by old and new wage structures. The few odd tubs the putters no longer fill explain, both actually and symbolically, the decline in productivity claimed by management (or at least that part not due to geological factors). The continuation of rules generated by bord and pillar working within the marra/cavilling tradition, on the other hand, explains why the hewers continue to fill *as many tubs as they do*, despite the abrupt removal of financial incentives and the increasingly difficult geological conditions. The generative rules for self-regulated productivity and extensive, even altruistic, cooperation within the marra group, common to both wage structures and therefore mutually reinforcing, ensure continued productivity more or less apace with what geological circumstances will allow. The change in generative rules between Wage Structures I and II tell the remaining part of the story. A time-based wage removes the inclination for the putter to fill a few tubs or for two hewers to fight over use of a tub; but coordination between task groups under bord and pillar working remains strong, as do the traditions for hard work and cooperation between marras, particularly hewers.

A northern pitman captures the importance of what I have called generative rules for self-regulated productivity, and what I wish to stress here: that *self-regulation* does not mean *downward regulation.*

> Within the [marra] team . . . men worked to each other's speed and shared particularly hard tasks. . . . Each member of the team was expected to keep up with his marras. . . . Marraships were formed in this way, according to capacity for work. . . . Many people have heard of the almost legendary "big hewer" in County Durham, and the hewer who could work as hard as ten ordinary men and perform wondrous feats of strength. . . . The same thing worked in reverse of course, when a team got a reputation as slackers. . . .
>
> A man can get a reputation as a bad worker as well as a good one. A whole legend can be built around a lazy or shirking miner, whose fame for being idle is complete. . . .
>
> It was said of Tony [a fictitious name of a miner at Wardley colliery] that once he got cavilled with a one-armed man. Well, old Tony didn't like to hurt his feelings so he worked with him for a week. When he went to collect the Master Note at the end of the week he saw that their yardage wasn't too bad and the wage was decent. Up comes the one-armed marra, obviously a bit embarrassed. He says to Tony, "Wey, ah reckon ah'll ask for the cavils to go in again and ah'll get a move." "Oh, that's all reet," says Tony, "the wage isn't to bad." "Ah know," says his mate, "but me one arm won't do for the two of wi."[48]

Geordie humor reflects—in this case in the words of a working pitman—the real and keenly felt work attitudes which are generated in purest form by the cavilling/marra structures under northern bord and pillar working. Output per manshift declines at Rainton, but not as sharply as failing resources and the abrupt removal of monetary incentives would lead us to expect in the absence of traditions of self-regulation which stabilize worker effort.

HORDEN

Summary / Description of Resources

If Durham were Nottingham, then at least as regards productive potential, Horden Colliery would be a typical pit. As it stands, with Durham a region declining in importance as its production lags behind that of the East Midlands and South Yorkshire coalfields, Horden is typical only of the string of highly capitalized pits which dot the eastern coast of the county, and whose faces extend two to six miles beneath the North Sea.

As the northern coalfield has suffered during the last half century, the importance of Horden and of the neighboring coastal pits—Blackhall, Easington, Dawdon, Vane Tempest, Seaham—has risen commensurately. The only possibility of maintaining employment in the industry, and indeed the likelihood of retaining a vital coal industry in the region at all, rests on the fate of these collieries.

Even when they are being optimistic, Coal Board and NUM officials offer a picture of mining in County Durham which represents a surrender of the great mining tradition of the northeast to harsh geological and fiscal realities. Colliery villages throughout inland Durham have been blighted by closures and will neither be renewed nor replaced. Rather, eight or ten collieries operating under the sea—automated, anonymous factories instead of family pits—will by the late 1980s represent the full extent of Durham mining. If the intent of this project is realized—to modernize and concentrate production effectively without vast dislocation of miners or negative effect on regional development more generally—then total production will remain stable. Productivity (output per manshift) will increase, and manpower decrease through "natural wastage" in certain operations, offset by the recruitment of young men as necessary. Of course, the historic place of coal at the center of the region's economic development and at the foreground of the people's image of themselves will be lost. The process is all but completed.

The importance of Horden in particular and the coastal pits in general is confirmed by Coal Board officials. When asked to characterize the trends in productivity, output, and industrial relations for the entire region, they quickly turn to what is clearly the burning issue for Durham productivity: the productivity of coastal pits. Between 1974 and 1976, unforeseen conditions, in the form of unexpected faulting under the North Sea, had intervened to threaten the NCB's plan for the northeast. The official spoke with resignation, having to acknowledge a flaw outside his control.

> On the coastal pits, we were very optimistic about offshore reserves, based on eighteen deep bore holes, which are sunk out and set by using tower mounted drills. They are enormously expensive, therefore the boring pattern is quite widely spaced. Unfortunately, [we] discovered [that] within the boring pattern, there is local geological disturbance, the effect of which in that locality is to diminish the coal seam, even divide up the coal seam.[49]

He confirmed that by October 1976 production throughout the Durham area was down 10 percent from the previous fiscal year, and 12 percent against the budget.[50] Geological conditions forced a reduction of the scale of operations at Vane Tempest, and have raised very serious doubts about the long-term future of Dawdon Colliery. The impact of geology on Vane Tempest and Dawdon, argues the official, "has been depressing on morale and probably on [the production] at other neighboring pits." He observes that in a daywage system, adverse mining conditions always slow down operations more than in a system of payment by results. It is particularly hard, under daywage agreements, to respond flexibly to geological disturbance by providing an alternative productive unit—new coal face—quickly.

Thinking of the difficulty at Vane Tempest, he concedes, "One operation [which is] slower under daywage is development work."[51] Without speedy work on the development of new coal faces, major geological interference cannot easily be overcome.

It is no surprise that the pitmen speak less of productivity and more about how the promotion of Horden as a cosmopolitan pit—with a new town, Peterlee, next door drawing its working population from the traditional village—has affected their laboring relations and their social existence.

"I'll tell you the biggest change," notes the lodge chairman. "Horden was a family pit once. Now all the villages [have] closed down. Langley Park [neighboring colliery] was the last colliery. . . . The biggest change is [that you have] 40 percent strangers. You used to say, 'How're you, Geordie.' Now you say—'Who's that?' "[52] The union official went on to say, with some bitterness, that it was the National Coal Board's policy to introduce experienced, very highly trained men onto face work at Horden. "You tend to get an older workforce, not young trainees. They aren't being set on. They are fighting for thirty positions on a new face. In the village, eighty wanted it." The NCB was putting on outsiders when there were local men who wanted the work—and face work was their only chance of upward mobility, possibly the only thing that would keep them in the industry and in Peterlee. To the Horden miner, a product of village and family pit, this was a source of anxiety and resentment. The Coal Board was actively violating the old ways, and forces were combining to destroy the village traditions, the life above ground, much as mechanization and new wage structures had affected the conditions of work and the laboring relations down the pit. As a lodge official put it,

> Peterlee. A town set up slap bang in the middle, Horden, Easington, etc. When I was a lad, you had to live

in with relations. Peterlee [before the new town development] was for the overflow. Now most [of the young lads] have shifted out of villages. [They've] decimated the villages. And run down [Horden] with mechanisation. There used to be ten thousand men. Now [there are] two thousand.

Horden is no longer the "biggest colliery in the world," the title claimed for it until the middle '60s and repeated to me by a ranking NUM area official who, despite his high regional standing within the union, calls himself simply, "a Horden man."[53] Nonetheless, since nationalization in 1947 output has never fallen below a million tons per year, and the saleable face OMS frequently places Horden among the top ten collieries in Britain.

Thus, given its size and position among the shrinking set of Durham collieries, even small fluctuations in Horden productivity have enormous repercussions for the total production profile of the northeast. Horden is not a small, anomalous pit allowed to survive into the last quarter of the twentieth century. Rather, this mammoth colliery on the coast of southeast Durham is the case which proves how exceptional the Durham system of production remains in comparison with the national pattern anticipated by the NCB in its centralizing strategies.

Horden is a straightforward NPLA pit, with a distinct daywage tradition grafted upon the rules generated by piecework under a cavilling/marra structure. It is a Nottingham colliery with Durham miners laboring in its seams. The systematic patterns of production at Horden both reinforce the regional patterns of Durham mining and underscore the more general comparative argument. In this way, Horden illuminates the particular influence of the Durham tradition of working, even where the technological, geological, and social context—and particularly, the wage structure—closely approximates the more "modern" conditions of the East Midlands.

Wage Structure I

Horden Wage Structure I conforms to the classic Durham cavilling/marra structure. The NUM area official, who worked in Horden from 1930 to 1967, recalls the particulars. Conditions were "very bad," the piece rate in 1930 amounting to just over a shilling per ton (for hewing) and a similar wage for putting a score of tubs (which at Horden was twenty-one tubs, rather than the usual twenty).

At Horden, as elsewhere, the putting and hewing operations set the fundamental division of labor and determined the locus of relations among the pitmen. The hewer "by means of a pick . . . felled the whole area of coal and filled it into tubs."[54] Working directly to extract the coal, the hewer represents the outsiders' image of the miner, and in nearly all collieries a similar sense of the hewer, as the central figure both down pit and in the union hall, is shared by the colliers. Typically, the putters are young miners who have not yet gone onto the face to become hewers. Their task is to provide the "chum 'uns" or empty tubs for the hewer, and to lead the "full 'uns" away, by pony, or if the face is too narrow, without any aid. A putter "might have four or five places to supply and never please everybody because all the workers want their tubs fetched back there first."[55]

As at Rainton, special relationships developed at Horden between a putter and several hewers; the hewer's pay would be directly affected by his ability to have an empty tub ready when needed, and the next full one led outbye immediately when filled. "I was a putter and a hewer," recalls the Durham official. "You serve[d] your time putting, then started hewing. [We] had a cavilling system. There used to be cavils in every quarter. Some, if you were lucky, you could have a good cavil; good flat, coal soft. If [you got] bad flats—you were working harder for less money."

This situation of inverse proportionality between effort and pay, combined with a declining rate of pay throughout the county during this period, resulted in an important improvisation on the general cavilling theme of worker self-regulation of the pace of production. At Horden, not infrequently, putters would "go slow," initiating a process of "restricting." They would provide only a small number of tubs to hewers during a shift—two to four, by one account—which represented a substantial reduction from the normal supply. Similarly, the hewer might restrict production so that putters would have considerably fewer than the typical thirty to forty tubs to put during a shift. In either case, the slowdown by one task group reduced the wages for all colliers on a given shift, and consequently forced a united front of workers against management in pursuit of increments in the piece rate to be paid for either task.

Thus in Horden, Wage Structure I generated a complicated pattern in the politics of productivity. The structured relationship between hewer and putter generated a "united front" of colliers against management, allowing for a limited diversity of interests between miners in different task groups. Indeed, as the NUM official recalls, "There used to be blood for money—fighting over tubs and a heck of a lot of risk taken." Individual putters, in order to promote their earnings, fought over scarce instruments of labor (the tubs), and reduced the earnings of their marras. At the same time, the payment-by-results structure—based on the separate labor of each task group, measured individually, and set by no common wage norm—generated conflict between the putters and hewers. But, what is most critical, the conflict between task groups was expressed in a particular form (restriction of output) which forged a common unity against management.

In 1957, the District Power Loading Agreement was introduced in an extremely selective manner. Yet the most powerful features of the cavilling/marra tradition were retained. Management selected men from among volunteers, and initially six men who cavilled together, a "set of men," were put to work in the Hutton seam on daywage, two to each shift. In this way, self-selection of team and team composition across shifts, key features of the marra tradition, were preserved within a new daywage structure. Management authority, which would eventually in the 1966 NPLA include decisions over manning, team composition, and positioning on the coal face, was initially limited to the selection of the "set of men" to go on the daywage agreement, the other responsibilities reverting to the miners themselves under the custom and practice typical of the cavilling/marra structure.

Taken on the average, wage levels on daywage and piece rate in Horden were "more or less the same." The relative level of wages between the two wage structures, recalls a miner who worked under this system, "depend[ed] on the previous cavil." At Horden, management did not employ the district daywage agreement—as had the Boldon management—in a "carrot and stick" strategy intended to influence productivity and industrial relations by threatening to return "less cooperative" workers to more difficult and less remunerative labor in the predominant hand-got piece-rate seams. Consequently, management had no way of countering the indifference toward productivity which is characteristic of daywage working, as Boldon management could do when the daywage pay level was substantially higher than the traditional piece-rate structure at the same pit.

Horden Wage Structure I may be summarized in this way.

1. Identification: cavilling-marra/DPLA structure.
2. Form and level of payment: time-based wage; level set at relative parity with colliery piece-rate norm.
3. Generative Rules
   3.1 Assignment of position on coal face: by cavil, despite management prerogative.
   3.2 Work pace and attitude toward productivity: relative indifference to productivity.
   3.3 Division of labor in primary work group: coordination between different task workers, limited to face team.

3.4 Relationship among shift and task groups: formal and practical indifference."

Wage Structure II

As the lodge chairman at Horden says, the contemporary
wage structure is "strictly power loading—there is no flexibility." A large, critical colliery, Horden must "go by the
book," unlike some of its irregular neighbors. As a consequence, it represents in all particulars the explicit formulations of the National Power Loading Agreement.

Horden Wage Structure II may be summarized in this
way.

1. Identification: NPLA daywage structure.
2. Form and level of payment: time-based payment at
nationally negotiated NPLA rates.
3. Generative Rules
   3.1 Assignment of position on coal face: strictly by
      management prerogative.
   3.2 Work pace and attitude toward productivity: rel-
      ative indifference to productivity.
   3.3 Division of labor in primary work group: formal
      cooperation.
   3.4 Relationship among shift and task groups: for-
      mal cooperation.

Systematic Pattern of Production

PRODUCTIVITY

The issue of productivity forces the usually placid lodge
chairman to allow some emotion to enter his voice. With
regional production down and the coastal pits carrying most
of the country's output burden, the question is highly
charged. "Is productivity down? That's what the management says. Not so. If the belt is going, we put coal on.
Conditions govern what you produce. You can't try to produce coal [when the belt is stopped]." This denial, made

in front of several prominent lodge officials, reflects both the Horden miner's pride and the official policy of the local union. But there is another side to the question of productivity, which the Horden lodge chairman also revealed—speaking now more as the miner and son of a miner and less as formal representative of the NUM.

> I suppose if there was money there, more risks [would be taken]. Before power loading fifteen or sixteen were killed every year. [There have been] four in the last two years. Before that, fifteen years without any killed. Before [when there was piece rate] five or six were killed before the holidays, coming up to Christmas. Always. Five. Four. Five. Six . . . killed each year. Tried for a bit extra (for the holidays). Took risks.

A second miner nodding his agreement, his face displaying the grim memories, adds the Geordie acknowledgment, "Wey-aye." A third miner agrees: "Your father, my father, my wife's father. . . ." Looking around the room, he concludes, "Not many escaped." Perhaps, as under any system which precludes explicit incentives to increase production, the Horden miners have reduced their effort to a degree.

Certainly, there are strong indications of decreasing productivity. Statistical evidence, although incomplete, reveals a picture of consistent decline in saleable OMS in recent years. G seam, which is four feet thick, with one retreating and three advancing faces (all equipped with powered supports and multi-task cutting-hewing equipment), provides the most appropriate source for reviewing recent trends in productivity at Horden. Typical of Horden mining, G seam is also the only seam whose faces were in continuous operation during the period for which a sample of weekly productivity figures is available. Comparisons of productivity measured in saleable OMS for the 1974–1976 period show a decline in productivity of 24.5 percent between 1974 and 1975, and a further decline of 17.9 percent between 1975 and 1976. Comparison for the single month of November during the same period, for which more complete weekly figures are available, shows an even greater rate of decline in productivity for Horden's G seam (see Table 4.3). Other factors, such as a changed blend with reduced ash content, may have reduced the saleable tonnage at Horden during this period without reflecting any change in the amount of coal coming off the belts or the miners' effort. But it seems likely that at least a portion of the reduced rate of output between 1974-1976 implied by the data is due to the miners' indifference to productivity under the national daywage agreement which pays them regardless. At the same time, the evolution of political and laboring relations under the contemporary system of production at Horden indicates the possibility of a more complex dynamic at work.

POWER RELATIONS

Horden dispays a pattern of power relations typical of NPLA pits. Disputes occur occasionally which are reminiscent of piece-rate struggles, such as those over payment for the presence of water or a high concentration of dust on the coal face. But with nationally negotiated time-based

TABLE 4.3. Productivity Trends at Horden Colliery for G Seam, 1974-1976[a]

	1974	1975	Percentage Change 1974-1975	1976	Percentage Change 1975-1976[a]
Annual[b] average	6.95	5.25	−24.46	4.31	−17.90
November[c] average	7.34	4.90	−33.24	3.58	−26.94

SOURCE: NCB Computer Services, Northeast Area, Weekly Face Results.
[a] All figures represent saleable OMS/tons.
[b] Annual productivity averages are based on a set of incomplete weekly figures for each year.
[c] November productivity averages are based on complete weekly figures for 1974 and 1976 and figures for the first three weeks of November 1975.

wages, anomalous conditions are merely inconvenient or, at the worst, dangerous; they have no effect on wages and therefore are dealt with as secondary issues. Sometimes conflict develops over the grade of work under which a miner is being paid, the NUM demanding an upgrading which would increase the man's earnings. But the size and prominence of Horden makes it a colliery where management and labor relations take place more within the letter of national agreements than is the case at many of the smaller inland pits. "Horden is strictly power loading," confirms the lodge chairman. "There is no flexibility. If we think a man [deserves] a higher grade, they will upgrade him. It never comes to a [serious dispute]."

Because "everything is by the book and controlled by [it]," the pressure exerted on management by the local NUM is of two types: either to ensure that national agreements which, for example, govern compensation for work performed under extremely wet conditions, are observed; or to urge action on individual requests—to get an injured man a light job or work on the surface, to allow a man to change his shift, etc.

But even at a colliery like Horden, everything is not completely in accord with the stipulations of the NPLA. No colliery in Durham, it seems, works entirely by the book. The rules for working which developed under the cavilling/ marra system continue to determine the pattern of laboring relations at Horden and in turn influence power relations in a way which is unique to Durham coalmining. There are two processes at work.

First, the men unilaterally introduced a system of rotating positions on the coal face, despite the clear prohibition of any such cavilling mechanism under the NPLA. A regional NUM official explains the procedure at Horden, confirming the continued effect of pre-NPLA traditions of laboring relations.

> The whole power loading team is on the face. Say two or three men have bad conditions. Although cavilling

is not allowed, men make arrangements among themselves. . . . We say we'll have a change around, make
an arrangement before anything starts up. [Otherwise]
a man might be doing twice as much work and more
arduous.

The NUM official adds that although according to the NPLA
men working together at a face are "a *team* of power loaders
. . . [and] are supposed to do all the jobs on the face [as a
team]," the miners make arrangements among themselves
so that there end up being "specialized jobs." Thus, central
elements of the cavilling/marra tradition—assignment of
task and of position on the coal face—have been reintroduced by Horden colliers despite the provisions of the NPLA.

Second, miners at Horden have introduced restrictive
practices, comparable to those which were initiated by
hewers and putters under Wage Structure I. The NUM
official, speaking guardedly, identifies this development in
power relations.

We could restrict efforts, [it] could happen any time.
I won't say "restriction," let's say "work to rule." We
also say, "we should work to rule all the time," but
still they take chances, still do things, take risks. They
carry on the same sort of thing [as when a putter or
hewer would go slow]. They try to force a point. There
is definitely a restriction on output.

Today such restrictive practices cannot influence wage levels or rates as they did under Wage Structure I, and are
employed instead to pressure the local management over
manning, grading, etc. or to influence national negotiations. Disagreements concerning overtime are a special case
and have also led Horden men to institute restrictions on
output. Should coaling operations be performed during
overtime? How much overtime should there be? Historically, these issues separate Durham miners from most other
miners in Britain. From the moment of its formation in
1888, the Miners' Federation of Great Britain, representing

miners in Yorkshire, Lancashire, Cheshire, the Midlands, and Fifeshire, campaigned for the establishment of an eight-hour working day through legislative enactment. Led by Durham men, the National Union of Mineworkers—which represented miners from the coalfields of Durham, Northumberland, South Staffordshire, and South Wales—opposed the eight-hour day movement within the coal industry. Durham miners opposed it for one central reason: for hewers it would mean an *increase* of one, and in many cases, one and a half hours per day.[56] NUM officials in Durham recall the outlines of this history as justification for their contemporary opposition to overtime. Having fought for a seven-hour day a century ago, before the rest of the country had even begun the struggle for an eight-hour day, Durham pitmen are still opposed to an increase in the typical hours worked by colliers. The opposition to extensive overtime in general, and especially with regard to hewing operations, unites otherwise diverse opinion in the Durham coalfield. Using hypothetical language to confirm the use of restrictive practices without technically admitting contractual violations, the DMA official explains, "There is a lot of organized overtime which we don't agree with. This could cause a restriction in output. [For example], we do not do preparations [during regular shift time]. So overtime is not worked, in effect. [They] have to do preparations that shift, instead of working coal, so the whole shift is lost."

Summary

Despite an apparent lack of flexibility at an important, showcase, high-producing NPLA pit, traditional rules which govern laboring and power relations—assignment of task and position on the face, self-regulating restrictive practices which limit output—re-emerge at Horden. While the fact of declining productivity seems certain, the explanation remains less clear. No doubt lack of financial incentive reduces laboring effort to some extent, although technical problems, as the miners suggest, and changes in the saleable vend, may be strong contributing causes of the decline in OMS. The generative rules of the cavilling/marra tradition continue to determine the general contours of the politics of productivity at Horden, despite the presence of the NPLA, and at least sporadically, they figure in the decline of productivity. As will become clearer with the presentation of the Nottingham colliery studies, despite its technological and geological features comparable to an East Midlands or South Yorkshire pit, the system of production which emerges at Horden under the NPLA marks it very definitely as a Durham colliery.

CONCLUSION

These five underground anthropologies demonstrate the decisive effect of the cavilling/marra tradition on the systems of production which have emerged in Durham collieries. These habits and traditions of working—the laboring relations of Wage Structure I—introduce a firm regional pattern which overshadows the diversity of individual colliery outcomes in the unfolding dialectic of control. They are the key to understanding the effects of the NPLA on regional productivity, and they remain the core determinant of the systems of production in Sacriston and Eden, where the NPLA was never introduced (see Table 4.4).

As anticipated, the introduction of the NPLA effected a shift in the primary focus of labor-management conflict from explicit issues of pay to the issue of control over the organization of production. In Boldon there is frequent conflict over manning. In Horden and Rainton workers have forced management to accept the reintroduction of traditional mechanisms for worker self-regulation, such as cavilling and restrictive practices which limit output. Thus the three NPLA pits display the predicted patterns in their power relations, with conflict focused on issues of control over the organization of production. In Sacriston and Eden, the two pits which have remained independent of the NPLA,

TABLE 4.4. Summary of Systems of Production in Selected Durham Collieries

	Wage Structure I	Wage Structure II	Productivity	Power Relations
Boldon	cavilling/marra; DPLA	NPLA	declining; rate unknown	conflict over manning
Sacriston	cavilling/marra	cavilling/marra, with spot-bargained incentive bonus	improving	minimal conflict: absenteeism, breakdowns, and supply of materials
Eden	composite longwall (piece rate)	composite longwall with incentive bonus	stagnant or slightly declining	minimal conflict; infrequent disputes over manning
Rainton Adventure	bord and pillar, cavilling/marra	NPLA	steady or slightly improved at point of transition; declining in post-1974 period	conflict over absenteeism; introduction of cavilling
Horden	cavilling/marra	NPLA	declining	conflict over grading, application of national agreements, and individual requests; reintroduction of restrictive practices and procedure for rotation of face positions

conflict is minimal, and such disputes as do arise conform to a different pattern. In Sacriston, with its terrible geological conditions, the main issue which separates men and management is absenteeism. Even more striking, Sacriston men dispute with management about insufficient or tardy supply of materials—a mode of "conflict" which would seldom occur under a daywage structure. At Eden, conflicts about manning take place, but they are not as serious and persistent as those at Boldon, for example, and involve the peculiarities of the composite longwall system as it challenges the single-task orientation of the cavilling/marra tradition.

In general, pre-NPLA habits and traditions of laboring relations determined the meaning which Durham miners attributed to the NPLA, and hence conditioned the contemporary evolution of laboring relations. Although the comparison between Durham and Nottingham will show more clearly the way in which relations among miners under the NPLA depend upon the miners' previous work habits and attitudes, a comparison of Durham collieries begins to suggest the pattern. Among the three NPLA pits, differences between Rainton Adventure and Horden best indicate the effect of antecedent patterns of laboring relations on contemporary habits of working. At Rainton, traditional rules for self-regulated productivity which, under bord and pillar tend to promote worker effort and initiative, continued to sustain productivity during the transition from piece rate to NPLA daywage. Moreover, a reintroduction of cavilling under Wage Structure II acted simply to reinforce traditional laboring relations, which remain cooperative, even altruistic. At Horden, where restrictive practices have traditionally been applied to force management to accept higher piece-rate levels, self-regulation reemerged under the NPLA as a weapon against management and a contributing cause of declining productivity.

I argued above that the effect of new wage structures on productivity depended on the power relations and laboring relations which developed under the complex interaction of succeeding wage structures—and that these patterns, which displayed regional trends but also varied from colliery to colliery, might either aid or inhibit productivity. Again, although a full explanation of the effects of the NPLA on productivity must await comparison with Nottingham, the Durham colliery studies offer initial supporting evidence for my proposition. In Sacriston, where the generative rules for working show the most marked complementarity between Wage Structure I and Wage Structure II, the effects of the new wage structure on productivity are the most positive. In Boldon and Horden where the traditional rules for self-regulation under the cavilling/marra system are least compatible with the generative rules of the NPLA, the effects on productivity are the most negative.

Moreover, the central proposition that the effects of new wage structures can best be understood in the context of preexisting patterns of laboring relations seems to be generally confirmed by the Durham colliery studies. The technological/geological conditions at Horden are the most advantageous, and yet productivity is declining. If the NPLA is the fundamental cause of this decline, then why did productivity at Rainton remain steady or even improve slightly with the introduction of the same national daywage structure? If the introduction of an incentive bonus scheme is responsible for improved productivity at Sacriston, then why does a similar scheme at Eden have such disappointing consequences?

These results, I believe, are not as inexplicable as they might at first appear. In each of the five Durham collieries—as for the area in general—the specific characteristics of the contemporary systems of production are largely determined by the particular way in which the cavilling/marra tradition affects power and laboring relations under succeeding wage structures.

In Chapter Five, I offer an account of the systems of production which have emerged in five collieries in the very different Nottingham coalfield. Nottingham displays another side of the complex effects of wage structures on the politics of productivity in British coal mining. The best laid plans of the NCB again confront a regionally diverse industry whose workers consistently apply their own meanings to management's every initiative.

CHAPTER FIVE

NOTTINGHAM COLLIERY STUDIES

INTRODUCTION

It is commonplace for people in Nottingham who are associated with coalmining to stress two particular features about the industry they know: that the men are hard-working and that both the rank and file and the union are prepared to cooperate with management so long as they get a fair return for their efforts. As a consequence, on both sides of the industry Nottingham men feel constrained by the NPLA and embittered by a wage structure which, they believe, rewards slacking and petty militancy while it fails to provide any incentive for determined production. A member of the area NCB Wages Branch explains the Nottingham attitude well, providing a hint also of the unflattering opinion Nottingham miners often hold about their northern comrades.

> In this part of the world, we never wanted the NPLA. Traditionally it's been, you work first and argue about money afterwards. You'd got a job to do, you do the job. If you're not satisfied with the money, argue about it the next Friday. In other parts of the world, there's not the same attitude to work. When people came down from other parts of the world, they didn't immediately settle into the level of performance we were doing. . . . You'll have heard of Spencerism. It's an attitude of miners in the area. They are more willing to work hard for the money. . . . I'd not been working long, for three shillings per cubic yard [of hewing] and filling any mucking. That was extra. It was the devil's own fight to get that included. Several of the younger

chaps said, "We ought to be getting more money." Then you got the answer: "We'll have to have bigger stints, do an extra yard." It was not a question of asking for an extra twopence per yard. We never wanted the NPLA here.[1]

If one takes "other parts of the world" as a euphemism for low-producing or more militant regions (particularly Durham), the contrast between the two regions in laboring and power relations, in the meanings attributed to the NPLA, and hence in attitudes toward productivity, becomes clear. Where Durham men institute restrictive practices and rely upon traditions of self-regulation to secure control over the process of production or to combat an unfavorable industrial condition, Nottingham men work harder and longer to secure management cooperation and higher wages in exchange for their higher productivity. This generalization is an oversimplification, no doubt, but one which holds much truth about the two regions; it is believed by miners and management alike, in Durham, in Nottingham, and throughout the country. The "attitude of miners" referred to as Spencerism by the NCB official, which grew up alongside what I have called the butty/chargeman structure, defines the essential regional differences between the East Midlands and the northeast. Taken together, the wage structure and the union attitude are the critical influences upon the laboring and power relations which set Nottingham apart from Durham in its response to the introduction of the national daywage structure.

By the late nineteenth century, the distinctive Nottingham approach to mining—more production, more cooperation—was becoming readily apparent. "[R]elations between the coal-owners and the union were considerably easier in Nottinghamshire than in most other coalfields," wrote R. G. Searle-Barnes. "The explanation of this is no doubt largely to be found in the more favourable geological conditions enjoyed by many Nottinghamshire collieries.

Better conditions made for bigger tasks, higher profits and higher wages."[2]

Most commentators (including Searle-Barnes) qualify their praise for the East Midlands geology by noting that comparable physical conditions accompany far lower productivity, for example, in South Yorkshire. None, however, doubts that relations between management and men in Nottingham had taken a distinctive turn toward cooperation. As early as 1893, in the midst of the first national strike called by the Miners' Federation of Great Britain (MFGB), which struggled vainly against an effort by coalowners to effect a wage reduction of 25 percent in response to falling prices, the Nottingham miners set a pattern of withdrawing from the struggles of the national union. Nottinghamshire coalowners, who were able as always to make higher profits than their counterparts elsewhere in the country, urged Nottingham men to return to work without reductions. As soon as the Nottinghamshire Miners' Association (NMA) consented, local pitmen returned to work more than a month ahead of colliers elsewhere in Britain and on considerably better terms.

When in the aftermath of World War I the government belatedly moved to decontrol the industry, the MFGB fought to retain a national wages pool and to eliminate district relativities. The owners held firm, demanding a return to settlements based on separate regional ascertainments. Again, Nottingham miners and the NMA were trapped by their unique advantages as a high-producing and remunerative district.[3] With no agreement either in hand or in sight, a lockout accompanied the passage into law of the Coal Mines (Decontrol) Act in March 1921.

In June, districts were balloted on a package presented by the owners and the government for district rates, which were to be supported in part by a £10 state subsidy. All areas would suffer reductions from the rates which had held during wartime controls, but district rates meant differential losses for the colliers. With Nottingham the most secure financially, NMA men would lose the least. Of course, a national pooling arrangement, such as that proposed by the MFGB, would require the subsidizing of the poorer districts by the richer, and the long-run transfer of potential earnings from Nottingham into other coalfields. Accordingly, local miners showed no great enthusiasm for the MFGB's cause. In the ballot on the district-rates-plus-subsidy package, Nottingham voted narrowly in favor of the national earnings pool. But fewer than one-third of the NMA members bothered to vote at all. In a mild preview of the breakaway to come five years later in 1926, the Nottingham miners held firmly, if unenthusiastically, with the MFGB and stayed voluntarily locked out despite their collective regional self-interest. Explaining the significance for what was to come, A. R. Griffin writes of the chilling effect of the lockout on the determination and the local power of the NMA.

> Many of those who did not take the trouble to vote in the ballot to decide whether to continue or end the stoppage, were busily at work on the dirt-tips and outcrops. And many of them were to drop out of the union in the months ahead when they found themselves called upon to pay stiff levies to pay off the mountain of debt accumulated during the lockout. Here was a dispute where Nottingham stood to gain nothing. In defending a principle (which involved the permanent subsidization of the poorer counties by the richer, with Nottinghamshire as the chief loser from the arrangement), their members had suffered hardship and their Association had been financially crippled.[4]

Comparable financial issues faced the Nottingham miners in the 1926 strike. This time, under the influence of George Spencer, NMA general secretary, lack of enthusiasm was translated into explicit opposition to the national stoppage. While nationally the miners held out against ever more certain prospects of defeat, Spencer, who had opposed the stoppage from the beginning (but initially worked for its support), began to lead a drift back to work which was initiated by the rank and file itself. By October 1926, roughly 70 percent of Nottingham pitmen had accepted the coalowners' terms and returned to work. Events then followed quickly on the course toward a Nottingham breakaway from the MFGB.

Spencer negotiated terms for men to return to work at a number of collieries and was expelled for these efforts by the MFGB. Immediately, he formed the Nottinghamshire Miners' Industrial Union (NMIU) and gained sole negotiating rights with the owners for the breakaway union. Bringing together the nonpolitical trade unionists and the most reactionary employers, the Spencer Union, in alliance with the National Union of Seamen led by Havelock Wilson, for a very brief time appeared to pose an important alternative to the "political" stance of the Trades Union Congress (TUC). The Non-Political Trade Union Movement of Wilson and Spencer quickly lost influence, however, when the TUC legitimized its own version of nonpolitical unionism by embracing the Mondist policy of cooperation and rationalization at its 1927 national conference. Nevertheless, in Nottingham the NMA was effectively crushed until 1937, and "Spencerism" acquired a permanent place in the Nottingham trade union lexicon. More important, the influence of industrial unionism—quick to accept rationalization and unwavering in its opposition to the integration of local industrial disputes into broader labor movement strategies—remained strong in the Nottingham coalfield.

A vision of Nottingham's separate path and a conviction that the area loses through participation in a nationally based wages policy are very much alive today. At the same time, the fear that Nottingham will break away again when the time seems ripe is routinely expressed by Durham miners, who fought the longest in the 1926 struggle and feel very keenly their reliance in national disputes on the industrial strength of areas such as Nottingham. Proud of their rank-and-file efforts to secure a share of power on the

coal face despite a lackluster area leadership, Durham miners resent their Nottingham kin. The more militant northern pitmen consider their Midlands counterparts to be too
zealous in a battle for self-interest, working docilely under
very favorable geological conditions and accepting a kind
of stewardship from the area union which they appear
unwilling to countenance. The contrast between the two
regions in the attitudes of miners, as in the productive
potential, is stark. Nottingham is a high-producing area
where men cooperate with management, and rank-and-file
energies are directed at securing better rewards and ensuring the consistent possibility of high wages. Durham is
a low-producing area, where the union may cooperate, but
where the miners struggle at the coal face to secure not so
much higher wages as a measure of control over production
and some redress against harsh working conditions.

As Searle-Barnes wrote, "Quite a number of George
Spencer's arguments were to be heard again long after
Vesting date. More important, however, the Union in Nottinghamshire carried over into nationalization the policy of
cooperating fully in production matters and claiming their
share of the resultant benefits."[5] One crucial argument of
Spencer's, his opposition to national wage agreements which
would hurt the earning potential of Nottingham miners,
finds expression in opposition to the NPLA which is voiced
throughout Nottingham. Len Clarke, the president of the
Nottingham area union (who rejects the term "moderate"
for the term "responsible" in placing himself within the
spectrum of NUM politics) claims, "The NPLA is a disaster,
both for wages and productivity."[6] A local NCB official,
admitting that Clarke "would be annoyed to be called Spencerite," nevertheless insists that "Spencer would have been
quite happy [with Clarke]."[7]

Today in Nottingham it is hard to separate the influence
of Spencerism from that of the butty/chargeman system of
working. NCB officials confirm the influence of the butty
system on the discipline and on the attitudes toward work
of contemporary pitmen. Clearly, rank-and-file traditions

reflect the earlier competition for scant work and the drive to high productivity generated by the butty structure. Of course, there is no cavilling and no rotation. On the contrary, in the same colliery men may work year after year under different conditions, for different levels of pay, and think nothing of it. Surely they will never think of introducing a lottery system to standardize chances, preferring rather to seek selection for a position according to their taste for hard work and their appetite for greater reward. The presence of "market men," who do not have positions in face teams and who are ready to step in and replace a flagging regular face worker, helps maintain the pressure for high production.[8] In combination, the tradition of market men inherited from the butty system and the system of nonrotational locations on faces of unequal earnings potential induce habits of high productivity.

A former face worker at Ollerton Colliery captures this Nottingham attitude toward work.

> Generally speaking, one side of the pit—the south side—had coal which was very good. It was cool, well-ventilated. There was a good working height. On the north and east, the other side, it was warm, dustier, not such good conditions: difficult cleavage, you couldn't cut so much. There were those who wanted to work on the money side, also those who were harder working. So there was a process of exchange. A man would get old, have an accident. There would be a vacancy. Sometimes the manager wouldn't allow it, often he would. A market man would come onto the north and east, then [when there was a new vacancy] he would move onto the south side. You would work harder on the south side, fill big stints. On some other faces, you could work just as hard and get less money. There is an old saying, "good coal makes good colliers."[9]

As the five colliery studies which follow will indicate, good coal and appropriate generative rules for high productivity make good colliers, even under "bad" wage structures.

Located in a more unified region, with conditions and traditions less varied than those found in Durham, Nottingham collieries show relative consistency in their laboring and power relations. This fact tends to confirm my hypothesis that systems of production within the industry conform to strict regional patterns. The specific conditions of work, the web of evolutionary custom and practice agreements, the character of the local union branch, and the potential (and actual) productivity vary from colliery to colliery. But in all five Nottingham collieries—to a greater or lesser degree, and more or less directly—the dialectic of control at the coal face reflects the influence of the butty/ chargeman structure on the system of production which evolved under the NPLA along lines which clearly distinguish the Nottingham from the Durham coalfield.

First, I present Thoresby Colliery, a "typical pit," where the butty system directly influenced the habits of working right up to the introduction of the NPLA. With high productivity, a trace of sectional divisions among classes of workmen amidst generally cooperative power relations, and strong branch pressure to increase overtime working, Thoresby shows the general Nottingham pattern, both in the evolution of power and laboring relations, and in the development of the contemporary system of production under the NPLA. Sherwood, the second colliery, is a showcase Nottingham colliery where, despite the absence of an explicit butty structure, very determined and high productivity accompanies a pattern of extraordinary cooperation by a union branch which Spencer would have particularly admired.

The third colliery discussed below, Bevercotes, shows the pervasiveness of Nottingham habits of sustained productivity and cooperative relations, even in the face of extremely trying geological conditions and an encounter with unsuccessful experimental technology and unique wage structure innovations. Fourth, Harworth, a colliery with a tumultuous past and a strangely calm present, indicates the tendency for Nottingham rules of working to generate

placid power relations and sustain steady productivity, despite a location on the edge of Yorkshire and the inheritance
of an unusual reputation for disruption. Finally, Teversal,
a colliery facing closure but with a unified branch determined to keep the pit alive, demonstrates that even in the
case of extreme hostility between management and men,
the rules for working generated by the butty/chargeman
structure lead to a pattern of steady productivity. Taken
together, these five underground anthropologies indicate
a distinct regional pattern to the systems of production in
Nottingham's collieries. In providing a stark contrast to the
Durham patterns, these studies illustrate the decisive effects which laboring relations under antecedent wage structures have had on productivity and on the power relations
which have developed under the NPLA. At the same time,
the Nottingham colliery studies show that even under the
most favorable circumstances, the imposition of centralized
bureaucratic structures is a process fraught with complications and contradictions.

THORESBY

Summary / Description of Resources

A regional NCB official calls Thoresby "as typical as any
pit" one could find in Nottingham—"average sort of size,
reasonably good labor relations, fairly stable."[10] A union
official proudly confirms the judgment, assuring me, "as
Thoresby goes, so goes the county."[11] Reflecting the nonconfrontational power relations and consistent productivity of the Nottingham coalfield, Thoresby has ties with the
historical evolution of local laboring traditions which are
unusually direct. The pit was sunk during the 1926 strike.
An aging miner recalls that in the early years (production
commenced in 1928), the "management stipulated that if
you were not in the Spencer union, you did not have a
job." Both the Spencer union, which emphasized full cooperation with management in return for job security, and

the butty system, which set the character of laboring relations, come up frequently in the conversations of Thoresby men and not only as momentary reminiscences. "The
butty system came with the sinking of the pit," confirms
the branch secretary. "[The system] was in effect until 1939
or so . . . just before the war." Miners assert, however,
that "a sort of butty system" was practiced during the war.
The chargeman—ostensibly a low-ranking official on each
face who was intended to supervise and coordinate work,
ensure continuous provision of supplies, etc.—became a
sub rosa NCB "little butty." One rank-and-file miner recalls
bitterly:

> On each individual face, chargemen used to pay out.
> At individual places: back of the office, in the field.
> . . . A group of workers would get a wage. It was up
> to the chargeman or butty. As much as thirty men on
> one paynote [weekly wage bill]. . . . They would de-
> cide between themselves what was paid. No one could
> tell us about it.

Remarkably, the current branch secretary insists that,
according to his predecessor, there were vestiges of the
butty system right up to the introduction of the NPLA. "To
all intents and purposes it had been abolished," recalls the
official, "[but] there was a tendency to appoint by management 'super-chargemen' who would get paid extra in
order to organize [a particular job]." On development and
work on junctions between the face and tunnels, the organization was left to these chargemen-butties. Their orders superseded those of officials who were ostensibly their
superiors such as overmen and "possibly" undermanagers.
    From the start, Thoresby was a highly productive pit,
with production of 600,000 tons the first year, the coal
"com[ing] right off the shovel." Spencerism dominated. In
1934, only three Thoresby miners belonged to the Nottinghamshire Miners' Association,[12] and an old miner, asked
to explain the development of the butty system, linked the
wage structure to the character of the union. Implying that

behind-the-scenes deals had taken place between Spencerite officials and butties, he asserted: "It was the Spencer Union . . . and even then you couldn't attend meetings. You didn't know when they were held. There were lots of committee meetings, but not many political meetings."

With the effects of the butty system more direct than in most Nottingham collieries, and its presence felt much more recently, the generative rules of the old wage structure are manifestly present in this, the most typical of Nottingham pits. Power relations are cooperative, and laboring relations are geared instrumentally to sustain steady productivity. After a short downturn in the immediate post-NPLA period, production stabilized. Considering the contemporary effect on industrial relations at Thoresby of the resilience of the butty system, the branch secretary pinpoints Nottingham's distinctive character. "I don't think there was the sort of unity you got in the North," he muses. "It was a rat race [here] before the term was invented."

Wage Structure I

As early as 1953, the first District Power Loading Agreement which applied to Nottingham specified that men who worked on power loaded installations were to be paid a daywage rate plus a completion-of-task bonus. The latter typically amounted to about 10 percent of the fall-back rate.[13] Since the operations were strictly cyclical, however, and there was little opportunity for effort to be reflected in production in excess of completion of the cyclical task (e.g., the undercutting of a strip of coal), the bonus provided little incentive. Accordingly, when the NUM sought an increase in rates in 1957 at a point when new conveyor technologies had brought an element of continuous (noncyclical) mining to the industry, the NCB pressed for a new agreement which would be based on the application of method study. According to a pathbreaking agreement negotiated in August 1957, a method study production norm representing roughly 75 percent of the theoretical performance was agreed upon. Performance above or below the norm affects earnings on a pro rata basis, subject to corrections due to anomalous conditions, unavoidable machine delays, etc. The new base rate was 60 shillings per shift and the payment for "optimum performance" (defined as 133⅓ percent of method study norm) was set at 80s. When one realizes that the 1953 agreement paid 49s. 11d. plus 5s. completion-of-task bonus, the character of the incentive—and the size of the wage increase—with the transition to the Nottinghamshire Power Loading Agreement become obvious. Despite vigorous objections to the characterization by regional NCB staff, the Board, not unreasonably, considered the Nottinghamshire divisional agreement (hereafter referred to as DPLA) to be a use of method study which, instead of controlling task norms, tended to promote and justify higher levels of performance to which a higher level of earnings pressed by the union would inevitably be linked.[14] A piece-rate agreement which rewarded high, competitive productivity under close management scrutiny of manning and manpower assignment, the DPLA augmented the generative rules of the butty/chargeman structure. It therefore represents an important stage within the evolution of Wage Structure I, which helped transmit the rules of the butty system to miners who were working in the period just before the introduction of the national daywage agreement.

Due to the anachronistic presence of the butty system at Thoresby up to the very introduction of the NPLA on 59's face in June 1967, the DPLA contract system generated particularly strong tendencies for competitive laboring relations and determined productivity. Until 1968, face workers, rippers, and craftsmen, whether on the DPLA productivity agreements or on separately negotiated contracts, bargained directly with the chargeman or the undermanager. The unions were completely removed from the process, a fact which removed with it any possibility of consistent payment for equal effort or productivity. Thoresby's branch secretary recalls the arbitrary and direct manner in which arrangements were made between management and men: "Trade unionists had nothing to do. Union officials [were] not allowed in with the chargeman and the under-manager. It was difficult to find out who was getting what or how [the contracting parties] arrived at a price. The chargeman was almost a butty."

The chargeman, ostensibly selected through a process of joint consultation between the NCB and NUM but operating at Thoresby outside the normal framework of collective bargaining, was not an outright butty, acquiring a global sum of revenues and determining the wage shares for an entire colliery. But by negotiating incentives through secret arrangements with distinct work teams, the chargeman engendered laboring relations which broadly reproduced those of the earlier period. One difference between the character of the incentives in the butty system and that of Thoresby's Wage Structure I was repeatedly emphasized by the branch secretary. "Since the war," he stressed, "we've had incentive payments. Before that, the incentive was keeping your job." While the difference is critical, the generative rules which condition the habits of working are roughly comparable.

Thoresby Wage Structure I may be summarized in this way.

1. Identification: butty-chargeman/DPLA structure.
2. Form and level of payment: piece-rate earnings with DPLA as fall-back rate; competitively negotiated contract rates.
3. Generative Rules
   3.1 Assignment of position on coal face: by management prerogative, variation open to discretion of chargeman.
   3.2 Work pace and attitude toward productivity: effort regulated in part by power loading equipment; positive attitude toward productivity.
   3.3 Division of labor in primary work group: by

management prerogative; exercised by chargeman in consultation with team leaders.
3.4 Relationship among shift and task groups: competitive.

Wage Structure II

Thoresby entered the era of power loading and of the
national daywage reluctantly. The branch registered a clear
preference for the contract system, which offered generally
high rewards for productivity over the certainty of predetermined power loading rates. A series of resolutions
passed by the Thoresby Branch reveal this tendency. On
14 July 1963 the branch asked the Nottingham area to ban
further mechanization, complaining that a new stablehole
machine was interfering with wages. Discussion reflected
opposition to power loading and a consensus that men
were "not working well on the Notts power loading agreement." Eight months later, on the eighteenth of March,
the men voted to inform management that there was "no
desire to participate at Thoresby in the installation of pow-
ered-supports." While allowing the introduction of power
supports on a new face in June 1964, the branch continued
for two more years to voice its opposition to each attempt
at technological innovation and wage structure rationalization. On 11 July 1965 the branch requested a meeting
with management to protest the displacement of men as a
consequence of a recent innovation in the chocking (roof
support) system; on September 12, the branch voted to
oppose the introduction of any Remote Operated Longwall
Face (ROLF) just in case the Board, recognizing Thoresby's
favorable geological conditions and steady production record, might be considering experimentation there.[15]

Not opposed to innovation per se, the miners were used
to coordinating production cooperatively within the framework of management imperatives. Hence, the opposition
to power loading and to ROLF seems to reflect the laboring
relations of the butty/chargeman structure and the pro-

ductivity incentives of the Nottingham power loading agreement. The pitmen fought to preserve the potential of high contract earnings. When this imperative required opposition to management plans for innovation, that was the path the men took. Likewise, when productivity required a "me first" strategy against another work group, Thoresby men fought along strict sectoral lines. Accordingly, on 4 March 1965 the Thoresby Branch approved a resolution to ensure that front rippers got individual prices for each ripping lip rather than a colliery-wide price. The present branch secretary explained the reasoning, so typical of Nottingham, which lay behind this resolution: "[The men] wanted individual prices for each ripping lip. One side of the pit might be soft stone, the other hard and so on." Every chance they were given, the Thoresby miners preserved the differentials which geological chance and uneven technological innovation offered them. Similarly, despite a gradual movement toward acceptance of uniform wage levels, the very approval of the NPLA at Thoresby, fifteen months later, once again reflected the sectional interests of particular groups of workers.

Early in 1966, the tide began to turn in favor of power loading. On January 29, the Thoresby men expressed "recognition of the changing pattern of the coal industry," and asked for the Nottingham area to instruct the NUM National Executive Committee to establish a fixed rate for all men who worked on power loading teams. Clearly, the sentiment of Thoresby men, under pressure from the national leadership of the NUM, was moving in the direction of support for the NPLA. They were, a union official recalls, "convinced by this point that machinery [was] here to stay." But how convinced were they?

In May 1966, the NPLA proposals were put to the branches for consideration. A well-attended meeting drew two hundred, but only fifty attended the meeting of May 8, which was called to debate the critical issue of a fundamental shift in the wage structure. "Apathy. It can't be underestimated," recalls the branch secretary. "People did not realize how drastic a change [the introduction of NPLA] would make." Since most of the faces were long life faces, the vast majority of workers would stay on the old contract agreement. Consequently, the NPLA would not have a great effect on face workers in the short run. But the NPLA would in practice become a fall-back rate for colliers on existing piece-rate agreements, and would therefore benefit men in cases of machine breakdown or faulting conditions on the face. The branch official explains that "even if a man was against it in total, there were parts that were a real advantage." The face worker was, therefore, of two minds concerning the virtues of the NPLA. His general opposition to the NPLA and support for potentially higher piece-rate earnings was balanced by the guarantee which the new agreement would provide during periods of poor contract earnings.

For one set of workers, however, the question of the NPLA generated no such ambivalence. The new agreement would also include craftsmen who worked on the face team during coaling shifts. Searle-Barnes assesses the effect of the NPLA on the interests of craftsmen.

> These were the men who reaped the most benefit from the National Agreement. Overnight, they secured a massive wage increase without any extra work or responsibility. This increase was as much as 30s. per shift for the skilled face fitter or electrician and over 40s. per shift for the almost unskilled power supports maintenance man, practically doubling his wages.[16]

With this windfall in mind, the craftsmen put their support behind the NPLA at Thoresby, and neutralized the power of the ambivalent face workers. The vote tied at twenty-four for and twenty-four opposed, the chairman breaking the tie in favor of the national agreement. Throughout the period of the gradual transformation of the butty structure into the NPLA, sectoral divisions—craftsmen vs. face workers, rippers in soft stone vs. rippers in hard stone—determined Thoresby's attitude toward management and toward national NUM initiatives for change. These divisions, and the generative rules for competitive high productivity, would continue to fashion the laboring and power relations in the system of production which emerged in the NPLA era.

Thoresby Wage Structure II may be summarized in this way.

1. Identification: NPLA daywage structure.

2. Form and level of payment: time-based daywage at nationally negotiated NPLA rates; these serving as fallback rate for men on faces in operation under Wage Structure I; thereafter, NPLA rates tended to be substantially below the more favorable contract rates based on performance.

3. Generative Rules

   3.1 Assignment of position on coal face: by management prerogative.

   3.2 Work pace and attitude toward productivity: relative indifference to productivity.

   3.3 Division of labor in primary work group: formal cooperation.

   3.4 Relationship among shift and task groups: formal cooperation, but competition generated by distinct sectoral interests.

Systematic Pattern of Production

PRODUCTIVITY

Using an old colliers' idiom, the branch secretary tries to capture the motivation and working habits of the men who worked Thoresby in the early days after 1926. "A man worked his soul-case out. . . . If he fell foul of the butty, God help him." Neither the incentives nor the need for such soul-destroying effort—or such fear—remain with the miners at Thoresby. Nationalization removed most of the fear of losing a job through victimization. The Thoresby official links reduced effort first to mechanization, which lessens the need for intense physical exertion, and second, of course, to the daywage structure which removed the financial incentive. Nevertheless, while Thoresby men no longer wear themselves out as did earlier generations, productivity data suggest Thoresby's adherence to the Nottingham pattern of high productivity, even under the NPLA. The manager confirms these trends. "The discipline is quite good," he insists. "[Thoresby is] typical of the Notts attitude. They have always been used to working hard. We get twice the national average in OMS."[17]

In Thoresby, the NPLA was introduced as new power loaded faces began operations in late 1967 and early 1968. On the first new face, 69's, the transition to a daywage structure caused special problems. "On the first face that came under the NPLA, it was unfortunate that the men had very high contract earnings," recalls a union official. "The NPLA meant a reduction of £10-£16 per week. That really put the cat among the pigeons." Nevertheless, both by the general accounts of management and union officials and according to the available productivity data, Nottingham patterns of high productivity soon prevailed. The second year of production on 69's saw a percentage increase in productivity of 23.1 (see Table 5.1). On the second NPLA face, 80's, OMS/ton rose from 8.9 to 14.5 in the first twelve-month period (an increase of 62.5 percent), before declining to 8.1, for five quarters of production. While it is impossible to assess the independent influence of the NPLA agreement on these productivity trends, it is possible to speculate that after an initial negative reaction to the new agreement which significantly reduced the earnings of face workers, Thoresby men began to accommodate themselves to steady productivity under the daywage agreement. Accordingly, productivity trends conform to a typical trajectory: first, an initial period of moderate production during which productivity is conditioned by squabbles over manning, and production is limited by geological and technological settling-in problems; second, a period of peak production during the best months of the life of the

TABLE 5.1. Productivity Trends at Thoresby Colliery for Initial NPLA Faces[a]

	First Twelve-Month Period (1)	Second Twelve-Month Period (2)	Percentage Change (1)–(2)	Subsequent Duration of Face (3)	Percentage Change (2)–(3)
Average[b] 69's face	11.58	14.26	+23.14	—	—
Average[c] 80's face	8.93	14.51	+62.49	8.13	−43.97

SOURCE: NCB, North Nottinghamshire Area, Face Data Bank, Weekly History of Face Performance.

[a] Productivity measured in saleable tons output per face manshift.

[b] 69's face was worked from the last quarter of 1967 through the third quarter of 1969. Productivity averages are based on a set of monthly figures which represent tonnage rates for the last month of each quarter during the life of the face. Hence (1) covers the period October 1967–September 1968; (2) October 1968–September 1969. Production ceased before December 1969.

[c] 80's face was worked from the second quarter of 1968 through the second quarter of 1971. Productivity averages are based on a set of monthly figures which represent tonnage rates for the last month of each quarter during the life of the face. Hence (1) covers the period January 1968–December 1968; (2) January 1969–December 1969; and (3) January 1970 until the face ceased coaling operations in March 1971.

face; third, a period of decline when men labor under reduced coaling potential. Although the evidence is incomplete and Thoresby does not offer the possibility of the
most telling comparison—an evaluation of two faces which
are identical in every respect but wage structure—on one
point the data seem persuasive. There is no indication of
a decline in productivity at Thoresby's coal faces owing to
the introduction of the NPLA.

POWER RELATIONS

When asked how often and under what circumstances
the miners at Thoresby are likely to walk off the face, the
branch secretary replies in a matter-of-fact way: "All the
time. But I usually manage to contain it." The answer reveals a lot about the habits of Nottingham mining. The
comparison of Durham to Nottingham does not hinge on
a caricatured alternative of militancy vs. docile acquiescence to authority. Rather, in comparing the two regions
one sees that rank-and-file sentiment is in both places powerful and artfully directed—but the objects of industrial
action are different, as is the effect of militancy on productivity. Industrial relations at Thoresby are characterized
as "good" despite men walking off the face frequently,
because work stoppages are generally contained within a
work group and are of short duration. Most important,
they are not directed against productivity, and indeed the
generative rules for working appear to sustain a pattern of
high-level and determined production.

With the introduction of the NPLA, initial conflict focused, as it often does, on the composition of the power
loading teams and on manning. With the interests of craftsmen and face workers sharply divided on the acceptance
of the national daywage agreement, conflicts between these
groups of workers marked the settling-in period of the
NPLA. The agreement called for method study of the number of colliers on the power loading team, but remained
ambiguous on the number of craftsmen required. While
craftsmen fought for the inclusion of additional fitters and

electricians, and of categories of craft workmen—for example, hydraulic chock fitters—who were not mentioned specifically in the agreement, face workers struggled to increase their own numbers. The secretary recalls that the face men who suffered a serious decline in earnings asked for more men to make up the team, thereby to reduce their effort and set up a situation where they could work short-handed and, in practice, receive increased wages. At the same time, management "covertly wanted to stipulate a norm. They wouldn't say they wanted two strips, but the inference was there." An accommodation was reached. The Thoresby men produced their two strips and, as the above data suggest, after these initial settling-in conflicts, productivity took an upturn on the NPLA faces. Although manning issues and sectoral disputes between craftsmen and face workers were never altogether resolved, the power loading agreement, confirms the branch secretary, "was accepted without so much struggle—there didn't seem to be a big struggle against it."

The day-to-day walkouts are most often caused at Thoresby by resentment over the proliferation of underground supervision which accompanies the NPLA. "With four supervisors where we used to have one," the generally placid branch secretary argues, the annoyance obvious in his voice, "it's a wonder we haven't had more walkouts than we've had." He accepts that it is "natural that deputies and overmen are pushing a greater amount of effort," but complains that the miners resent the imposition of directions and control over face operations and the deployment of men when "very often [the deputies] could be wrong on why production is not there."

Thoresby men feel that when the capacities are there, the production is there. They object more to managerial tampering than to management's concern with productivity and output. Actually, the most significant industrial relations issue at Thoresby throughout the period of the NPLA is fought by the miners on the side of the NCB. Against the dictates of both national and Nottingham area

NUM resolutions, which restrict overtime to one coaling shift on weekends and not more than an additional half-hour at the end of a day's 7¼ hour shift, face workers want to increase overtime working.[18]

The problem of overtime has been felt at Thoresby from the very start of power loading. With no incentive increment for the face worker and minimal overtime working—frequently national guidelines have eliminated all coaling on overtime—differentials have narrowed, according to the branch secretary, "to such a degree that men working EBG [nonface work elsewhere below ground] make more with overtime, have higher gross wages than face workers." He is bitter that the wage structure makes it difficult to attract development men and provides "no incentive to get face workers of the right calibre and development men." He complains, "there are no differentials that reflect the fact that the face worker is important." The branch presses the area NUM for a relaxation of the overtime restrictions to allow five hours during the week plus one day on the weekend. Meetings of the Thoresby Branch when overtime is mentioned on the agenda "fill the hall."

At the same time, issues of overtime have brought the Thoresby union and management into a gentleman's conspiracy over the scale of wages to be paid for extra-shift workers. In the past, when a major underground job was scheduled for overtime, e.g., the laying of tracks for an underground transport system, the branch used to insist that face workers, who had little chance of overtime, be brought in. Recently, the area directed that colliers working during the weekend would have to be paid at the level (grade) appropriate to their regular underground classification. Informally, the management has manipulated the categorization of tasks by exaggerating the work done to ensure the higher rate of pay for face workers performing other tasks (e.g., dinting, the digging out of the floor when the strata has heaved). Thus, NUM restrictions on overtime have forced an unusual level of cooperation between the Thoresby Branch and the colliery-level NCB. The secretary admits, "the management aren't the bad lads they used to be. More often than not, they've been through the mill. [There is] a lot to be desired about them from our point of view."

Frequent localized walkouts or no, the relations between management and men at Thoresby are generally good, and for a very simple reason. Lost time means lost money, and the Thoresby Branch secretary, who is working such long hours that he greets the night shift coming off and the afternoon shift going on, dedicates himself to maintaining the production necessary for a full pay packet at the end of the week. "I've got a phone at home," he explains. "I'd rather they ring me. I'll straighten it out rather than lose money. . . . Last week. It's happening all the time. An argument with the gate end deputy about how the job should be done. The men simply got up and left. . . . I didn't know about it until they were out and bathed and gone home. They just lost money from the time they got up the pit. To me that's a tragedy." So, while the power relations at Thoresby are filled with little tragedies, the overall perspective is positive. The union goes by the conciliation procedures and, at least in a small way, has been forced by NUM overtime policy into cooperative relations with management. This, despite constant walk-outs, represents in pure form the Nottingham pattern of power relations.

Summary

A typical Nottingham pit if one can be found, Thoresby works quietly and well. The Board, looking to Nottingham as a mainstay of national production, presses Thoresby to set the positive pattern. There was therefore, by one account, "an arse-kicking session" with management because of a shortfall of 9,000 tons recently. But the Thoresby men seem to acknowledge the "burden" of this position. The branch secretary says with a rueful pride, "Thoresby pulls out Notts as Notts pulls out the country." More than favorable geological and technological conditions, the generative rules of working contribute to Thoresby's role. The historical nearness and the strength of the butty tradition mean a disciplined positive attitude toward productivity and an instinctive tendency toward cooperation with management. Both characteristics find an unusually able and knowledgeable architect in the current NUM branch secretary. Thoresby's consistency is therefore not circumstantial, but the explicit result of Nottingham's traditional laboring and power relations as they function under the NPLA.

SHERWOOD

Summary / Description of Resources

An official NCB mimeographed introduction to Sherwood Colliery, dated 1962, summarized the improvements in OMS which followed from a major colliery reorganization. This reorganization centered on the development of a conveyor haulage system to replace the use of wagons and locomotive, and also on the development of the thicker and generally productive Deep Soft seam to replace the uneconomic Dunsil seam.[19] Between 1954 and 1961, the colliery had increased saleable output from 495 thousand tons from ten face panels to over 625 thousand tons from just three panels. During the same period saleable face OMS tripled from 66.9 cwt. to an exceptionally high 192.9 cwt. But technical improvements are not the key to productivity at Sherwood, as management readily admits. In this same document, the NCB observed: "Whilst the reorganization laid the foundations for improvements by providing a more efficient transport system and tub handling facilities, all the improvements obtained in the Deep Soft seam cannot be claimed as a direct result of this."[20] Listing nearly a dozen additional factors, including face mechanization and maximum utilization of power loading machines, the Sherwood Colliery management recognized also the "[e]xcellent cooperation of workmen who readily accepted new types of machines and systems of work" and the "[g]reater control of face efficiency [which] ensure[d] maximum face productivity."[21] With a "we've been lucky so far, knock wood" approach, the report concluded with a section on the future:

> Having reached the present standard of efficiency, one asks the question, where do we go from here? It is envisaged that output will remain static and that improvements in efficiency will be forthcoming from the installation of stable hole machines, walking supports, ripping machines, high horsepower conveyors and so on. . . .[22]

A rare exception to the rule of excessive optimism in NCB public relations brochures, Sherwood's restrained projections proved very modest. By the mid-1970s, weekly face OMS regularly fell in the 350-400 cwt. range, and in one remarkable week, ending on 21 December 1974, the face OMS at Sherwood was 477.2 cwt. With the colliery pouring into NCB coffers an operating profit of over £3.94 million in 1975-76,[23] the Sherwood men and management were clearly doing nearly everything right. A Nottingham area NCB industrial relations official says simply, "Sherwood is a typical family pit with a very stable labor force, in an old, urban area. Everything goes well. There is never trouble. It has the highest OMS [in the North Nottingham area] although, geologically, it is working in very indifferent conditions."[24]

Sherwood is the rule that proves all other Nottingham collieries to be exceptions. With a crisp tradition of contract wage structures which generated rules for high and very determined productivity, the transition from the incentive structure to the daywage left productivity on a rising trajectory. Even in the ripping operation, where adequate mechanization was slow to follow the introduction of power loading on the face operation and the NCB complained of decreased performance combined with inflated manning of teams, Sherwood productivity held firm. Power relations are still positive, in a firm neo-Spencerite mold, the men more virulently at odds with the NUM overtime restrictions than with any NCB policy, save that of the daywage itself. Sherwood is a manager's dream, despite a strong and unified NUM branch—or indeed because of the steady contribution of the union to cooperation and productivity. This colliery symbolizes the NCB's best hope for the NPLA under typical geological and technological conditions.

Wage Structure I

If Sherwood ever worked under the butty system, the historical memory has dimmed. Before power loading, the colliers worked on piece-rate contracts, until the introduction of the Nottingham power loading agreement in 1957. Given the enthusiasm at Sherwood for incentive agreements, it is perhaps not surprising that, despite the miners' ambivalent feelings toward an era when job security was minimal and the physical burden of the work far greater than today, Wage Structure I is remembered more fondly than elsewhere. "The old contracts weren't popular," begins the branch secretary on a cautionary note. "It was not a popular system at all. You always had the feeling of being robbed . . . of not getting what you were entitled to."[25] But, warming to the subject and appearing to focus on the ever-present issue of incentives and wage levels, the Sherwood union official executes a right-angle turn on the subject. "Having said that," he laments, "they [the old contracts] were a means of increasing wages. You worked as hard as you wanted to and controlled your own living standards." The branch secretary, who consistently reflects Sherwood sentiment, went on to criticize the National Power Loading Agreement and, gaining steam, he concluded: "The other [contract] system was not popular, but much preferred [to the daywage]."

Regulating production upward in the classic Nottingham pattern rather than restricting and controlling production downward, as Durham men might, the Sherwood colliers

made a great success, also, of the DPLA. Having introduced an Anderton Shearer Loader in July 1956, Sherwood
went immediately on the Nottingham Agreement in 1957,
which included a daywage minimum and a pro rata bonus
for production in excess of 75 percent method study standard. Whereas elsewhere pitmen objected to the introduction of method study techniques or attempted to inflate
manning requirements regardless of method study norms,
at Sherwood little controversy accompanied the introduction of the district agreement. The union secretary accompanied the method study team to "observe and if necessary
give advice on the timing measurements." The NUM branch
members took a positive interest in these studies and, according to management sources, "[a]t no time was there
any reluctance on the part of the workmen or the union
representatives" to accept the application of method study
techniques.[26] Accordingly, Sherwood represents a textbook
example of the piece-rate contract/DPLA wage structure.

Sherwood Wage Structure I may be summarized in this
way.

1. Identification: DPLA/contract structure.
2. Form and level of payment: piece-rate earnings on
separate task contracts with fall-back area DPLA rate.
3. Generative Rules
    3.1 Assignment of position on coal face: by man-
        agement prerogative, exercised in consultation
        with union and according to method study re-
        quirements.
    3.2 Work pace and attitude toward productivity: ef-
        fort regulated in part by power loading equip-
        ment; very positive attitude toward productiv-
        ity.
    3.3 Division of labor in primary work group: by
        management prerogative, exercised in consul-
        tation with union and according to method study
        requirements.

3.4 Relationship among shift and task groups: ostensibly cooperative.

Wage Structure II

Asked to explain the change in performance at Sherwood with the transition to the NPLA, the colliery manager observed: "It's partly a habit to get the shearer through the face as quick as they could. I didn't notice such a big change when the NPLA came in." There is no reason to doubt his judgment about productivity or his attention to the habits of working which, for Sherwood men, consistently generate disciplined high productivity. From another perspective, the branch secretary's constant plea for a return to an incentive structure reflects this urgent pride in keeping the coal coming off the face at the greatest rate possible within the bounds of safety. "We have to produce what we earn," is the way he rephrases the miners' age-old claim—a fair day's pay for a fair day's work—to reflect Sherwood's unique drive for production.

The issues of deployment and manning reenforce the impression of Sherwood as a showcase colliery for the NCB wage structures. Two critical clauses of the NPLA require, first, that the "selection of men who are to comprise a power loading team shall be made by management, after consultation with the union," and second, that members of the work team "shall fully cooperate with management with the object of achieving the best possible utilisation of power loading machines throughout the full time of each shift."[27] While the letter of the contract unambiguously requires the cooperation of the union and the workers in accepting the interchangeability of workers among different tasks, the practices in many collieries are altogether more clouded. Rarely will a ripper, for example, do face work.

Not so at Sherwood where deployment is by the book, and the letter of the contract is also the spirit the union takes into its work. With obvious pride the branch secretary confirms the willingness of his men to discuss deployment with management, stick by their decisions, and make the NPLA work by accepting interchangeability. "In some pits, say you are a ripper and there is no job: you go down to do ripping even if the job is not available. Here we always run the NPLA like it's meant to be run. We do any job as long as there is no loss in pay." The management does not need to call in market men to "go on ripping or go on chocks," and there is no destabilizing assignment and reassignment of jobs so that men, "by the time they get underground have swapped back and forth." On the contrary, Sherwood expresses the NCB's fondest hopes for systematically planned and coordinated production with the NPLA, through flexible deployment which would not be disputed since wage issues were not involved. Time and again the branch secretary expresses his belief, at the level of an ethical obligation, that the union, since it is a party to agreements, must abide by the agreements. Deployment is a critical case in point.

> We say: it doesn't matter what job a man does. As long as the man is making money, what difference does it make? We take the attitude, as long as you are marching you are out there fighting. Here, there is no objection [to redeployment]: we go anywhere as long as the money is right. . . . [there is] strong interchangeability.

As the productivity data will reveal, the Sherwood men—despite dismay over the withdrawal of incentives and the loss of differentials and absolute wages by rippers in particular with the introduction of the NPLA—have made the daywage structure a success to a degree which even the NCB itself fails to recognize. With the geological and technological conditions no better than the Nottingham—or for that matter the Yorkshire—norm, the habits of working generated under Wage Structure I and doggedly pursued under Wage Structure II provide a large part of the explanation for the colliery's exceptional success.

Sherwood Wage Structure II may be summarize in this way.

1. Identification: NPLA daywage structure.
2. Form and level of payment: time-based payment at nationally negotiated NPLA rates.
3. Generative Rules
    3.1 Assignment of position on coal face: strictly by management prerogative, exercised in cooperation with branch officials.
    3.2 Work pace and attitude toward productivity: quick pace and positive attitude toward productivity, despite formal unconcern with output.
    3.3 Division of labor in primary work group: full (and not just formal) cooperation.
    3.4 Relationship among shift and task group: full (and not just formal) cooperation.

Systematic Pattern of Production

PRODUCTIVITY

According to insiders' conventional wisdom, the ripping operation, where exceptional effort is required and technological innovation has consistently lagged behind that found in the face coaling operation, best displays the decline in performance effected by the NPLA. Writing in 1969, as the results of the introduction of the daywage on power loaded faces were being evaluated by the NCB, Searle-Barnes explained the apparent negative effect of the NPLA on the completion of the ripping task:

> When existing faces finished and face rippers were incorporated in power loading teams on new daywage faces, they incurred, almost without exception, a significant reduction in wages. It was unlikely to average less than £5 per week and could amount to nearly £15 per week. It is hardly surprising therefore that on every new face ripping tasks, expressed in inches of advance

per manshift, have failed to reach the average ripping
task achieved on faces still operating on an incentive
basis. . . . On the vast majority of new faces . . . ripping tasks have been far below those achieved on incentive faces.[28]

At Sherwood, on the contrary, despite a great loss in relative and absolute earnings suffered by rippers with the
introduction of the NPLA, no fall-off in task completion
rate is evident. Likewise, general performance in coaling
operations on comparable faces, worked by the same primary teams, indicates increased productivity throughout
the period of implementation of the NPLA.

The resilience of the ripping teams' productivity is perhaps the most remarkable evidence of Sherwood's rules of
working. The performance in the gate ends, even more
than that on the coal face, suggests Sherwood miners' unique
combination of ostensibly contradictory attitudes: on the
one hand, utter dismay at the withdrawal of incentive wage
structures; on the other hand, uncanny devotion to the
ends of high productivity through consistent effort, whatever the wage structure.

In February 1971, when the 12's face ceased production,
work teams moved off contract and onto the new 32's face
where the NPLA was introduced, the geological and technological conditions remaining roughly similar (see Table
5.2). Measured in average advance in inches per manshift,
the performance of the Loader Gate ripping teams held
firm, with the average advance 12.9 inches for both the
12's and the 32's panel, considering the entire life of the
face in each case. Remarkably, in the Supply Gate, the
average advance actually improved 17.1 percent from 12.1
inches per manshift on the 12's panel to 15.8 inches per
manshift on the 32's panel. Although there is no clear explanation for *improved* performance in the Supply Gate, the
increased performance per manshift may be due to the
reduction of the ripping team from five to four men, with
the introduction of the boom ripper and the dirt slusher to

TABLE 5.2. Comparison of Performance of
Ripping Teams Before and After the Introduction of the
NPLA at Sherwood Colliery

	Leader Gate Rip	Supply Gate Rip
12's (Pre-NPLA) Average advance (inches/manshift)	12.9	13.1
32's (NPLA) Average advance (inches/manshift)	12.9	15.8
Percentage change 12's–32's	0	+17.1

SOURCE: NCB, Sherwood Colliery, Weekly Performance Charts Arranged by Task and Face.

NOTE: Performance is measured in inches advanced per manshift. All averages were compiled by Sherwood Colliery NCB officials and are based on weekly data for the period covering the full life of each face: for 12's face, February 1965–February 1971; for 32's face, January 1971–March 1974. For 32's face the periods from 12 November 1972 to 17 March 1973 (when there were serious geological problems in the gates) and from 15 January 1972 to 4 March 1972 (when work was interrupted due to a national strike) are omitted. At Sherwood, 32's face replaced 12's face, the general features which influence productivity are broadly similar (except for the wage structure), and the ripping operations were performed by the same (or nearly the same) work teams.

complete the mechanization of the ripping operation. The sustained effort by rippers despite a complete loss of their differentials in comparison to face workers—as late as 1968 rippers routinely earned one-third more than face workers—remains an impressive indication of Sherwood's habits of working. The branch secretary, discussing the difficulty of getting young colliers to volunteer for ripping and then keeping them up to the traditional level of productivity, warns, "Differentials have been destroyed. In destroying differentials, you've destroyed the incentive." Incentive or not, the performance has remained steady. Particularly in the absence of explicit payment by results, one is drawn for an explanation to the notion of Nottingham habits of persistent high productivity, which are particularly pronounced at Sherwood. There is no other way to explain the steady performance of the ripping teams, where both NCB and NUM officials least expected to find a constant level of productivity.

A comparison of productivity by face teams who moved from contract earnings on 12's face to the NPLA on 32's, reveals a like pattern of sustained productivity (see Table 5.3). Despite a downturn in the average face OMS/CWT during the second annual production period of 32's face (due to adverse geological conditions which plagued productivity throughout the subsequent life of the face), productivity on the NPLA face exceeded that of the same work team on the incentive face by 40.3 OMS/CWT (or 15.1 percent) for the total life of the two faces. Within the range of discrepancies in production which may be attributed to incidental geological anomalies and to minor changes in technological capacities, the data therefore indicate a pattern, on both ripping and face work, of sustained and determined productivity under the NPLA at Sherwood.

POWER RELATIONS

"I firmly believe in the maxim 'respect commands respect,' " explains the branch secretary. "A lot of people say, 'Why in bloody hell should we call the manager mister.' All I can say is, he calls me mister." Starting from the premise of respect, further conditioned by habits of cooperation and the potential of consistent high productivity, the power relations at Sherwood are decidedly nonconflictual. The branch secretary admits that there is a "strong memory of Spencer's union and always will be." Accordingly, there is no branch which more closely follows the Nottingham rule of full cooperation in production matters in exchange for such benefits as may be won from management through good relations. Indeed, the situation may

TABLE 5.3. Comparison of Productivity by Face Teams Before and After the Introduction of the NPLA at Sherwood Colliery[a]

	First Annual Production Period	Second Annual Production Period	Subsequent Production Period to Exhaustion	Total for Life of Face
12's Average[b] Face OMS/CWTS	243.7	292.7	—	266.4
32's Average[c] Face OMS/CWTS	378.9	256.2	263.4	306.7

SOURCE: NCB, Sherwood Colliery, Weekly Performance Charts.

[a] Productivity is measured in saleable CWTS output per face manshift.

[b] For 12's face, the first period runs from 4 April 1969 to 28 March 1970; the second period runs from 4 April 1970 to 6 February 1971, when the face ceased coaling production. All dates represent the last day of a week to which the production records refer. Figures represent complete weekly records for production for the annual periods considered. The early life of the face, from the start of production during February 1965 to the week ending 29 March 1969, is omitted for lack of appropriately detailed data.

[c] For 32's face, the first period runs from 13 February 1971 to 25 March 1972; the second period runs from 1 April 1972 to 31 March 1973; and the subsequent period runs from 7 April 1973 to 30 March 1974, when the face ceased coaling production. All dates represent complete weekly records for production for the annual periods considered and for the life of the face except for the following; the weeks ending 30 January 1971 and 6 February 1971 are excluded as settling-in periods during which the face was not in full operation with regular team members; the period from 12 November 1972 to 17 March 1973, when there was little or no production due to bad geological conditions in the gates; and the period from 15 January 1972 to 4 March 1972 when work was interrupted due to the national strike. At Sherwood, 32's face replaced 12's face, the general features which influence productivity are broadly similar (except for the wage structure), and the two faces were worked by the same work team.

go one step beyond the common view of cooperative management-labor relations. The secretary insists that the union
expects the management to do its part to facilitate production. As he explains, the branch is prepared to keep the
management to its half of the high production bargain.

> At Sherwood we have a sense of an honest day's work
> for an honest day's pay. . . . If management does
> something and the men believe it's going to stop them
> from producing coal, we will go into management and
> say, "What's your game? Your job is to make condi-
> tions to allow us to produce coal."

Management will hardly object to power relations oriented this way, nor will the branch generate many areas
of conflict. The manager, asked to characterize the issues
which force confrontation at Sherwood, claims that there
are "no daily disputes," and that there has been only one
walkout "in memory." The issue which led to a walkout,
confirmed by the branch secretary, involved a disagreement over the appropriate job classification ("grading") for
the workers who survey the face (the "lines' lads"). The
secretary, reassuring me that he "wasn't proud to do it,"
called the men out on strike. Perhaps realizing that his
acknowledgment of discomfort in the face of confrontation
might be misconstrued as a sign of timidity or excessive
moderation, he explained that the men were also in dispute
for two years over an issue of release time from work for
NUM members who were asked to greet a visiting digni-
tary. Having reached no agreement over an incident in May
1974, the branch secretary cautions that for the time being,
"if the Queen comes, she won't meet anyone in the NUM."

The issue, while not telling in itself, seems important to
the Sherwood Branch. The secretary uses the example to
illustrate Sherwood's militancy, despite its unparalleled cooperation on matters of production. "Sherwood is not the
most militant colliery in the country," allows the branch
secretary, "but we stand together better than anyone else."
Later, he confirms the central point of his illustration, ex-

plaining again for emphasis why none of the men would entertain any dignitaries while the impasse remained.

> When Sherwood men say they're not going to do something, they really mean it. No man who received a letter to come would come. There is strength and strength, in being militant. [Generally] the pits called moderate are the most militant: the men stick together through thick and thin.

Both this statement and the secretary's subsequent illustration of militancy by reference to the issue of overtime working reveal a lot about power relations at Sherwood.

As the dual nature of the overtime controversy indicates, militancy at Sherwood works to ensure high wage levels in return for consistent effort, and it is directed as often against the NUM as against the NCB. Against management, the branch insists that an entire team must work any overtime shift and share the benefit of increased weekly earnings. Management has agreed to this principle, despite the advantages to the Board of assigning men only as needed to perform particular tasks. The struggle against the union on the issue of overtime, however, promises to continue without resolution.

Area NUM policy limits coal production to "the period of a workman's five normal shifts."[29] Moreover, according to the policy, any overtime "required in the interests of safety" which would result in coal production outside the 7¼ hour shift periods requires prior authorization by the area NUM.[30] At Sherwood, coal is produced by a uni-shearing system (i.e., a machine which undercuts the coal in one direction), whereas most cutting equipment shears the coal back and forth along the face. This situation opens the way for conflict between the Sherwood Branch and the area NUM.

Sherwood face workers routinely return the machine to a "place of safety" and shore up the roof supports during overtime.[31] The men on the day shift, therefore, work one hour overtime daily, and the men on night shift work two additional hours. The branch secretary insists that since the men cannot, for reasons of safety, leave the machine "where it stands" at the end of 7¼ hours, there are two additional possibilities. Either Sherwood men abide by the NPLA and fully cooperate with management, the result being a fair complement of overtime, or they do not begin work on an additional strip if, in the judgment of the face team, there will not be time by the shift's close to return the machine to a safe position. Since the latter strategy would reduce coaling time by as much as two hours each shift, the choice of the former strategy seems obvious for Sherwood men. Habits of high, determined productivity and cooperative power relations with management require it. Not only that, but as the branch secretary admits, the securing of illicit overtime is "the only way face workers have for increasing earnings." The area union, meanwhile, repeatedly calls Sherwood on the carpet for violating the overtime policy.[32] No resolution of the intraunion conflict seems imminent.

In a truly Spencerian argument, the Sherwood secretary insists that full cooperation with management to ensure production, even when it pits branch against area NUM, has its concrete rewards. There are benefits, says the secretary with an air of shared conspiracy, which only Sherwood men have won: nine hours of pay despite eight hours of work for men driving "locos" above ground; the upward shifting of gradings for several sets of workers who may thus secure wages in excess of national agreements; the payment of machine drivers as chargemen, etc. High productivity secures an atmosphere in which cooperation rewards cooperation. This pattern seems fixed and inviolable at Sherwood, and yet the men, maintaining habits of determined productive effort despite the removal of financial incentives, seek a more explicit and certain pay-off for their high productivity.

Summary

Sherwood colliers produce a piece-rate tonnage under a daywage agreement. The branch wants the imbalance between pay and productivity redressed, regardless of national policy. The secretary has tried to negotiate a separate contract with the Nottingham area NCB which would provide a productivity bonus. He laments the opportunities passed up at the national level, noting what an incentive agreement, such as that defeated at the national level in 1974, would have meant to his men. "I would calculate that my men have lost £3,000 per man," states the branch secretary boldly, producing detailed figures based on weekly tonnage compared to standard performance. "That's a lot of money. . . . This pit can afford [to pay] it." The finances aside, the NCB blankly refuses to negotiate a separate incentive scheme with Sherwood. "If the agreement is not [reached] legitimately, it is not worth doing at all," argues a high-ranking regional NCB official. "All you do is set the hares running elsewhere."

The branch secretary spiritedly insists, "I do not really consider myself in Spencer's tradition," and decries the proclivity of national union officials to assert that Nottingham will "go back to Spencerism." But the parallel is plain. The Sherwood Branch today, like Spencer's union, argues that management can be persuaded to pay at a level commensurate with what Nottingham can produce with determined Nottingham miners. The Spencer tradition of high productivity and full productive cooperation in exchange for positive financial considerations, which is alive throughout Nottingham, remains particularly powerful at Sherwood. Of course, even Sherwood is not truly Spencerite, for there would never be a breakaway. But it is the quintessential Nottingham pit in performance as in the politics of productivity.

BEVERCOTES

Summary / Description of Resources

The NCB works hard to embellish mining's new image. From time to time a newspaper article on the miners' newest wage demand or the Board's latest plan for coal will include a reassuring photograph. It has become a set piece: a miner, virile and handsomely tousled after a hard day at the pit, smiling vacuously. A little overworked to be sure, but cleansed by his honest labors, the young pitman has his attention focused apparently on the dance that night at the miners' welfare (workingmen's club) or on the hot meal awaiting him in the canteen on his way home to the color telly. The NCB public relations department has even produced a promotional pamphlet for recruitment which features multicolored day glow pits and colliers on fast motorcycles with pretty girls in tow. Among the selling points mouthed by such a "disco-collier" after his first day down the pit is the notable platitude: "Unless you're a ruddy genius you've got to aim for something steady— where you're turning out something that's *really* wanted . . . like COAL!"[33]

Beneath this Fleet Street and Hobart House fantasy of the "new" coal industry, Bevercotes Colliery reveals a lot about the practical failures of modernization through technological innovation and the disappointing results of nearly unlimited capital investment in the face of insurmountable geological difficulties. With seams which are 5½ feet high Bevercotes was, as one management official put it, thinking about the narrow seams of Durham mines, "a Geordie's heaven."[34] It was the Coal Board's pet project when full-scale production began in 1967, an offshoot of the white-hot technological revolution, the "most modern pit in Europe." While pit ponies still labored in Rainton and a dozen other collieries in Britain, the operations at Bevercotes were to be remote-operated. A central controller sitting underground before a futuristic console of dials and gauges would direct the operation for a specific "control sector" of the underground installation. By push-button control, he would regulate the remotely operated longwall faces; the underground transport of coal, men, materials, and dirt; access and egress through two mine shafts; and operations both in the coal preparation plant and in surface and underground ancillary operations. The "cutting horizon" of the power loading equipment—shearer loaders taking a twenty-four inch strip of coal with each run—would be "determined by a radioactive source." Power supply equipment for the face operation and machinery for the gate would be transported by a rail-mounted structure which ran along a chain conveyor, all controlled by remote signal and called a "pantechnicon." There was no end to the innovations intended for this twenty-first century operation. Information regarding the operational state of the "plant"—you can hardly call this subterranean dwelling a "pit" and the official brochures seldom apply the word "colliery"—would be transmitted by visual eight-light indicators in a "mimic display unit" in the control centers. Manning would be through an electronic deployment system. The position of each workman would be transmitted to the control console, deployment boards would be set up for scanning these positions, and the information reproduced on punched tape as the basis of a time-keeping account for each collier. From the punched tape the divisional computer facility would "produce the weekly payroll without further direct labour."[35]

Most important, a space-age technology required a compatible, and equally innovative, wage structure. Even the ROLF Agreement completed in 1965 and designed precisely for operations such as that envisioned at Bevercotes would not do, since the NCB officials wanted their capital investment at Bevercotes to have the advantage of a continuous twenty-four-hour-a-day, seven-day-a-week operation. Accordingly, Sidney Ford, NUM president, spoke for both sides of the industry when, amidst grumblings from the Nottingham area, he assured the press in October 1966 that the NUM supported both aspects of the experiment at Bevercotes:

> The N.E.C. [National Executive Committee of the NUM] today considered the position of Bevercotes Colliery. As you will know, Bevercotes Colliery will incorporate

the latest techniques of coal getting and the National Union and the Board hoped it could be used to experiment not only on coal getting operations but with new concepts of wages and conditions of employment. To this end we sought to draw up an agreement setting out the wages and conditions of employment at Bevercotes which was completely different to the existing National Agreements.[36]

The NUM executive continued to seek such an agreement and ultimately prevailed, producing local and Nottingham area consent for a special Bevercotes wages structure which operated for three years. But the agreement was scrapped in 1970, never becoming the prototype for national agreements as the NCB hoped. Likewise, by the end of the initial three-year experimental period, technological failures and unanticipated geological problems had shattered the Bevercotes dream.

When I went down the pit in the summer of 1976, the control rooms were empty and unused, the face operations performed by conventional power loading methods and paid under existing national power loading agreements. As the branch secretary put it, "Technologically they tried to run before they could walk."[37] Repeatedly, I was told stories of technological buffoonery and public relations gimmickry. When a member of the royal family was on hand to witness the inaugural operation of Bevercote's ROLF system in January 1967 he was—so the story goes—witness to an elaborate fraud, since the coal had been supplied from a neighboring colliery and placed upon remote-controlled conveyors. Bevercotes' own power loading equipment, it seems, was not in working order. The system was constantly breaking down. The shearer, for example, operating by sensors triggered by radioactive isotopes, failed to distinguish between a thin band of dirt running through the middle of a seam and the top edge of the seam. As a result, the machine was set to the wrong height and the coaling operation was crippled. Shearers, experimentally directed by laser beams along the face, failed to accommodate themselves to sudden changes in the position of the face, which traversed sharp inclines and shifted from side to side.

Technological difficulties were compounded by extraordinary geological misfortune. As a member of the NCB staff at Bevercotes recalled bitterly, "Twenty-foot faults. They don't tell you about twenty-foot faults." Beyond the very irregular wanderings of the precious band of coal among the worthless strata, the NCB also was caught unawares by the persistent cross-cutting of deposits of shale with the coal. As a result, men on each coal face operating in 1976 at some point along the face encountered a thickness of a foot or more of oil. Conditions on the face are worsened by heat as great as ninety-five degrees in the gate ends where arduous ripping operations are performed. From the original four-quadrant design for the colliery, less than one-half of a single quadrant is workable.

No longer the wave of the future, Bevercotes has passed through its unique initial wage structure which allowed continuous operation according to the "continental system," and has operated since 1970 under existing national agreements. With this separate history, it is no surprise that the details of Bevercotes' systematic pattern of production depart from the general Nottingham mold. But the general patterns in the politics of productivity are seen. Since both Wage Structure I and Wage Structure II were time-based wages which generated relative indifference to productivity, power relations reflected conflict over control of production. Within the generally inflexible format of a nationally monitored showcase agreement, conflict focused on incidental grievances and on spot-bargained incentives to promote productivity, a pattern which in general remained intact in the post-NPLA period. Since the habits and traditions of laboring relations under the Bevercotes Agreement complemented those of the NPLA, both the power relations and the productivity itself remained stable within the limits set by adverse geological conditions and persistent technological miscalculations.

Wage Structure I

In Bevercotes alone, Wage Structure I was not inherited, but imposed. After work was discontinued on two short-lived faces which operated by piece-rate contracts in 1960-61, the colliery faced entirely new technological and wage prospects as the experimental reopening in January 1967 approached. From the beginning, Bevercotes was set apart from other ROLF installations. In agreement with the NCB, the NUM National Executive Committee insisted that Bevercotes "would incorporate the latest techniques of coal-getting and would be used to experiment with new concepts of wages and conditions of employment."[38] Private minutes of the Nottingham area NUM reveal a sharp and growing conflict between the area and the NEC over control of Bevercotes' fate. While national officials of the NUM argued strenuously that fierce competition from alternative sources of energy made it imperative that the coal industry have the opportunity of experimenting with new ideas both in the field of automation and in industrial relations,[39] Nottingham wavered and Bevercotes Colliery declined the honor.

With initial presentations from the Board rejected by the Nottingham NUM in May (and subsequently in August) 1966,[40] the National Executive of the NUM admitted blandly that "[s]ome difference of opinion" had initially arisen between the Nottingham area and the NEC over "the character of the administrative arrangements to be operated."[41] To assuage their worst fears, the NUM president assured the press that there was "no question of Luddism, nor any question of the NUM or its members preventing Bevercotes from commencing production."[42] The NEC publicly pressured the Board to open the colliery according to the agreed national ROLF Agreement and forsake its design of seven-day production. Privately, however, they insisted that the subsequent statement by the NCB that they intended to follow this prescription—that is, to open the pit under the existing ROLF Agreement—was taken unilaterally and was therefore unacceptable.[43]

The NEC further inflamed opinion in the Nottingham coalfield by insisting that the negotiations about a separate agreement for Bevercotes were definitely a national matter, although as a compromise certain details might be left to the Bevercotes men to decide. The area issued a strong protest to the NEC, urging members of the National Executive to visit Nottingham and answer objections, but Will Paynter, secretary of the NUM, pointedly refused. In a January 1967 letter he confirmed that the principles contained in the Bevercotes Agreement were to be extended to collieries in other parts of the country, a consideration which emphasized the national character of the experiment and the NEC's sole authority for negotiating the agreement.[44] Under this pressure, and with an upward revision of the rates to make the agreement more palatable to Bevercotes men, Nottingham acknowledged, but never endorsed, the agreement. A union official at Bevercotes recalls bitterly:

> It was Bevercotes and Notts against the Bevercotes agreement. It was imposed on us. Bevercotes was chosen because of the [character of the] pit. We had to go along because it was national policy. [In the colliery branch meeting] only one voted against the Bevercotes agreement. We were given such a story, we agreed to it.

The NEC had committed Bevercotes Colliery to starting production in January 1967 under the special agreement for an experimental period of three years. Nationally the NUM and NCB agreed that Bevercotes would work three coaling shifts per day and eighteen coaling shifts per week, against the five-day norm throughout the industry. Local discretion was limited to the narrow decision as to which three shifts during the weekend would be nonproductive.

According to the agreement, miners were paid a weekly wage for four, five, or six scheduled appearances in a week, the pit thereby remaining in continuous production and capable of coaling operations, potentially, every day of the week.[45]

While elsewhere in the industry men received a 20 percent bonus for completion of a full five-day work week, at Bevercotes the incentive for full attendance was posed negatively. Where a pitman failed to make a scheduled attendance, reductions from the weekly wage were made in strict proportion to the number of days he was rostered to work: if rostered to work four days he was docked one-fourth of the weekly wage for each absence; if rostered to work five days, he was docked one-fifth, and so on. Management retained strict control over the deployment of men, retaining full authority over the selection of teams, setting of the roster, and determination and selection of men for overtime and nonscheduled additional shifts.[46] Equally galling to the men, there were no premiums paid for the performance of additional shifts, the overtime rate remaining approximately one-fifth of the weekly salary.

Union members recall Wage Structure I with great relief at its passing, but also with a measure of satisfaction at having survived an ordeal for which only they had been chosen. "We were a bit annoyed when we were called a white elephant," recalls one official. Blaming problems of production, reasonably enough, on technological and geological miscalculations, a leading member of the branch is nevertheless unequivocal in his estimate of the most prominent feature of the Bevercotes Agreement, the system of shift rotation by management-determined rota.

> The shift situation was ridiculous . . . seven on and two off, the colliery only closed one Sunday in three in a productive sense, the craftsmen still working. The craftsmen worked as many as ten [shifts] on a trot, the others seven. With no overtime premiums. It was pretty

hard going onto the bus [for the trip to the colliery] on a Saturday night and seeing lads going out.

While the men express much bitterness about work under the Bevercotes Agreement, they complain as much about the inflexibility of the agreement (a factor heightened by the presence of an unusually strict colliery manager who insisted on going by the book) as about the rotational system in itself. They recall that the manager would list a man's shifts for an entire year on a card, then change the rota at a moment's notice, send a car for a man, and deduct wages if he refused to attend. "That manager was inflexible," recalls a branch official, "even on Christmas [he would send a car]."

Contractual precision about management prerogatives over manning and the organization of production and fixed weekly rates meant that antagonism toward a manager who, whatever the true circumstances, was universally believed to be obstinate and hardwilled, was expressed directly in conflict over payment for anomalous conditions. While these conditions abounded, in the form of faults, excessive heat, and the presence of oil on the face, the second clause of the agreement expressly stipulated that its provisions "will supersede all existing arrangements, whether rising from agreement, custom or practice, relating to the wages and conditions of service."[47] With this unusual contractual provision for the exclusion of custom and practice, and with a guaranteed weekly salary obviating the traditional basis for additional compensation for anomalous conditions, an inflexible management had sufficient grounds for going strictly by the book. Accordingly, disputes were regularly left unsettled at the pit level and subsequently considered at the second level of the conciliation procedure provided for in the agreement, namely, at a joint committee representative of the union and the Board at the area level. The result, from the union's perspective, was doubly unsatisfactory. Recalls a branch official: "All you could do was complain about anomalies.

The agreement was so specific there was nothing you could do. But the committees never met. So we were left with anomalies *and* with the agreement, too."

The fact of disappointing productivity through Bevercotes' experimental period remains, of course, overdetermined. Geological and technological externalities, as well as factors internal to the wage structure and the power and laboring relations, doubtless contributed to the inauspicious productivity record. During 1967, the first year of production under the Bevercotes Agreement, in no month did productivity at Bevercotes exceed the average for the North Nottingham area. Worse, considering the yearly average, Bevercotes' productivity was barely two-thirds that of the area (although somewhat higher if the first three months of the agreement are omitted from the compilation on the assumption that they reflect settling-in problems). Certainly the Board could not have viewed this result as a reasonable return on investment. The situation was worsened by the inconsistency of production, at whatever level of OMS, suggested by the number of days worked per month which, during this period, never came close to fulfilling the promise of seven-day coal-getting (see Table 5.4). The record does not provide any measure of the independent influence of the wage structure upon productivity and power relations. It is reasonable to speculate, however, that relative indifference to productivity generated by a strict time-based wage, combined with hostile power relations, may have contributed to the disappointing record of production under the Bevercotes Agreement. It also seems likely that inflexibility in management response to both the wage implications and more general industrial relations implications of unexpected geological and technological problems contributed to the workers' relative unconcern with productivity. Paid neither by results nor compensated for their efforts under difficult and unpleasant circumstances—eighteen inches of oil and ninety-five-degree heat, to cite an extreme but not infrequent face condition—the

TABLE 5.4. Productivity at Bevercotes Colliery
During the First Year of Experimental Operation (1967)
Compared to the North Nottingham Area Average with
Reference to Days Worked

	Average Productivity for Bevercotes[a]	Average Productivity for North Nottingham Division[b]	Days Worked
February	3.70	9.82	12
March	3.79	10.06	7
April	2.14	9.82	17
May	9.72	9.75	16
June	8.16	9.45	24
July	7.51	9.04	18
August	7.81	8.59	10
September	7.96	8.41	23
October	6.40	8.81	20
November	6.20	9.02	17
December	5.38	9.38	18
Yearly average[c]	6.25	9.30	
Adjusted average[d]	7.39	9.06	

SOURCE: NCB, North Nottinghamshire Area, Face Data Bank, Weekly Listing of Face Performance.

[a] Represents productivity measured in saleable tons output per face manshift; figures for November and December include average productivity for the 5's face (the only ROLF installation during that period).

[b] Represents productivity measured in saleable tons output per face manshift for all mechanized faces in the North Nottingham Division, excluding Bevercotes and including the following collieries: Bilsthorpe, Blidworth, Clipstone, Harworth, Mansfield, Illerton, Rufford, Sherwood, Shirebrook, Thoresby, Warsop, Welbeck.

[c] Represents the eleven months during which Bevercotes operated under the experimental Bevercotes Agreement.

[d] Represents the period May–December, an adjusted frame of reference which represents eight months of relatively effective work at Bevercotes after an initial settling-in period of three months for the experimental operation.

men had little incentive to produce coal during exceedingly trying times.

Bevercotes Wage Structure I may be summarized in this way.

1. Identification: Experimental Bevercotes Agreement.
2. Form and level of payment: weekly payment at nationally negotiated rates at or above NPLA level, but without overtime premium or bonus for completion of five-day work week (rather, substantial financial penalty for absence from any shift assigned in work rota).
3. Generative Rules
   3.1 Assignment of position on coal face: management prerogative, strictly preserved.
   3.2 Work pace and attitude toward productivity: effort regulated by ROLF operations, hindered by adverse geological and technological conditions; relative indifference to output.
   3.3 Division of labor in primary work group: by management prerogative.
   3.4 Relationship among shift and task groups: formal and practical indifference, within context predetermined by ROLF operations.

Wage Structure II

Despite an offer by the NCB in April 1968 to increase all the weekly rates by 13 shillings,[48] determination grew among Bevercotes men that the special agreement ought to be discontinued. Accordingly, in December 1969 the Bevercotes Branch voted decisively—320 against, 133 in favor, with one spoiled ballot paper—to end the existing Bevercotes Agreement.[49] In the apparent hope that the miners would withdraw their opposition to the experimental agreement, the NEC repeatedly asked the Nottinghamshire area officials to inform the men that there was an excellent likelihood that the agreement would be improved. Despite entreaties, the men were not persuaded and in January

1970 the Bevercotes Colliery Sub-Committee agreed to recommend that the NEC take steps to terminate the agreement.[50] The NEC endorsed the decision and terminated the agreement as of 2 May 1970, whereupon Bevercotes went under the general national power loading agreements.[51]

While asserting that the Bevercotes Agreement could have been saved had people at the national level worked hard enough to resolve problems, and particularly those problems associated with the unpopular shift rotations system, branch officials are proud of their decisive defeat of the experimental agreement, and feel that they saved their comrades from a very unpleasant wage structure. "Had it been a success, we'd have had to go right through the coalfields. Some of the militant areas can thank Bevercotes that [rotational shift work] is not in their area." Instead, the men at Bevercotes returned in all details to the formal structures of the National Power Loading Agreement.

Bevercotes Wage Structure II may be summarized in this way.

1. Identification: NPLA daywage structure.
2. Form and level of payment: time-based wage at nationally negotiated NPLA rates (substantially below Bevercotes Agreement rates).
3. Generative Rules
    3.1 Assignment of position on coal face: by management prerogative.
    3.2 Work pace and attitude toward productivity: relative indifference to productivity.
    3.3 Division of labor in primary work group: formal cooperation.
    3.4 Relationship among shift and task groups: formal cooperation.

PRODUCTIVITY

The persistence of anomalous geological conditions, amidst a retreat from space-age coaling technology, continues to

fashion Bevercotes' productivity. From the reintroduction
of the NPLA until late in 1972, work at Bevercotes was
limited to the development of new tunnels and roadways.
Productivity has remained sporadic, and conditions de-
plorable throughout the subsequent period, as faces have
been developed only to be found unworkable shortly after
production was undertaken. Neither of the faces being
worked in April 1972, for example, remained in operation
in June 1973. When I went down the pit, I avoided looking
at the work on 57's face which, in operation for approximately one year, had men working, as the NCB training
officer put it, "in shocking conditions, up to two feet of
oil." Productivity had risen from 221.3 (saleable face output
in hundredweights per manshift) for the month of June
1975 to 314.9 the following December, and 421.3 for the
last week of March 1976.[52] But with production having
reached the worst patch of oil, the face was nearly worked
out. Production was beginning on the neighboring 59's
face, which I visited. The story is generally the same with
each of the half-dozen seams worked under the NPLA:
settling-in period, followed by rising productivity, followed
by crippling geological conditions which force the NCB to
transfer the operation to a neighboring face or seam and
to experiment with the development of additional faces in
a separate region of the colliery. Within this pattern, the
influence of wage structures and traditions of working on
productivity is difficult to assess. As elsewhere in Nottingham, management asserts that there are "low statistics
for rippers [and] constraints [on the overall operation] put
on by ripping." The current manager complains of the
problem of a "bottleneck" being formed around ripping,
but registers no disappointment with the men's effort under the face conditions, which he described repeatedly as
appalling.

POWER RELATIONS

While the geological and technological factors dominate
the perceptions of management and men about productiv-

ity, and render speculation about the effects of wage structures and traditions of laboring relations somewhat remote, the power relations seem especially revealing. Experimental or not, Bevercotes displays the distinctive industrial relations patterns of a Nottingham pit. Under the extraordinary conditions of Bevercotes, the relations between management and men are especially notable for their generally pacific, noncombative quality.

The current branch secretary stresses, "Industrial relations depends on who the general manager is—the attitude to an agreement, productivity, this sort of thing." Union officials confirm the positive change in attitude under the existing manager, asserting that "relationships are good," whereas in the past, under Wage Structure I, inflexibility led to conflict. The branch secretary asserts, "As far as [this branch] is concerned, we have been prepared to fight. This lad [i.e., the current manager] has recognized it. This one cooperates." But when was the fight and what were the issues and object of the struggle?

Beyond objections to rough handling by the first manager and despite a regional reputation for militancy, Bevercotes pitmen have generally accepted their unusual fate with good grace. Not wanting the original experimental agreement and resenting the shift rotation system, the men persevered, and then years later accepted an average weekly drop in wages of approximately 25 percent to join the rest of the nation's collieries on the NPLA. Appealing to the Nottingham area NUM Council in 1966, that "vigorous steps be taken to get all outside contractors who are doing work that should be done by the NCB labor, out of the industry,"[53] a decade later union officials unanimously agreed that they are a "necessary evil." The union representatives grant that the outside contractors are not liked, but that there is "never a problem down the pit."

The generally unproblematic character of underground relations is important. Neither when they were forced onto the Wage Structure I, nor when they lost substantially in the pay packet to make the transition to Wage Structure

II, did conflict down the pit substantially influence productivity as far as one can tell. Nor did power relations lose their focus on the personality and approach of a particular manager. Remarkably, there is no hint of any action by the branch or by individual colliers under Wage Structure I to challenge the authority of the manager over the determination of work teams and shift assignment under the unique rotational system.

Likewise, there is no evidence of restrictive practices, such as were practiced at Horden Colliery in County Durham, to limit overtime working; overtime has been introduced under Wage Structure II to circumvent the bottlenecks caused by the ripping operation. Observes a branch official, "We cooperate with overtime when it is necessary. We make sure it is necessary. Our policy is totally in line with the national policy. It's got to be legitimate. We don't encourage any kind of fiddling here."

So the union as much as the current management seems flexible, even allowing face workers to drive the underground transport vehicles when necessary, and allowing colliers to work different tasks on different pay grades as necessary to turn over the face. "They can't complain to us about being noncooperative," asserts the branch secretary. Such conflict as arises today concerns compensation for horrid working conditions. "It's been ninety-three degrees with a strata temperature of one hundred plus humidity," recalls one of the men. "[W]ith certain jobs in the gate ends where it's hottest, [the] men [are] bent over with exhaustion." With conditions such as this, it is not surprising that power relations focus on ex gratia payments and concessions: from 12½ p. to £2.00 per shift bonus for anomalous conditions; the provision and laundering of additional protective clothing; agreements for "wet riding," i.e., acceptance that men working in oil and water can leave the pit and bathe ten or fifteen minutes ahead of shift time; occasional rest periods during shift time; the provision of "barrier cremes" for protection against dermatitis, etc.

These local gentleman's agreements provide the basis for

generally nonconfrontational power relations despite "frayed tempers" and "blow-ups" under the extremely adverse and unpleasant conditions which often exist on the coal face. When conditions are unbearable, men simply stay home. As a result, in March 1976, for example, the average attendance per day for face workers and rippers stood at 203 of 253 workers, a ratio which the NCB termed "insufficient to fully man the face and development programmes."[54]

Summary

Despite diverse provocations, laboring effort seems relatively constant and power relations positive under trying circumstances. The branch's unity finds expression in spot-bargained agreements for anomalous conditions, rather than in confrontational postures or intricate schemes to challenge management initiatives. Where Durham miners challenge the authority of management and struggle to reinstitute formidable rank-and-file checks on the Board's contractual power to control all the details of production, Nottingham miners repay flexibility with hard work and constructive fair play in the performance of their assigned tasks. Thus, the dialectic of control unfolds differently in the two regions. Assessing the lasting influence of the Bevercotes Agreement, the Nottingham voice of the Bevercotes branch secretary comes through clearly:

> [The experimental agreement] did some damage. On one or two occasions, we've had it said—that's a pit with the continental system. It's a stigma. [We're] still considered a lone wolf. If we had complaints, the [area and the national] union attitude was: "It's your problem—you get on with it."

United by their differences from the rest of the coalfield under the initial Bevercotes Agreement, the branch concentrates on making do under difficult circumstances. They get on with it. Accepting with little question the day-to-day authority of the NCB, management and men preside cooperatively over the continuing failure of the glorious Bevercotes experiment.

HARWORTH

Summary / Description of Resources

History has deserted Harworth, the most tumultuous colliery of the interwar period, leaving it to a complacent, even static present. Between 1926 and 1935, Spencer's breakaway from the MFGB, the Nottinghamshire Miners' Industrial Union (NMIU), consolidated power in the county, holding sole bargaining rights with Nottinghamshire coal-owners. When the MFGB, sensing an upswing in the industry's prospects, sought a national flat rate addition, Nottingham remained the sticking point in the campaign. "Nottinghamshire holds the key position in the industry," claimed Ebby Edwards, general secretary of the MFGB. "Wages are high, conditions and other things good, and yet they are one of the weakest links in the Federation."[55] Edwards, wondering whether the Nottinghamshire miners were "prepared to fight,"[56] soon discovered a battle of unexpected proportions being waged at Harworth, and one which threatened to erupt into a national work stoppage.

In the part of the country around Harworth, in the outlying reaches of North Nottinghamshire, the division between Nottinghamshire and Yorkshire runs deep. Despite roughly equivalent geological and technological potential, the NCB's expectations about the two areas are as distinct as the political attitudes of Len Clarke and Arthur Scargill, the leaders of Nottinghamshire and Yorkshire, respectively, who then comprised the extreme right and left wing of the NUM National Executive.[57] Nottingham registers steady production and is the voice of cooperation on income policies, for example, at the level of national policy. Yorkshire represents class politics and provides the seedbed for confrontation—from wildcat strikes which mushroomed into the national work stoppage in 1972 to flying pickets at Grunwick in the summer of 1977 (where Scargill was arrested).

Historically, Harworth's remoteness from the geographical core of the Nottinghamshire coalfield, its association with the confrontational industrial politics of the North, and its development under the guidance of a notoriously tight-fisted mining company—all these factors marked Harworth for distinction when national attention focused on Nottingham as the MFGB struggled to restore its power in the afternoon of the 1926 debacle. Griffin recalls the atmosphere which fed confrontation at Harworth.

> . . . Harworth, a newish colliery owned by the Barber Walker Company. Harworth is in North Nottinghamshire, quite close to the Yorkshire border; and the mining village built by the colliery company—Bircotes—acquired a character of its own. Physically, Harworth belongs to the South Yorkshire coalfield (and indeed, the Yorkshire Miners' Association had members employed there at times), whilst a high proportion of the labour force came from Durham. Bircotes was a raw place in the 1930s; a soulless village inhabited by people whose roots were elsewhere. Further, it was a company village: the houses were owned by the company; so was the land; the church, the parish hall, the Salvation Army Hut were all erected on land provided by the Company; and even the Curate-in-Charge looked to Barber and Walker for his £400 a year.[58]

Throughout 1935, the balance of support for the MFGB-affiliated Nottingham Miners' Association and the Spencer breakaway NMIU shifted in favor of the more confrontational NMA. At the beginning of the year the NMA could count only seven members out of a work force of over two thousand. By the end of the year the Harworth branch of the NMA had 157 members, and by the summer of 1936, while the NMA pressed for a countrywide ballot to oust the Spencer union, and Harworth membership doubled to 302, the leadership of the branch was taken over by a Com-

munist activist. In the meanwhile, traditional conflicts between the miners and Barber, Walker Company intensified, particularly around the issue of "dirt deductions,"
i.e., automatic reductions of up to 5 cwt. 7 lb. from the
tonnage per tram of coal loaded (and thus figured in piece-
rate earnings) regardless of the actual weight of impurities.
In this context of heightened confrontation, everyday conflicts escalated into a massive showdown.

On 31 August 1936 the management refused to see representatives of the NMA branch to discuss a claim that a
Barber, Walker deputy had physically assaulted two youths
employed at the pit. The next day, two colliers who were
ordered to "stand snap" (break for a meal) ahead of schedule in order to save working time during a haulage breakdown refused, and on September 2 they talked over a
hundred men into staying off the afternoon shift. Management continued to refuse any appeals to negotiate with
the NMA, and incrementally the dispute deepened. The
colliers who walked off on September 2 lost their jobs, and
the face workers subsequently voted 785 to 136 to begin a
strike. In October, the confrontation intensified around the
issue of dirt deductions; by November, a ballot of Harworth
men to determine their choice of union (the disparity
doubtless inflated by Spencer's orders that his supporters
not participate) registered 1,175 for the NMA and only 145
for the NMIU. On December 11, the MFGB instructed all
NMA members who were not already on strike to hand in
their notices, and for the next six weeks the whole issue
of national recognition and the authority of the MFGB was
focused on isolated Harworth, where never more than six
hundred Industrial Union and scab workers were escorted
to the pit by police, amid growing harassment and violence
by both parties.

Men who lived through it, with the notable exception of
the current Harworth branch secretary, swear that the
impressions of the winter of 1936 will never leave them.
"The miners' welfare was built by Barber, Walker," re-
counts an NCB official from another colliery who, as a

youth turned out of his home by the colliery owners, remains bitter about the events in Bircotes. "It was a natural place. . . . The first thing [the striking miners] did was to pick up bricks and throw them through the windows. They wrecked the place." But the branch secretary—who is vilified by some as an "opportunist" and a "nonentity"—insists that the men care nothing for the events four decades ago, and do their jobs like pitmen anywhere else in Nottingham. When asked to discuss the effects of the Harworth controversy on the attitude and work habits of the current Harworth miner, he explains: "There is no lasting effect of 1936-37. . . . I don't think the attitudes are different. We have not lost the 'tag' but there is no truth to it. . . . The history of 1936 . . . [is] remembered by outsiders more than insiders—[not] Harworth men."[59]

If the effect of Harworth's history on contemporary pitmen is in dispute, there is nevertheless a consensus about the evolution and the characteristics of the system of production at the colliery. In May 1937 the NMA and the NMIU merged on terms extremely favorable to Spencer, and work resumed at Harworth and at other Nottinghamshire mines under a contract that included a five-year no-strike clause. The Harworth spirit was shattered. "Of course," recalls a local NCB official who lived through the Harworth strike, "the village was broken up and the natural leaders were scattered far and wide." Board officials speak of the "Yorkshire influence" in contemporary Harworth, by which they mean a lower average productivity under conditions which are comparable to those of the higher-producing pits in the heartland of the Nottingham coalfield.[60] But, more important, the fighting spirit of 1936 seems very remote at Harworth today. A high-ranking NCB official allows that Harworth has "very stable industrial relations."[61] So, while one can only speculate about the concrete effects of Harworth's extraordinary history on its unexceptional present, productivity data and interview accounts point to an intriguing pattern of connections. Not the power of the confrontation in 1936 but the mark of the defeat in 1937 seems to linger in the power relations in contemporary Harworth. At the same time, the generative rules of the butty-charge-man system, practiced under the strict hand of Barber, Walker, color the contemporary laboring relations. As a result, productivity is low but remarkably steady under both incentive and daywage structures. Despite its north-ern location and its tumultuous heritage, Harworth is most definitely a Nottingham and not a Yorkshire pit.

Wage Structure I

The harsh rule of Barber, Walker continued right up until nationalization in 1947, and indeed, the rules of the butty-chargeman structure continued long past the demise of private ownership. By the close of the 1930s formal butties had disappeared; by 1943, after a decade of disputes and a three-day walkout of the men over arbitrary dirt deduc-tions, a system of deductions based on the actual average weight of dirt per tub (called "clotching") reduced the level of controversy at Harworth.[62] But traditional contract work remained the rule throughout the period leading up to the DPLA, with the number of men for the job, their position on the face, and their stint determined by the chargemen. While the colliers retained some direct control over the determination of wages—rippers might go "a man light" and share out twenty shifts' pay among nineteen men—features of the old butty-chargeman system remained in-tact. The wages were paid out by the NCB and not out of the butty's own revenues, but the chargeman continued his predecessors' practices, "paying out of the tin" on Fri-days. The chargeman also measured out the stints. He maintained control over the pace and the details of pro-duction, and he arranged overtime, fixing payments for abnormalities and for the performance of ancillary tasks such as road laying, extra packing, or provision of timber.

Harworth men and NCB officials recounting the histor-ical evolution of wage structures at Harworth make little distinction between the butty-chargeman system of working and production under the DPLA. Bartering continued under the incentive-dominated power loading agreement, with the chargeman's task gradually transferred to the deputy. But the imperatives for high, disciplined productivity remained. "A chap who didn't pull his weight was pushed out of the contract," recalls an ex-collier who is now a member of the regional NCB staff. "If he was behind on a stint, had the 'Monday morning feeling,' other chaps would come and help him, 'give him a dig.' If it occurred regularly, eventually they'd put the squeeze on him. They don't want the man on the team."[63]

The fear that the chargeman or deputy might "fetch in a market [man]"—replace a member of the team by a non-assigned new man or by one who was looking for upgrading or redeployment—complemented the imperatives of the *pro rata* incentive structure of the DPLA. Together, the fear of removal from the team to nonface work and the monetary incentives of the district agreement guided the efforts of the work team, generating habits of positive self-regulation to ensure consistent productivity.

Harworth Wage Structure I may be summarized in this way.

1. Identification: butty-chargeman/DPLA structure.
2. Form and level of payment: incentive structure pitched at moderate level, based on spot-bargained contracts, augmented after DPLA by standard power loading fallback rate.
3. Generative Rules
   3.1 Assignment of position on coal face: by management prerogative.
   3.2 Work pace and attitude toward productivity: generally disciplined and positive attitude toward production, generated both by the incentive structure and by the coercive powers of chargeman/deputy.
   3.3 Division of labor in primary work group: initi-

ated by group, with firm supervision of deputy/
chargeman.
3.4 Relationship among shift and task groups: formally cooperative.

Wage Structure II

The transition to Wage Structure II, the National Power
Loading Agreement, was opposed by the Harworth men
who were conditioned to incentive-governed productivity.
"I'd like to get back to local incentive systems," asserts the
generally undogmatic branch secretary. "We had a power
loading agreement in Nottingham with incentives. Harworth voted against the NPLA." In the classical Nottingham pattern, Harworth men reacted to the daywage
structure not by regulating productivity downward but by
demanding overtime. The branch secretary is dismayed,
professing amazement that men will work more than five
days per week. He calls the Harworth face workers' thirst
for overtime one of his "pet aches." "There has been a mad
race for overtime since [the introduction of] the NPLA,"
he laments, explaining that under the Nottingham power
loading agreement of Wage Structure I, the "men's attitude
used to control overtime." Although traces remain of the
tradition of spot-bargained piece-rate contracts for extra
work—clearing the gate, dinting, shoring up the roof,
fetching timber—Harworth in general conforms to the Nottingham characteristics of the NPLA.

Harworth Wage Structure II may be summarized in this
way.

1. Identification: NPLA daywage structure.
2. Form and level of payment: time-based daywage at
nationally negotiated NPLA rates, augmented by spot-
bargained piece-rate agreements for ancillary tasks.
3. Generative Rules
    3.1 Assignment of position on coal face: by man-
    agement prerogative.

3.2 Work pace and attitude toward productivity: formal indifference to productivity; more positive
attitude conditioned by butty-chargeman tradition, sustained to a degree by deputy's role in
initiating informal agreements.
3.3 Division of labor in primary work group: formal
cooperation.
3.4 Relationship among shift and task groups: formal cooperation.

Systematic Pattern of Production

PRODUCTIVITY

Complaining of the "Yorkshire influence" on Harworth,
a high-ranking official of the NCB contends that productivity at Harworth is "lower than anywhere else . . . [be-
cause it is] next door to Doncaster." The Nottingham wisdom is that South Yorkshire and North Nottinghamshire
have nearly identical geological and technological poten-
tials, but that the discipline of the Nottingham miner makes
a big difference in terms of output. Harworth is "staffed
by non-Notts people, many from Doncaster," explains the
NCB industrial relations official. "It's a typical Doncaster
pit except for the industrial relations which are much better.
[It is] accepted that the norm of task is much lower than
in the rest of Nottingham, although [it has] among the best
face conditions."

These remarks of the NCB official, however, reveal only
half the story of Harworth productivity. True, this Nottingham colliery, which is geographically situated within
the Yorkshire coalfield and populated by an unusually high
proportion of northern pitmen, produces well below the
norm at Welbeck Colliery, for example, a pit with comparable face conditions, which is located physically and
"spiritually" within the Nottingham coalfield. Incomplete
monthly productivity figures for face OMS measured in
saleable hundredweights for the period from June 1973 to

March 1976 indicate a Harworth colliery average productivity which is barely two-thirds that of Welbeck: 199.66 as compared to 296.22.[64] Nevertheless, given a downwardly adjusted task norm for Harworth, the productivity is reasonably close to the target and—what is most important—performance remains relatively stable during the transition from Wage Structure I to Wage Structure II.

A comparison of productivity for the first two face teams who made the move from the contract system to the NPLA indicates that performance, when measured against a projected standard, held reasonably steady (see Table 5.5). In the first case, men moved from the 70's face where they had worked under Wage Structure I to the neighboring 72's face where they worked under Wage Structure II. Comparing productivity during the entire course of production for each face, one finds an increase from 83 percent of standard for 70's to 89 percent of standard for 72's. A similar comparison for 56's and 57's reveals a decrease in performance, measured as the percentage of actual extracted coal to standard, from 90 to 85. Thus, Harworth provides one example of an improvement on standard (plus 6 percent) and a second example of an equivalent decline of performance compared to standard (minus 5 percent). Taken together, the two cases tend to sustain a hypothesis that the Nottingham pattern of consistent productivity applies to Harworth as to other collieries despite Harworth's comparatively low productivity norm. The NCB's dismay with productivity at Harworth, therefore, seems only half-justified, the other half perhaps attributable to Harworth's unique historical "tag."

POWER RELATIONS

Whatever its tumultuous past, there is no mood of conflict evident at Harworth today. The branch secretary speaks with pride, as if it were his own accomplishment, of the "remarkable" change between the ways of private ownership and the pattern of relations between men and management today. "You used to have to give notice [to the

TABLE 5.5. Comparison of Productivity of
Face Teams Before and After the Introduction of
the NPLA at Harworth Colliery[a]

	First Annual Production Period	Second Annual Production Period	Subsequent Production Period to Exhaustion	Total for Life of Face
70's[b]				
Average E/S% (Pre-NPLA)	90	103	74	83
72's[c]				
Average E/S% (NPLA)	98	73	—	89
56's[d]				
Average E/S% (Pre-NPLA)	79	87	95	90
57's[e]				
Average E/S% (NPLA)	85	—	—	85

SOURCE: NCB, Harworth Colliery, Weekly Output Calculations.

[a] Productivity is measured as a ratio of actual weekly saleable tonnage extracted (E) to standard—method studied norm or target—tonnage (S), expressed as a percentage. Figures represent complete weekly records of production for the life of each face.

[b] For 70's face, the first period runs from 25 August 1962 to 27 July 1963; the second period runs from 17 August 1963 to 27 June 1964; and the subsequent period runs from 18 July 1964 to 3 June 1967. Periods were chosen to reflect the natural breaks in production determined by annual summer holidays. All dates represent the last day of a week to which the production records refer.

[c] For 72's face, the first period runs from 3 June 1967 to 22 June 1968; the second period runs from 13 July 1968 to 3 March 1969, when the face ceased coaling production. Periods were chosen to reflect the natural break in production determined by annual summer holidays. All dates represent the last day of a week to which the production records refer. At Harworth, 72's face replaced 70's face, the general features which influence productivity are similar (except for the wage structure), and the two faces were worked by the same work team.

[d] For 56's face, the first period runs from 25 December 1965 to 31 December 1966; the second period runs from 1 January 1967 to 30 December 1967; and the subsequent period runs from 6 January 1968 to 24 August

manager] in writing to ask for an interview. Today you can walk in at any time," explains the union official. "The relationship is man to man although there is still a little bit of the them and us." Oddly enough, while the branch official stresses the previous omnipotence of management, a member of the Nottingham NCB industrial relations department recalls the shoe, in those days, being on the other foot.

> Harold Phillips, the branch secretary at Harworth where there was the big strike in 1936-37 for recognition. He was a big man, in every sense of the word. His authority was more pronounced than managers. Phillips had an inner sanctum. You knocked, waited to come in. You didn't just come in. . . . Authority. There is no doubt he had greater real power than any management structure.[65]

The NCB official further explained that with the introduction of the NPLA, the Harworth Branch never regained the same authority. When the daywage structure was introduced, Phillips was approaching retirement age. He made it clear, however, that he would have given up the job anyway, complaining that the reality of representation was no more than a mere shadow of what it had been. Phillips had no interest in being branch secretary, it seems, when all the union officials did was "blow up trivial issues into major ones."[66]

The reduced range of activity of the Harworth Branch, with questions of actual remuneration taken out of its hands by the national agreement, seems very clear. One NCB

1968, when the face ceased coaling production. All dates represent the last day of a week to which the production records refer.

e For 57's face, the first period runs from 16 November 1968 to 23 August 1969, the period representing the entire coaling life of the face. All dates represent the last day of a week to which the production records refer. At Harworth, 57's face replaced 56's face, the general features which influence productivity are similar (except for the wage structure), and the two faces were worked by the same work team.

official who is particularly critical of the current branch secretary claims, "If you went among Harworth miners at the welfare [workingmen's club] you'd find them totally different, different animals." But as far as branch activities are concerned, Harworth men seem cooperative and politically placid. Despite or because of the memories of the 1930s, they approach industrial relations today in the typical Nottingham manner.

With no cavilling/marra tradition for worker self-selection of the team, the branch representatives and the management, for example, look at manpower needs at the start of a new face and reach an agreement about the composition of the new team and the number of "market men" to be brought in. Never wishing to equalize chances at preferred locations down the pit as do the Durham miners, the Harworth men refuse to change positions on the face or to alternate face teams onto more or less favorable faces. They assert that "a face could be bad for three weeks and good for four months," so that swapping to get a good face makes no sense. Indeed, the anti-cavilling sentiment runs so deep at Harworth that management-induced switching of face positions is, according to the branch secretary, "one of the main causes" of conflict between management and men. "The men don't like being displaced," he explains with some heat. "We had a [disturbance] last night. On one conveyor face there was a mechanical breakdown. The men claimed there was enough work without being transferred. The men walked out." What requires explanation is not so much the *level of militancy*, a concept which is too general to add much to an understanding of underground power relations, but the *sources of conflict*. In Durham, the miners force management to allow rotation of faces, while at Harworth the men walk out of the colliery to make sure that they do not give up their claim to a particular piece of underground turf.

It is equally typical of the Nottingham pattern of power relations that when asked to discuss the causes of tension with management the Harworth branch secretary time and again drifts into a criticism of the NPLA. It was bad for Nottingham because it reduced the area's well-deserved benefits in comparison to other regions, and it was bad for the industry because it reduced differentials in a way that contradicted the traditional relations among classes of workers. Admitting that five rippers now do the work of four in the past, the branch secretary complained bitterly of the "suffering" inflicted on rippers by the agreement, and its effect on recruitment for this, the most difficult and dangerous underground job. "It's hard to get men to do ripping. You've got to beg and pray. Always before [the young lads would ask], 'Can I have a rip?' " Accordingly, the Harworth Branch works cooperatively with management to arrange for face workers and rippers to get weekend work. They are paid the highest underground rate (A rate) for noncoaling work associated with face work and are paid double after 2 o'clock on Saturday. To the Harworth secretary this seems small compensation for men robbed of the greater potential of an incentive agreement.

Summary

When asked to characterize what is special about Harworth, the branch secretary explains that all the miners live in the new Harworth village and, as a consequence, deep bonds form among them.

> Harworth: 1100 coal board houses and 1100 NUM workers. We work, live, and play together. . . . One man [walks] out, everyone is out. It makes a difference. Take Bevercotes, there is no village at all. Or Sherwood. The number of men who live together is very different. They only see one another when they are at the pit. At Harworth, we are all resident in the village. There is complete unity in the way we live and work. . . . If there are small disputes, it very soon spreads. . . . Those on the next shift making inquiries: "Does that job want [i.e., need] some unity?"

Obviously proud of the now quiet, remote village, Harworth men seem wary of past controversies, and happy enough to live in the relative industrial harmony of the present. They work at their steady pace, accepting an unusually low productivity norm, but by and large sticking to it whether under an incentive scheme or under the NPLA. With apparent indifference to their collective past, they express their unity around issues, such as overtime and unwillingness to shift underground locations, which mark them as typical Nottingham miners, not the Harworth men who gained such fame (and notoriety) by challenging Barber, Walker in 1936.

Teversal

Summary / Description of Resources

NCB officials state simply that Teversal is near closing, the final exhaustion of workable seams expected shortly. Accordingly, the area industrial relations officer admits in a noteworthy understatement, "There are particular problems and disputes."[67] Teversal is "a bit like Langwith,"[68] a colliery whose closing in neighboring Derbyshire threatened, in the spring of 1976, to erupt into a national overtime ban, sometimes the first step toward an industry-wide work stoppage. In the end, Langwith was closed uneventfully, as the Derbyshire NUM took its cue from the national NEC and backed off from the dispute.[69] But Teversal men are determined to fight in a way that Langwith did not. They count on forcing the "Nottingham area [to] do for Teversal what Derbyshire did not do for Langwith."[70]

Teversal is a proud family pit, the men more spirited and more closely knit than at any other colliery I have observed. With over a third of the labor force at age fifty-five and above, there is a marked "fathers and sons" quality to the pit and the village, located in a remote outreach of the county. One of the older members of the branch explains why Teversal men will fight to keep their geologically harsh, undercapitalized pit open. "People who are working at the pit have worked nowhwere else. Shift them, they are not going to settle. Most of the men are forty, forty-five—over 40 percent will leave the industry." Members of the branch executive speak together around a table in the canteen— fresh, brash young pitmen and the respected elder spokesmen, joking back and forth, displaying the special unity of Teversal while trying to explain it. A second official adds, "I was a foreigner at another pit." A third concurs, "I don't think you can find atmosphere at other pits like this. That's why they want to split it." A younger pitman adds, bragging really, "They call us the backwoodsmen."

These "backwoodsmen" have another unique claim, beyond the associational qualities of the colliery and village. "Do you know what pit this is, lad?" a union official asked me at the outset of my first meeting with the Teversal Branch. He explained that Teversal is the "Tevers Hall" which provides the background in D. H. Lawrence's *Lady Chatterley's Lover*. Intrigued by my ignorance of their history, the men proudly explained that Lawrence, a Nottinghamshire man, had grown up nearby. Transported for a moment from the immediate fears of closure, they discussed and disputed the particulars of the novel, promising to take me around to point out where the gamekeeper's cottage was and where Chatterley's wheelchair had stuck in the mud, humiliating the impotent Clifford—the colliery's owner, after all—in front of his wife's lover, a former pitman.

Of course, the NCB cares nothing for this heritage and little for the men's sentimentality about keeping Teversal at work. Branch members hope, nevertheless, that regional Board officials, whom they discuss derisively, cannot afford to ignore the consistent high productivity of the doomed colliery. The colliers, who work at a steady pace naturally, conditioned as they are by the generative rules of the butty-chargeman/DPLA structure, hope to buy the life of the colliery by keeping it in the black. Thus, Teversal's determination to stay alive reinforces the rules for working of

Wage Structure I to ensure the same high productivity under a national daywage structure, even though the men would prefer to see the NPLA daywage replaced by local incentive agreements.

Wage Structure I

Teversal has followed the traditional Nottingham pattern of contract earnings under Wage Structure I, both with the butty-chargeman and the DPLA wages structure. "The chargeman paid out. . . . He could take ten bob [shillings] for your two," recalled a branch official who reviewed the history of the butty structure at Teversal, under both the room and pillar system and the longwall system, the latter introduced in 1939. Actual incomes varied enormously depending on the contracts, but the complaints were always the same and typical of the butty structure. The weighing of tubs of coal, which determined the weekly wage, cheated the hewers of their wages and preserved the butty's profit.

> They'd get kids to knock tubs so coals would come off, so other men would get two or three tubs a week picking up our coals. We had check-weighmen: the men paid one, the company one. The management one said the coals were too small. We had screens. We had to fill off the coal with screens [which] separated out the slag [small bits of coal]. If you were caught filling with a shovel—it was a five bob [shilling] fine. Half your wages. . . . Sometimes the butty was on three stalls. He might take a week's holiday and still get more than them that [were] working on [the coal].

While nationalization brought a definitive end to the butty system per se, the competitive patterns of contract workings, still subject to the whim of the chargeman, remained until the NPLA era. "We used to pit man's ability against a machine," recalls a union official who negotiated contracts with the Board in the days when mechanization was very uneven, leaving the stablehole operator untouched.

The deputy would set charges and "fire the holes," which broke up the coal on the face, the men loading the coal out by shovel and setting the timber alongside new hydraulic support. The unusually difficult geological conditions, explained the pitman, reinforced the butty tradition, giving the chargeman considerable latitude in determining wage levels by manipulating compensation for anomalies.

> Very, very often we used to encounter bad geological conditions in stable holes. The chargeman . . . had to negotiate and come to satisfactory agreement for some allowance for abnormal conditions. At the end of the week it led to frayed tempers between men and management and the unions. If he didn't get an understanding [which was] dependable, you found out your abnormal allowance was nothing compared to what you were expecting. Then there was serious trouble, men refusing to come to work.

Difficult geological conditions and a "divide and conquer" attitude among officials led, in this settling-in period of nationalization, to conflict among work teams. The miners who hand-filled the coal and those who were applying early machinery worked under the same conditions, and under essentially the same contracts. Here is where the element of men racing the machine enters.

With the cutting machines advancing from three-four feet of coal per minute along a fourteen-fifteen foot stretch, the five or six men who worked—by hand—in the stable-hole "had to advance almost three times faster, four feet of coal in a ten-yard length, hand-filled, cut with an old hand-cutting machine." But there was an additional reason for extreme haste, which more directly influenced relations among work and shift teams. "Speed determined the rates of pay," recalls the branch secretary. "So, the less time you could take on the coal face, the more you could take home. Overtime came out of your own earnings." The rules of working were simple: work as fast as you can and don't worry about the impediments to productivity which will face men on the next shift.

Accordingly, hostile, competitive relations developed between those who undercut the coal on one shift, and those who filled it off into the tubs (later conveyors) on the next shift. The cutting shift would often leave "gumming"—the grit turned out by cutter picks which rotated around the four-foot, six-inch jib. With the "relationship between officials and workmen far from good," the management demanded that all the gummings be cleared up. As a consequence, the fillers had an "obstacle before [we] got started. . . . We would very often get a full load of gumming" and the controversy erupted over the rate of pay. "Then it was my word versus the district deputy," recalls the branch official who negotiated rates for gumming. "The rate drawn up for gumming was six, seven, eight pence per yard. [This led to] opposition amongst men."

Tensions also developed between good and bad cutting teams who might attack the strata by different strategies. Again, erratic geological conditions led to "frayed tempers and arguments about satisfactory allowances." In the Dunsil seam, colliers' wits and physical capacities were tested by unusual conditions: "weight breaks" in the roof caused by the inadequacies of a roof support system which relied on a widely spaced steel bar prop system; and "potholes," cone-shaped displacements in the roof, a kind of zig-zag break in the strata. A man who worked under these conditions recalls the problems caused by "potholes."

> At front of the actual solid coal, this is where you would see them. You knew then you was in for trouble. They'd go as much as twelve and eighteen feet high, always the same shape. Once they'd come down, you used to get fatalities. . . . Potholes, something which you couldn't beat, because it was something that beat you.

Struggling under these extreme geological conditions, tensions grew among miners on successive shifts whose tasks suggested different remedies to the immediate problems. At the same time men and management struggled over the determination of price lists for the range of tasks, such as "gumming up," required of colliers, and over special allowances for anomalies. These problems were in some ways exacerbated by the introduction of the DPLA, which also had the unexpected effect of generating conflict over manning.

With the introduction of power loading, the Teversal Branch was obliged, despite consistent objections, to comply with method study assessment of the manpower requirements for each face. The method studies were detailed and precise. More important, they gave rise to constant bickering over manning, while they sustained the traditional butty rules for determined high productivity. Working time was minutely divided down to the level of individual operations—for example, "[t]ravel on manrider twice, including walking between cars: 13.64 mins."[71] Similarly, standard performance per manshift was charted to the hundredth of a yard advance and manpower was allocated down to one-third of a person per shift. Not only did the pitmen at Teversal object in principle to the introduction of method study of their potential performance, but the particular practices of contract working under method study forced the branch to argue about manning in order to maintain wage levels.

The union official who bargained with the NCB explained the complicated "double jeopardy" arrangements which conditioned the battle over manning under the DPLA. The men were paid a rate per yard advanced (against a fall-back rate, initially, of 65 shillings). This value (representing the contract price per yard multiplied by the quantity of yards advanced) was divided equally among all men working on the cutting and filling shifts. "The Board might say," explained the official, "it's a two-shift system. You can work it out on forty-five men: twenty-two on one shift and twenty-three on the other. We want two times twenty-three." If the Board insisted that the standard be forty-five for the two-shift cycle (and not forty-six), "you got five additional shifts than what you wanted."[72] These five additional shifts would be listed as "time worked outside of contract shifts," and—in a throwback to the butty system where men essentially paid for their own overtime working—the original members of the team would be doubly penalized. First, the gross earnings of the team would be reduced by a value representing the contract price per yard times the quantity of yards advanced in five shifts. Second, the gross earnings would have to be shared with an extra man.

There is a further wrinkle to this system of working, which becomes particularly important at Teversal where geological conditions are so irregular. The DPLA contract system allows for the addition of shifts to the standard weekly estimate when abnormalities require an extemporaneous alteration of method study standards. But the deputy retains enormous discretion over the implementation of this option, and thus can exhort (or coerce) high, determined productivity in exchange for the "favor" of recognizing abnormal conditions. As the branch secretary puts it, it was "arbitrary whether it was 'extra men' or an 'abnormality.' " Accordingly, down to its last days under the DPLA, Wage Structure I generated rules of working which sustained high productivity while, at the same time, miners were pressured to consider competitively the distinctive needs of their own work groups.

Teversal Wage Structure I may be summarized in this way.

1. Identification: butty-chargeman/DPLA structure.
2. Form and level of payment: incentive structure pitched at moderate level, based on spot-bargained contracts, augmented after DPLA by standard power loading fallback rate.
3. Generative Rules
   3.1 Assignment of position on coal face: by management prerogative, exercised by chargeman/ deputy.

3.2 Work pace and attitude toward productivity: generally disciplined attitude toward production, generated both by the incentive structure and by the capacity of the deputy to manipulate financial consequences of manning decisions, particularly under abnormal geological conditions.

3.3 Division of labor in primary work group: initiated by group, with supervision of management.

3.4 Relationship among shift and task groups: formally cooperative due to shared gross earnings based on two-shift yardage total; but groups nonetheless divided over responses to adverse geological conditions, responsibilities for ancillary underground tasks and, potentially, over problems of manning.

Wage Structure II

There is little regard for the NPLA at Teversal, a pit typical of Nottingham in the preference of its members for an incentive structure. Members of the executive committee of the Teversal Branch explain that the NPLA generated resentment during the long transitional period when some colliers continued working under their contract while others, entering new face panels, worked under the power loading agreement. As a consequence, the "natural" correlation between hard work, good bargaining, and high wages evaporated. Relativities among work groups went awry. "It was a ridiculous position," recalls a branch official. "In a lot of cases men on power loading were getting more." Miners on a contract in a bad district (relying on a fall-back rate of 65s.) were ill-suited by the traditional Nottingham attitude to accept men on a daywage contract in the same district receiving 86s. 9d. (the initial Nottingham NPLA rate), independent of productivity. Somehow, the fact that "men on a contract in a district that was good could make £7-£8," seemed less problematic.

Today, the Teversal men remain unreconciled to the NPLA, preferring proposals for a productivity agreement. Thus, when the branch secretary says with some heat, "Power loading is the best thing that ever came out for the union," he is not referring to its implications for the pattern of working. He states explicitly his one positive reaction to the NPLA: it made the national strikes of 1972 and 1974 possible. Nevertheless, despite a passing acknowledgment that a daywage may mean safer work habits—here the branch secretary quotes former NUM Secretary Will Paynter's famous endorsement of the daywage, that it would mean that miners could "stop leaving [their] skins on the face"—Teversal opposes the NPLA. The treasurer of the branch complains that the NPLA has sown the seeds of disunity by weakening interest in the branch and by undermining the rules of unity within the work team which dated from a time when miners had to fight constantly for the wage against butty and deputy.

> When I first joined the Union, we had to negotiate the contract every week. The NPLA took a lot of interest out. [Before] there were contracts for packing, stinting, ripping. If there was trouble, the team came out in a block. At Teversal, it was always one out, all out. A family pit. Only since powerloading, [you've] had individualism.

Branch members seem to be arguing that the unity is not expressed in the work teams, but at the level of the colliery qua family pit struggling to keep the collectivity intact. Indeed, because of the hostility that the issues of potential closure have generated between management (both pithead and regional) and miners, relations are strained, and there is no room for the kinds of tacit agreements which are common elsewhere. At Teversal, therefore, the NPLA seems to be run by the book.

Teversal Wage Structure II may be summarized in this way.

1. Identification: NPLA daywage structure.
2. Form and level of payment: time-based daywage at nationally negotiated daywage rates.
3. Generative Rules
   3.1 Assignment of position on coal face: by management prerogative.
   3.2 Work pace and attitude toward productivity: formal indifference toward productivity.
   3.3 Division of labor in primary work group: formal cooperation, possibly individuated.
   3.4 Relationship among shift and task groups: formal cooperation.

Systematic Pattern of Production

PRODUCTIVITY

In January 1967, men began switching over from the 6's face to start development work on the 8's face. In February, 6's (a contract face) ceased production and 8's began working with the same face team under the NPLA. Unfortunately, a clear comparison of productivity on the two faces is not possible for two reasons. First, the change in wage structure accompanied a transition from a hand-filled face (6's) to a fully power loaded face (8's). Therefore, direct comparisons of production would not necessarily isolate the influence of wage structure on worker initiative or laboring habits. Second, I secured the data on productivity at Teversal from a resourceful colliery official, the NCB having officially discarded records for Teversal which were more than five years old. While the records are undoubtedly accurate—they are in the original hand of the surveyor—they do not conform to the standard categories which were used subsequently. Accordingly, I had to rely on different indices of productivity for each face.

The data which are available, however, indicate a pattern of steady productivity at Teversal (see Table 5.6). Figures for OMS for 6's face indicate little variation in productivity

TABLE 5.6. Compilation of Productivity by Face Teams Before and After the Introduction of the NPLA at Teversal Colliery

	First Quarterly Production Period	Second Quarterly Production Period	Third Quarterly Production Period	Fourth Quarterly Production Period	Subsequent Production Period to Exhaustion	Total for Life of Face
6's[a] OMS (Pre-NPLA)	97.3	102.1	100.6	91.8	96.8	97.4
8's[b] E/S% (NPLA)	128	78	114	102	94	104

SOURCE: NCB, Teversal Colliery, Surveyor's Reports and Colliery Output Weekly Summaries.

[a] Productivity for 6's face is measured in OMS (face CWTS/manshift). Figures are based on a set of complete four-week and five-week (monthly) colliery surveyor's reports. The first period runs from November 1964–January 1965; the second period runs from February–April 1965; the third period runs from May–July 1965; the fourth period runs from August–October 1965; and the subsequent period runs from November 1965–August 1966. Although the face commenced coaling on 12 October 1964, October 1964 is omitted as a settling-in period. Likewise the period from September 1966 to the end of production in December 1966 is omitted because of distortions attributable to face shortening and difficult roof conditions and because of the lack of complete OMS data.

[b] Productivity for 8's face is measured as a ratio of actual weekly saleable tonnage extracted (E) to standard—method studied norm or target—tonnage (S), expressed as a percentage. Figures are based on complete weekly records for the periods considered. The first period runs from 22 April–22 July 1967; the second period runs from 29 July–14 October 1967; the third period runs from 21 October 1967–29 January 1968; the fourth period runs from 27 January–20 April 1968; and, the subsequent period runs from 20 April–22 June 1968. All dates represent the last day of a week to which the production records refer. The period from 4 February–15 April 1967 is omitted, since the fall-off in performance (to 14 percent of standard) could not meaningfully be attributed to changes in workers' effort associated with the wage structure. At Teversal, 8's replaced 6's face, and the two faces, which were in the same (Waterloo) seam and had comparable geological conditions, were worked by the same team. It should be noted, however, that 6's was hand-filled, whereas 8's was power loaded.

throughout the life of the face, despite complaints by management of serious absenteeism in the closing quarter. The first and last periods of production indicate a variation of average OMS of a scant 0.5 cwt. and the average production for the total life of the face varies but 0.1 cwt. from that of the first quarter of production.

Although it would be extremely useful to know the standard envisioned by the NCB for 6's face, reasonable inferences of positive productivity can nevertheless be drawn. Weekly comments of satisfaction by the surveyor tend to reinforce the record of productivity, which seems all the more impressive in light of repeated references to difficulties with the condition of the roof and associated geological disorders. In the case of 8's face where the method studied standard is known, the data indicate that actual extraction of coal exceeds standard, over the life of the face, by 4 percent. This is a record which the NCB can hardly fault, and one which supports the hypothesis that Teversal reflects Nottingham's typical generative rules of working and its habits of determined productivity under the NPLA as well as under the less exceptional case of an incentive-based contract structure.

POWER RELATIONS

All other issues pale before that of closure, a prospect which makes the power relations at Teversal extremely tense. The branch secretary confirms with resignation, "I suppose we shall have to make a big issue [out of the future of the pit]. The Board is waiting for all the pressure to come from our end. We got to keep putting the pressure on." With this in mind, in January 1976 Teversal Branch instituted an overtime ban, in an effort to force the NCB to agree to develop a new seam (the Clowne seam) to keep the colliery working. According to private notes by a branch official from a series of special meetings, attitudes between management and men hardened during the five-week job action, and the dispute generated a series of spin-off confrontations: windingmen refusing to wind men down, the colliery manager outlawing use of the canteen for branch meetings, proliferation of contradictory claims by NCB and NUM engineers about the cost of developing the Clowne seam for Teversal. The branch claims that the NCB has withdrawn a promise to develop the seam and fear that another Nottingham colliery or even one in neighboring Derbyshire will work it, while Teversal is closed. Indeed, the Teversal men, the "backwoodsmen," affirm that "action against the area union" must be part of their strategy.[73] At the same time, they insist that the area NUM will "be watching the [closure] issue very closely. Notts is not Derbyshire when it comes to a fight." Beleaguered, Teversal men speak of a "con" by the NCB, one official promising development under conditions of sustained productivity, another threatening closure despite all.

In the meanwhile, while the future of the pit is undecided, branch officials deal with other issues—manpower, grading—as the formal national agreements require, through long conciliation procedures. Convinced that conciliation procedures are to the advantage of management, the branch, nevertheless, follows the line of least daily resistance on many of the small issues. Unwilling to risk the decline in productivity that would signal the definitive demise of Teversal, the union observes icy, proper relations within an irrevocably politicized atmosphere, hoping the big fight can, somehow, be won in time.

Summary

Caught between militancy and the desperate hope that a record of high, consistent productivity will be rewarded by the NCB, the Teversal men execute an uncertain strategy, pressing, like Sherwood, for more overtime working in between threats of overtime bans. They complain that the bigger pits are allowed to work overtime, while the smaller pits are made to toe the line. Teversal is being squeezed out, they argue, because the NCB and the NUM have agreed to a national policy of rationalizing the industry through concentration of production in bigger units. They sense that the manpower is being run down through "voluntary wastage" and that ineffective managers have been passed through Teversal ("a training ground for gaffers"), all to the detriment of a pit whose men are desperately trying to keep the colliery producing efficiently. "If your future is in doubt," remarks a branch official, "then everything that comes to light, you're suspicious. . . . They've not replaced the last two undermanagers. They're trying to run the pit down."

Pressed by the branch secretary at an official Colliery Review Meeting in 1976, the NCB refused to give assurances "that if the OMS stays good, we should go for the Clowne seam." The branch secretary laments, in response, "How can we expect to work a pit with all this uncertainty?" But work it they do, in true Nottingham fashion. Conditioned by the generative rules of the butty/chargeman structure, steady productivity is doubly certain at Teversal. It was there, initially, during the transition to the NPLA despite opposition to withdrawal of incentives. It is more certain, now, in a hopeless effort to keep Teversal open by keeping it remunerative. Fixated, quite naturally, on the closure issue, power relations have soured as at no other Nottingham pit. But even amidst growing conflict, ironically, Teversal—for its own separate reasons—conforms to the Nottingham pattern. Embittered relations do not get in the way of productivity; loss of morale is not reflected in declining production. Pushed to the edge, notified by NCB officials that the Clowne seam will not be developed by Teversal,[74] facing dissolution of the community, Teversal branch officials try, nevertheless, to preserve a positive sense of the colliery. While in Durham that might require a show of defiance, in Nottingham the Teversal branch official opts to soften his account of Teversal's militancy to make it clear that whatever the branch has done—they have been forced to do. "It's a very happy pit," he reminds me. "Don't get the feeling it's a bad pit."

CONCLUSION

As the five underground anthropologies demonstrate, neither the patterns of laboring and power relations nor productivity trends in Nottingham show a close resemblance to the systematic features of production observed in the Durham collieries. Influenced by the butty/chargeman structure, the Nottingham pitmen responded to the NPLA in a way which markedly differs from the reaction of Durham miners, whose attitudes were, I have argued, conditioned by the fundamentally dissimilar cavilling/marra structure. If these observations are accurate, then disparate regional traditions of laboring relations have severely damaged the *national* design of the daywage structure as the dialectic of control is battled out work group by work group. Generalizations about productivity and productive relations must now be made at the regional level—and then made only with careful reference to distinctive traditions which have endured at individual collieries. Thus, antecedent patterns of laboring relations influence the meanings which workers attach to NCB initiatives, and unfailingly generate responses which challenge the management's design for the performance of work under a national daywage agreement.

The clearest result to emerge is that the NPLA effected a shift in the locus of labor-management conflict from issues of pay to the problem of control over production. Thus at Nottingham's most typical pit, Thoresby, despite generally positive power relations, conflict arises over the composition of face teams and in response to what the miners consider to be excessive underground supervision (see Table 5.7). At Sherwood, a model colliery in both its power relations and its exceptional productivity, questions of grading have caused the only work stoppage in memory.

As predicted, structural features of the NPLA have generated some degree of uniformity in miners' responses, particularly when NCB initiatives bring to the fore problems such as increased underground supervision and method

TABLE 5.7. Summary of Systems of Production in Selected Nottingham Collieries

	Wage Structure I	Wage Structure II	Productivity	Power Relations
Thoresby	butty/chargeman; DPLA	NPLA	high	cooperative conflicts over composition and manning of teams, and underground supervision; conflict with union about overtime
Sherwood	DPLA/contract	NPLA	very high	extremely cooperative; incidental conflict over grading and nonproductive issues; severe conflict with union about overtime
Bevercotes	Experimental Bevercotes Agreement	NPLA	erratic	cooperative; conflict over compensation for anomalous conditions; gentleman's agreements as part of compensation
Harworth	butty/chargeman; DPLA	NPLA	steady	cooperative, placid; occasional "anti-cavilling" controversy; gentleman's agreement about overtime and grading
Teversal	butty/chargeman; DPLA	NPLA	steady	conflictual over potential closure (with use of overtime ban); cooperative on matters of production

study determination of manning. On these issues, the conflicts at Thoresby are parallel to those which occur at Boldon
and Horden in County Durham. In important additional
ways, however, Nottingham and Durham miners part
company in their response to the NPLA. In Durham, the
most distinctive responses to the introduction of the daywage structure came at Rainton where the miners effectively exerted pressure for the reintroduction of cavilling,
and at Horden where the miners reintroduced practices to
restrict production and to rotate positions at the coal face.
In Nottingham, colliers have characteristically responded
to the introduction of the NPLA by pressing management
(and the NUM) to increase overtime and revise upward
the gradings of specific classes of miners. The issue of grading has been a problem for political relations at Sherwood
and Harworth, and in the latter colliery the pitmen have
introduced an "anti-cavilling" perspective on the question
of assignment of face locations. Throughout Nottingham,
but particularly at Sherwood, Thoresby, and Teversal, the
question of overtime has been the focus of power relations.
Thus, regionally specific responses to the introduction of
the daywage (cavilling and restrictive production practices
vs. questions of overtime and grading) modify the otherwise uniform shift in the locus of conflict from issues of
pay to issues of control over production.

In both coalfields the habits and traditions of laboring
relations under Wage Structure I directly conditioned the
evolution of laboring relations under the NPLA. The reintroduction of restrictive practices and rotational schema for
the selection of face teams under the NPLA reflected the
traditions of laboring relations in Durham, particularly at
Rainton, where the bord and pillar system generated unusual habits of altruistic cooperation among the colliers.
Likewise, the lasting effects of the competitive, high productivity of the butty system may be recognized in the
attitudes toward production, and in the continued use of
the mechanism of market men, in Nottingham collieries.
While productivity declines at Rainton as closure ap-

proaches, not only the fight to oppose closure, but the resilience of the generative rules for working under the butty-chargeman/DPLA structure ensure steady productivity at Teversal. In Sherwood, where under Wage Structure I cooperation among classes of miners for the upward regulation of production was typical, these habits of cooperative relations among different grades continue to generate extremely high productivity even among rippers, despite the lack of financial incentive. There is also, at Sherwood, an unusual degree of cooperation with management on the sticky matter of deployment. This may well reflect the history of laboring relations which, without the explicit presence of the butty system, did not, at Sherwood (in contrast to Thoresby), set classes of workers at odds with each other. At Thoresby, with the interests of task groups divided under the harsh pressures of the butty-chargeman/DPLA structure, differences between craftsmen and face workers continued to generate conflict among the men during the settling-in period of the NPLA.

Finally, productivity under the national daywage structure was conditioned by antecedent habits and traditions of laboring. The effect of the NPLA on productivity, therefore, was largely determined by the transitive characteristics of the cavilling/marra and the butty/chargeman structures. Since worker self-regulation can in practice have either an upward or a downward effect on productivity, the effect of the generative rules of the cavilling/marra structure in Durham varied according to colliery-level specifics. Thus, an incentive structure at Eden accompanied stagnant or slightly declining productivity, while an incentive structure with cavilling at Sacriston tended to improve productivity. But the generative rules of working associated with the butty/chargeman structure affect productivity in a far more uniform way. Strange and unforeseen geological and technological problems have led to an erratic pattern of production at Bevercotes, and—the odd colliery in every way— the men have no direct historical link with the butty or DPLA structure. Even at Bevercotes, however, there is no evidence of poor productive effort by the men. In every other colliery studied here, production is steady, despite uncertainty over closure (Teversal) or accusations of "Yorkshire influence" (Harworth). At Thoresby and Sherwood where the influence of the butty/chargeman generative rules for working is particularly strong, productivity is unusually high.

The systems of production which have developed under the NPLA in the Durham and Nottingham coalfields differ from each other in regionally characteristic ways. While differences in geological fortunes and technological innovation should not be ignored, the effects of wage structures on productivity and power relations can best be attributed to the specific evolution of preexisting patterns of laboring relations and, notably, to the lasting effects of Durham's cavilling/marra and Nottingham's butty/chargeman structures. Amidst such contradictory responses along sectional lines, rationalization through national uniformity seems the least likely of outcomes.

CHAPTER SIX

CONCLUSION

True to their understanding of Weber, academic social scientists have stressed the need for greater insight into the inner rationality of administrative organizations, while Marxist theorists have mainly considered the broad structural characteristics of the capitalist state, presupposing a close connection between state activities and the reproduction of class relations. Too often, their attention to the character of the state within a class environment simply counterbalanced the one-sidedness of conventional academic concern for the internal dimensions of bureaucracy and the highly observable features of their institutional structures. Accordingly, the explicit relationship between the *internal* organization structure and the *external* evolution of class forces and the mediate expressions of class power (parties, unions, etc.) has seldom been raised as a serious issue.

ORGANIZATIONAL STRUCTURE AND CLASS POWER

The problem has recently come to the surface, however, in part because some Marxist theorists remain troubled by Lenin's warning that the "old State machine" must be smashed and not, as Kautsky and modern social democrats would have it, merely captured and repopulated.[1] For those inspired by Lenin, yet haunted by the manifest failure of the Soviet bureaucracy to allow "the *mass* of the population to [take] an *independent* part . . . *in the everyday administration of the State*,"[2] theoretical concerns about organization and state theory are motivated by the need to understand how class power informs the organs of state administration. At the same time, the not inconsequential prospects of Eurocommunist or committed socialist regimes in Western Europe add urgency to the programmatic divisions between adherents of the evolutionary and revolutionary approaches. The breach grows not only from disagreement over the content of transitional policies, but also over how they should be articulated and implemented, and how they may be kept both democratic and effective.

Thus the problem which Göran Therborn has referred to as the "form of the organization of the state" gains significance, and Marxist theory has attempted to absorb the best of Weberianism by investigating the dynamics of bureaucracy (modes of decision-making, handling of tasks, allocation of resources, patterning of personnel and responsibilities, etc.) in terms of the class character of the state.[3] If the organizational form which defines a capitalist state today can be identified, then perhaps the appropriate structure for a transitional state—one that is at once democratic and administratively capable—can be applied tomorrow.

Unfortunately, despite Therborn's claims, there may be no "real causal relationship between the forms of state organization and the particular class relations to which they are linked."[4] To keep to the case at hand, I can see no clear causal relationship between the forms of administration of the British coal industry and the capitalist relations of the lackluster "mixed economy" into which it was thrust. For the moment, Weber's argument that private and public administration are internally homologous seems closer to the mark than the alternative proposal that the form of organization bears the explicit markings of the capitalist state, for which it is uniquely suited. While there is more to the bureaucracy-state relation than Weber specified, the lack of explicit causal relationship is a problem for Marxist theory which should be clearly faced.

Lucio Colletti wrote in his notable analysis of Lenin's *State and Revolution*:

> For Lenin, the socialist revolution has to destroy the old State because it must destroy *the difference between governors and governed itself.* For Kautsky, the State and bureaucracy, i.e. the difference between governors and governed, cannot be suppressed and will always survive. For Lenin, the revolution is the end of all masters; for Kautsky, it is merely the arrival of a new master.[5]

Clearly, Kautsky intends that the new master will be a socialist-dominated parliament, while Lenin proposed in principle a "masterless" democracy of the soviets. The problem with the latter, what Colletti calls "the self-management of the mass of producers," is not that it is utopian, per se, but that it is one-sidedly utopian and hence implausible.[6] Alongside the vision of a true democracy, socialism requires the institutionalization of effective coordination, or at the least, Engels' "administration of things." If the administration is to take place at the level of the state, then whatever the transformative designs of the new masters, some bureaucracy will have to stay.

The response of the French left to the problem of the class character of the administrative bureaucracy which was embodied in the Common Program—the ritual affixing of the word "democratic" before every example of state administrative activity—is not good enough.[7] The promise of democratic governance obscures the certainty of hierarchical coordination and hence the "undemocratic" character of any (even partly) centralized administration. At the same time it draws attention away from the obvious: that whatever the division of the spoils among Socialists, Communists, and radicals—or the disagreements that would tear apart such an alliance—there would be a coterie of new masters, and the populace at large would not take part in the everyday administration of the French state. Whatever one might want to say about the class character of a Eurocommunist regime or a determinedly socialist regime committed in principle to democratization and decentralization, there would invariably be a fundamental continuity in the form of state organization (the modes of decision-making, etc.).

THE NECESSITY OF CENTRALIZED BUREAUCRATIC ADMINISTRATION

After a nominal change in power, who will be the new master? How will the rules which the new regime promulgates, the norms it observes, the powers of coercion it preserves, condition the reproduction of class relations and influence the balance of class forces? These will remain the central questions throughout the initial transitional period. Whatever the outcome of this set of battles, some new master—party or parliament, organs of dual power or direct executive leadership—will require administrative assistance. If the "destruction of the bourgeois State machine is not the Ministry of the Interior in flames,"[8] it is also not "small is beautiful" decentralism and community control.

In a sense, both Kautsky and Lenin are wrong (or misleading): the former because the existence of a leftist parliament and new bodies in the old bureaucratic offices does not ensure a new class basis for the state nor secure it against capitalist counterattack; the latter, because we have to know an awful lot more about the principles which will replace the logic criterion and the structure criterion of the Weberian bureaucracy. Of course, conventional bureaucracy may rightly be attacked for its lack of internal democracy and its insulation from mechanisms of representation, whether democratic-centralist or parliamentary in form. But the class character of the state is not determined by the form of organization or level of democracy, however construed. A transformation of the class character of the state need not require the massive internal reconstruction of a more or less Weberian bureaucracy, even though it should introduce a period of the most far-reaching debate about new principles of representation, norms of accountability, levels of concern for the felt needs of disparate groups in the society, and so on. Without altering the form of organization, however, administrative bureaucracies can be set up to do the bidding of various classes and fragmentary coalitions representing diverse masters.

Owing to this class "openness" of the bureaucracy with regard to its logic or structure, neither the search for a singular capitalist-specific form of state organization nor excessive attention to the inner workings of bureaucracies seems promising, if the intent is to understand the connections between centralized bureaucratic administration and the changing balance of class forces within the context of existing capitalist relations. The crisis-ridden path of capitalist development can be understood far better from the concrete study of the initial determinations of state policy and the effect of policy implementation on the balance of class forces, and from a consideration of the capacities of state agencies to make their policies work and to make them stick.

One should not infer too much from a single case, nor leap carelessly from analysis of the nationalized coal industry to problems of state bureaucracy in the abstract. But both the political and economic centrality of the coal industry give it an undeniable importance, and the strict adherence by the NCB to the Weberian model of the modern bureaucracy adds a theoretical significance to the practical NCB problems. Weber's perception that bureaucracy is the common basis of organization within state administration and private industry and his assumption of harmonious codevelopment led him to neglect the complications which arise in the transmission of state policy. These complications do not follow as a matter of logic or necessity from the modes of decision-making followed by a bureaucracy but from contradictions, such as those I have discussed in terms of the British coal industry, which result from the dialectic of control which attends centralized bureaucratic administration. Problems result from the active response of those groups affected by policy to the spreading domination of the state, and not from a particular internal organizational structure.

In a general way, the class character of NCB policy initiatives is determined not by the institutional logic of administration, but by the structural context of the nationalized industries within capitalist Britain, and by the struggles between workers and management which are endemic to the capitalist labor process. This does not mean, of course, that policy initiatives undertaken by the boards of the nationalized industries cannot influence the context and generate conditions which may contribute to a realignment of class forces in Britain or (as Jenkins and the others had hoped) promote greater equality in incomes. Had the postwar balance of power been substantially more on the side of the working classes, then by 1966 the goals of the boards of nationalized industries might have been to transform work relations rather than to generate a surplus of revenues, and wages policy might have been fundamentally designed to reduce differentials among classes or workers.

How shall the public sector behave: as a beachhead against the bourgeoisie or as a halfway house for moribund private enterprise? The question is not, How, administratively (by what organizational structure), does the state command the heights? but rather, Who gives the commands and what sort of battle is waged? The constituency and (both foreseen and unexpected) effects of actual exercises in state power, rather than specific organizational forms, mark the class character of the state. The limits set by the capitalist economy in a national and international context, and the balance and organizational capacities of class forces, determine the effectiveness of state policies implemented today and condition the subsequent evolution of state-society relations.

State policy can fail because of poor design or implementation or because of more fundamental problems in centralized bureaucratic management. When the design is elegant and the implementation imaginative, and the failure arouses the native militancy and taps the full organizational potential of Britain's most determined working class activists, then policy initiatives undertaken by the Board of a nationalized industry can, indeed, create the possibility of an important shift in the immediate balance of class forces. As I will explain, more was at stake in the failure of the NCB then a decline in productivity and a change in the power relations at Britain's coal faces.

THE NPLA AND THE CENTRALIZATION OF CONFLICT

The NPLA, the cornerstone of the NCB's strategy for rationalization, conceived and administered by the "perfect Weberian bureaucracy," failed because of contradictions located in the complex play of state-society relations under contemporary capitalism. The Board was willing to offer a guaranteed weekly wage in return for firm management control over the face operation and over EMS. NCB officials reasoned that incidental stoppages and disputes would be reduced and that miners would accept flexible strategies down the pit more readily, since wages would no longer be tied to individual work strategies. Management reasoned rightly and planned well, but were not equipped to understand the full range of consequences which followed from the simple, uniform, national time-based wage structure. A centralizing policy was torn apart by the centrifugal pressures of a regionally distinctive industry. A policy which was designed thoughtfully to reward a simple instrumental reaction—cooperation in return for a guaranteed wage—succumbed before the complex meanings attached to it by workers who had long been influenced by laboring relations which occasioned responses that management had not foreseen. Accordingly, a policy designed to rationalize and harmonize a basic industry with unusual economic and political centrality served instead to undermine capitalism. The coal industry remains unstable, the workforce volatile.

Reflecting the contradictory processes of bureaucratic state administration, the new wages policy deepened the existing tension in the coal industry between the centralizing tendency of NCB policy initiatives and the regional character of work traditions. This being the case, the industry is best understood, in some sense, by reference to the decentralized pattern of its evolution, that is, as a set of regionally specific, locally differentiated and experienced fragments, rather than as a unified national enterprise. Nevertheless, the NCB endeavored through its policies to arrest the natural decentralizing tendencies of these regional influences and to rationalize the industry from the center. Curiously, the NPLA was a three-time loser: first, because, as the Board acknowledges, national productivity declined; second, because what I have called the politics of productivity at the coal face shattered the national design of the agreement; and third, because industrial conflict which had previously been decentralized and uncoordinated now erupted in national confrontations with strong class overtones.

With the introduction of the NPLA, the focus of industrial conflict shifted dramatically. Prior to the NPLA, local agreements for piece-rate price lists led to disputes over anomalies and to frequent work stoppages, but the participants were usually concerned with the conditions of a particular contract for a class of workmen in a single colliery. Industrial action might extend to the shift group or to the workmen in the colliery at large, but it would rarely transcend these natural limits. The built-in division between pieceworkers at the face and those working for a daywage in jobs "back-bye," which was seldom bridged, also tended to contain conflict. Likewise, the possibility of coordination among collieries was remote; and between regions, where differences in wage levels and in relative bargaining strength remained great, concerted action was extremely uncommon.

The NPLA, however, rationalized the basis for coordination of industrial action both among classes of workers and among regions.[9] Face workers, now dependent on the national negotiation of NPLA wage rates, lost their capacity to force wage increases through independent action at the coal face. Equally important, for the first time the interests of the face worker and of the miner working elsewhere below ground were linked, since all their wage rates were set by a single comprehensive agreement.[10] Most important, the face workers' unique power within the industry was directed away from the coal face, toward the arena of national negotiations. Since agreements were uniform, the division of interest among miners in different regions was vastly diminished.

Therefore, as a result of the NPLA, the industry entered an era of increased interregional and, ultimately, national militancy which began with rank-and-file strikes in the Yorkshire coalfield and culminated in the national walkouts of 1972 and 1974. In October 1969, a movement for higher wages for all classes of workers and for a reduction in the hours of work for surface workers spread from Yorkshire to Scotland, Wales, and Kent, leading to a two-week period of unofficial strikes by 150,000 miners in 130 collieries. In the first application of "flying pickets" since 1926, Yorkshire miners picketed moderate Nottinghamshire pits, displaying a technique which would later epitomize the fact that the 1972 action was rank-and-file dominated. Then, unwilling to wait for the culmination of the five-year transition period detailed in the 1966 agreement, Yorkshire miners struck in November 1970 for immediate parity among all regions, this time sending their squads to Derby, Lancashire, and Durham as well as to Nottingham.[11] In November 1971, sparked again by Yorkshire miners, the NUM began a national overtime ban, the initial stage in a growing industrial conflict which, in January 1972, culminated in the first national miners' strike since 1926. With more control from the NUM executive and more explicit nonindustrial stakes—including the question of the survival of the Heath government—the drama of a national miners' strike was repeated two years later.

What NCB manager or Tory minister would not have longed in the winter of 1974 for the halcyon pre-NPLA days of spot-bargain bickering and uncheckable wages drift? But the centralizing effect of the NPLA on industrial conflict was decisive, even as its effects on local industrial relations were, as I have shown, much more diverse and problematic than management had envisioned. Ironically, the NCB's best efforts to rationalize the industry's wage structure provided the basis for unified national struggle without ever offering the possibility of enhanced industrial performance. Such are the consequences of state policy implementation through centralized administration.

The NPLA and the Decentralizing Tendencies of the Politics of Productivity

Simultaneously, the NPLA effected a fundamental shift in the power relations in the British coal industry. While in general the primary focus of labor-management conflict shifted from issues of pay—the character of the bargain for anomalous conditions, the rate of the payment-by-results contract—to issues of control over coordination of production, the fundamental change in the locus of conflict had two distinct dimensions. First, structural features of the NPLA generated a level of uniformity in miners' responses to management prerogatives. Thus, at Thoresby, for example, in Nottingham, as at Boldon and Eden in Durham, conflicts erupted over increased underground supervision and method study determination of manning. But second, and more important in demonstrating the character of regional variations which are usually neglected in NCB accounts of the effects of the NPLA, there were distinct differences in worker response to management initiatives in Durham and in Nottingham. In Durham, at Horden and Rainton, the distinctively regional responses to the introduction of the daywage were very evident in the reintroduction of cavilling and traditional restrictive practices. In Nottingham, on the contrary, conflict between management and men under the NPLA has taken the characteristic form of disagreement over grading (at Sherwood, for example) and pressure for changes in overtime policy (at Sherwood, Thoresby, and Teversal). In the sharpest contrast to the Durham tendencies, Harworth has actually engaged in "anti-cavilling" controversies with the NCB to ensure that the management prerogative to determine the positioning of face teams under the NPLA does not result in any unwanted rotation or equalization of chances among Harworth face teams. Thus, the work relations and political struggle which ensue correspond neither to the process of individuated capitulation to the norms of capitalism which Burawoy anticipates, nor to the foreordained pattern of class conflict writ large, which Edwards sees as the necessary concomitant to the capitalist labor process. Rather, we see fluid and indeterminate episodes in the dialectic of control.

Further, the colliery studies indicate that the effect of the NPLA on laboring relations was conditioned fundamentally by the generative rules of previous wage structures, particularly by the influence of these rules on the customary performance of work and on attitudes toward productivity of the working pitmen. The character of the relations among workers—whether there was competition or cooperation in selection of the most favorable face positions and work tasks, whether members of a work team tended to perform the overall task cooperatively or compete for individual high productivity—reflected the pre-NPLA traditions in their distinctive regional patterns. In Durham where the cavilling/marra tradition influenced post-NPLA laboring relations, unusual habits of cooperation remain, most notably at Rainton, where the continued presence of bord and pillar working generates anew the traditions of altruistic cooperation among men who share a stall, even though their wages are no longer linked to joint production. In Nottingham, where the butty/chargeman tradition conditioned the working relations of miners and their attitudes toward production, the tendency for high, competitive productivity has led Sherwood rippers to perform extremely well despite the withdrawal of financial incentives. At the same time, differences of interest between face workers and craftsmen continue to divide Thoresby pitmen.

Much as the power loading machinery which provided the underlying rationale for the NPLA altered the technological basis of the industry, the new wage structure thus transformed the complex web of relations among working miners and between miners and managers which developed directly out of the production process. Focusing on the distinctive laboring relations, emphasizing the importance of regional differences, and grounding my general arguments in the details of ten colliery anthropologies, I have offered a more comprehensive account of the effects of the NPLA than any attempted to date. I have presented precise data from individual teams who worked through the period of transition from piece-rate to daywage structures, and these data support the view that distinct regional traditions and current practices of laboring relations have ensured a diversity in the patterns of productivity under the NPLA. Neglecting the regional patterns and forgoing examination of disaggregated data of the sort I have offered, NCB officials, on the contrary, consistently speak of "the effect of the NPLA," as if the consequences of the agreement were uniform and consistent.[12] Accordingly, the Board has concentrated its evaluation on annual changes in productivity: up 6.6 percent in 1967; up 9 percent in 1968-69; down because of the national strike in 1971-72; up 9 percent in 1972-73; and as yet never regaining the 1973 peak of 45.8 cwt.[13] Of course, attention to national averages of this kind may be useful in registering the industry's overall success and, particularly, in defending requests for government financial support. But aggregate OMS figures are essentially misleading because of the serious disparities in regional patterns of production, especially if the data are used as prima facie evidence for the radical alteration of a national wages policy.

Productivity Agreements and the Future

The NCB's latest hope for renewed success—scrapping the NPLA for a set of productivity agreements—relies too heavily on aggregate national data as justification for a wholesale rejection of the principle of time-based wages. As if ignorant of their own earlier claims that a daywage reflected the realities of modern technology and accorded management the firmest possibility for a rational planning approach to production, the NCB has reversed its public relations initiatives. Beginning cautiously in 1974, the Coal Board introduced bland "for background only" acknowledgments that the industry had experienced some problems in achieving high levels of efficiency in some jobs.[14] By 1977, Sir Derek Ezra, chairman of the NCB, citing a two-year decline in national OMS from 45.0 to 43.6 cwt. stridently warned that "without an effective production incentive scheme the industry would have difficulty in meeting demand."[15]

After an extraordinary campaign by the NCB and the NUM executive, the failure of a national productivity scheme in 1974, accusations of flagrant disregard of union procedures, the modification of Phase Three of Callaghan's "social contract" to meet the NCB's requirements, and the rejection of a productivity agreement by a national pithead ballot of NUM members[16]—finally, in the winter of 1978, all NUM areas agreed to pit-based productivity schemes. National negotiations would set the general terms of the agreement and the fall-back rates for particular grades of workmen, while the specifics of the wage package would be hammered out locally, based in principle on method study determination of standard performance. Assuming a pose of studied optimism, in April 1978 the Board linked financial solvency in the industry to the "early success of the productivity scheme."[17] Ezra neglected to mention the possibility of two-tiered industrial conflict.

THE CONTRADICTORY PATH CONTINUES

From the daywage to the production incentive plan, NCB wages policy seems fraught with problems and a decreasing likelihood of success. First, the NPLA leads to centralized conflict in conjunction with regionally fragmented, unforeseen, and not particularly successful patterns of production. Then, blind to the implications of the ambiguous results of the daywage, the Board comes to rely on a less centralized wages policy, centered on pit-based productivity schemes negotiated at the area level. Since a centralized and uniform wage structure has led to diverse regional outcomes, it is not clear that a regionally based plan will uniformly and consistently improve productivity.

I suspect, despite NCB assurances to the contrary, that the effects of the bonus scheme on productivity may be quite limited. An NCB study of the consequences of the incentive agreement in North Nottinghamshire reveals that during the first quarter of operation output was some 8.8 percent higher than would have been expected under the NPLA. However, the area statistician who authored the study acknowledged that, given the higher wages paid out as a result of increased output, a break-even point for the incentive scheme would have required an increase of about 8.7 percent.[18] This thin margin of success (0.1 percent) hardly augurs well for the productivity agreement, particularly when one considers the "commando results" which inflate productivity in the early days of almost any new wage agreement and the high-production attitudes of Nottingham miners who long sought the new agreement and surely wanted to make a success of it.

The NCB statistician admitted that the improvement in output nationally was much lower than in Nottingham and declined to suggest that the incentive scheme raised productivity, concluding only that in general the decline in output had been halted.[19] National data for 1979-80, the first full year of operation under the incentive scheme, indicate an increase in OMS of 1.5 percent, compared with 2.2 percent for 1978-79.[20] These figures do not justify the official fanfare accorded the agreement, particularly since it is quite possible that the all-important ratio of earnings to output (EMS/OMS) has not moved in the Board's favor, and that nationally the break-even point for the incentive scheme has not been reached.

Very likely the effects of the incentive scheme on productivity will vary widely, and outcomes, as in the case of the NPLA, will depend largely on specific regional differences in the previous evolution of laboring relations. Durham miners may tend to increase efforts as necessary to secure what they consider an appropriate level of earnings, then restrict productivity while insisting that wage levels remain steady. Alternatively, the NCB may discover that because of traditions which generated habits of high and determined productivity under the NPLA, Nottingham miners are already working close to capacity. If that is the case, the projected increase in OMS of 10 to 15 percent might remain out of reach, except perhaps for a few initial bursts of extraordinary effort which could not be sustained for long. At the same time, comparisons of other regions— Scotland to Derbyshire, Wales to Kent, Yorkshire to Northumberland, etc.—might suggest equally diverse regional practices and trends in productivity.

The same might also be true for patterns of work relations and conflicts originating at the coal face, and it is here, in the politics of productivity, that the incentive scheme will be won or lost. A Durham industrial relations official struck the balance well. "Productivity has improved markedly," he observed in August 1980. "On the other hand, we've had increased disputes."[21] Of course, the disputes are localized once again, as they were before the introduction of the NPLA. They tend, naturally enough, to be about the revision of task norms and the renegotiation of the output standard which will trigger bonus pay. The incentive scheme invites battles of self-interest and dampens collective expressions of militancy. As Joe Whelan, the new Nottingham area general secretary and the most powerful left-wing voice on the area executive, put it, "The incentive scheme has knocked a lot of the tradition of militancy out of the miners and that was what it was designed to do."[22] Dave Douglass, the rank-and-file activist recently elected to the NUM's Yorkshire executive, put the productivity agreement in historical perspective. He began by recalling the nineteenth-century wage system which linked a proportion of the miner's wage to the local selling price of coal. "When we had a sliding scale," said Douglass, "we had a county union. When we had the NPLA we had a national union. Now with pit-based incentives we have no union at all. The paraphernalia of the union still exists, but I wonder if the motivation of the union is still here."[23]

In the 1980 annual NUM conference in Eastbourne, Arthur Scargill referred to pit closure lists drawn up by the NCB under government pressure as "Tory blackmail," and added: "If this woman in No. 10 wants a fight it will be of her own choosing."[24] But of course Thatcher does not want the kind of fight that Heath fought (and lost) to the miners in 1974, and the productivity agreement, for now at least, is her security against one. Scargill's defeat as a newly elected national NUM president urging a strike over wages and closure threats in 1982 has probably persuaded him of this point. But the long-term prospects are by no means certain.

Two possibilities for the future remain and each is shocking to the Jenkinsite social democratic vision of state ownership. So far, a downward spiral of militancy has attended hard-nosed NCB industrial relations strategies and the revival of old-fashioned capitalist practices such as quick dismissal for absenteeism (a plausible if unsavory tactic while there are long waiting lists of youths ready to go down the pit). The public sector becomes a meaner, stronger capitalist sector bent on defeating working-class initiatives and preserving the class balance. This resonates poorly with the social democratic vision of state ownership as equalizing lever and public control from the commanding heights as agency of social transformation.

While the Thatcherite dream of successfully intimidating the union seems to hold for the moment, a second response to the incentive scheme may emerge to endanger the current strategy. The dialectic of control is by no means played out, and I suspect that the Coal Board has moved too precipitously to surrender the principles of the daywage. In the end, it may be that by their latest initiative the NCB has created the worst of both industrial relations worlds. While the bonus component of the wage structure encourages the advancement of diverse regional and local interests, the common nationally bargained base rate requires collective negotiation for uniform daywage minima and for the terms and conditions of working. Thus, the productivity agreement has secured the return of uncheckable wages drift and ensured that localized bickering returns to a coal industry which may again be plagued, at the same time, by prospects of fierce national conflict, whether over the annual wage agreements or in response to threats of a new wave of colliery closures.

There is an additional factor which may occasion wider dispute. This Conservative government, committed in principle to "nonintervention," interferes far more in Coal Board affairs than has any government before. One NCB official who is a party to national Coal Board decisions confirmed that for the first time the Board is summoned to monthly accountability meetings at the Department of Energy, and added, as if to protect management from blame for strategies to come, "Major policy decisions are being made by the government."[25] As miners sense this change and accommodate their strategies to the new political order, they may key their responses all the more to the government and to Thatcherism, fighting battles with higher stakes on broader class lines.

While the everyday administration of the state will not be in immediate jeopardy, the contradictory processes of centralized bureaucratic administration will be displayed in a more direct way than usual, as rationalizing strategies backfire with uncharted implications for capitalism. Nothing highlights the class character of the state more dramatically than "flying pickets" or the spectacle of miners leading a crowd to demand that a power plant be shut down. With Scargill installed as NUM president and the possibility that a resurgent Triple Alliance may be preparing for a new 1926 in hopes of a different outcome, it will take far more than an alteration in the inner rationale of administrative bureaucracies to ensure that the events of 1972 and 1974 do not become but the first acts of a deepening drama.

NOTES

In exchange for permission to review an extensive set of documents, I agreed to limit my citations to a statement of the kind of document (e.g., memo, briefing, letter), a statement of the general subject of the document, and attribution of date to month and year. All notation of NCB materials conforms to this formula. I have similarly protected the identities of interview subjects.

Chapter One

1. Roy Jenkins, "Equality," in *New Fabian Essays*, ed. R.H.S. Crossman (New York: Praeger, 1952), p. 83.

2. Israel Berkovitch, *Coal on the Switchback: The Coal Industry since Nationalisation*, with a Foreword by Sir Derek Ezra (London: George Allen and Unwin, 1977), p. 56. See also: Great Britain, Laws, Statutes, etc. *Coal Industry Nationalisation Act, 1946*, 9 and 10 Geo. 6, ch. 59, First Schedule.

3. NCB, Brief on Wages Policy 1947-1974, January, 1974.

4. NCB, Supplemental Agreement to the Revision of the Wages Structure Agreement of 20 April 1955 [NPLA], Recital Clauses (c-e).

5. I found this sentiment to be very general. See, for example, interviews with NCB officials, North Nottinghamshire Area Headquarters, Edwinstowe, 24 March 1976 and 22 April 1976; interview with NUM officials, Nottingham Area Headquarters, Berry Hill Lane, Mansfield, 13 April 1976; interviews with NCB officials, Northeast Area Headquarters, Team Valley, Gateshead, 30 July 1974 and 8 August 1974; interview with NCB officials, Eden Colliery, Durham, 31 July 1974; interview with NUM officials, Durham Area Headquarters, Red Hill, Durham, 19 January 1977.

6. I was given complete access to the entire set of files maintained by the Wages Branch of the Industrial Relations Department for the period between 1965 and the time of my research

in the autumn of 1976. These materials included an extensive set of memos, briefings, minutes of working parties, etc., concerning the implementation of the National Power Loading Agreement in 1966, the Wilberforce Enquiry during the national strike of 1972, and the Enquiry into Pay Relativities which followed the strike of 1974, and all annual wage negotiations between 1971 and 1976. These materials had never before been made available to anyone outside the NCB.

7. NCB, General Purpose Committee, Memorandum on Wages Policy for Industrial Employees, March, 1949.

8. See: NCB, Working Party on Wages, Draft Interim Report on Second NUM Wages Claim 1951, August, 1951; NCB, Draft Report on National Wages Policy, July, 1951; NCB, Brief on Wages Policy 1947-1974, January, 1974; NCB, Memorandum on Systems of Remuneration in the Coal Mining Industry, August, 1951; NCB, Memorandum on Control Over Price Lists and Piecework, August, 1951; NCB, Working Party on Wages Policy, Note by Member on the Regulation of Wages in Accordance with Productivity, July, 1951.

9. For the most comprehensive NCB inquiry see: NCB, Memorandum on Wages Policy for Industrial Employees. See also: NCB, Brief on Wages Policy 1947-1974; NCB, Memorandum on Systems of Remuneration; NCB, Memorandum on Control over Price Lists and Piecework; NCB, Working Party on Wages Policy, Note by Member on the Regulation of Wages.

10. See: NCB, Memorandum on Wages Policy; NCB, Working Party on Wages, Draft Interim Report on Second NUM Wages Claim 1951, August, 1951; NCB, Draft Report on National Wages Policy, July, 1951.

11. NCB, Memorandum on Wages Policy.

12. NCB, Brief on Wages Policy 1947-1974; NCB, Note by Member on the Regulation of Wages.

13. NCB, Yorkshire Division Industrial Relations Department to General Secretary Yorkshire Area NUM, March, 1966.

14. NCB, National Industrial Relations Department to Divisional Industrial Relations Directors, August, 1965; NCB, Exchange of Memoranda among members of Industrial Relations Department, November, 1965; NCB, Draft Memorandum Industrial Relations Department to Chairman, Board Members, and Area General Managers, October, 1965.

15. NCB, Brief on Wages Policy 1947-1974.

16. See: Great Britain, National Board for Prices and Incomes. Report No. 12, *Coal Prices* (Cmnd. 2919, February, 1966, par. 56).

17. See, for example: NCB, Brief on Wages Policy 1947-1974; NCB, Memorandum by Member of Industrial Relations Department for General Purposes Committee on NPLA, March, 1966.

18. Max Weber, *Economy and Society*, 3 vols., ed. Guenther Roth and Claus Wittich (New York: Bedminster Press, 1968), 3:956-58.

19. Erik Olin Wright, *Class Crisis and the State* (London: New Left Books, 1978), p. 217.

20. For an excellent account of the implications of the neo-Weberian model, see: Charles Perrow, *Complex Organizations: A Critical Essay* (Glenview, Illinois and Brighton, England: Scott Foresman, 1972), pp. 145-176. For the original works in question, see: Herbert A. Simon, *Administrative Behavior*, 2nd ed. (New York: Macmillan, 1957); James G. March and Herbert A. Simon, *Organizations* (New York: John Wiley and Sons, 1958); Chester Barnard, *The Function of the Executive* (Cambridge: Harvard University Press, 1938).

21. Ann Swidler, "The Concept of Rationality in the Work of Max Weber," *Sociological Inquiry* 43:1 (Spring 1973), 41. See: Peter M. Blau and W. Richard Scott, *Formal Organizations* (San Francisco: Chandler Publishing Company, 1962); Arthur L. Stinchcombe, "Bureaucratic and Craft Administration of Production," *Administrative Science Quarterly* 4 (September 1959), 168-187; Michel Crozier, *The Bureaucratic Phenomenon* (Chicago: University of Chicago Press, 1964); R. K. Merton, "Bureaucratic Structure and Personality," in *Reader in Bureaucracy*, ed. R. K. Merton and others (New York: Free Press, 1952), pp. 361-371. I am indebted to Swidler for many of these references which appear in the extremely lucid article cited above.

22. See: Robert Michels, *Political Parties* (Glencoe, Ill.: The Free Press, 1949); Jürgen Habermas, *Legitimation Crisis*, tr. Thomas McCarthy (Boston: Beacon Press, 1973). I exclude Habermas from my general criticism of internalist treatments of bureaucratic institutions.

23. Marshall W. Meyer, *Change in Public Bureaucracies* (Cambridge: Cambridge University Press, 1979), p. 158.

24. See: Hans Van den Doel, *Democracy and Welfare Economics*, tr. Brigid Biggins (Cambridge: Cambridge University Press, 1979), pp. 125-132. Van den Doel provides a comprehensive catalog of studies which focus on the behavior of bureaucrats, stressing in

particular the contribution of W. A. Niskanen, *Bureaucracy and Representative Government* (Chicago: University of Chicago Press, 1971). For earlier examples, see: A. Downs, *Inside Bureaucracy* (Boston: Little, Brown, 1967); J. K. Galbraith, *The New Industrial State* (Boston: Houghton Mifflin, 1967).

25. Weber, *Economy and Society*, 3:1394.

26. Weber, 3:971-72.

27. Weber, 3:1394.

28. See: Meyer, *Public Bureaucracies*, pp. 157-160. Stinchcombe, in fairness, links bureaucratization to fairly precise environmental factors such as level of urbanization, the density of social life, and the presence or absence of a money economy. See: Arthur L. Stinchcombe, "Social Structure and Organization," in *Handbook of Organizations*, ed. James G. March (Chicago: Rand McNally, 1965), pp. 142-193.

29. I am indebted to Anthony Giddens for this idea and for the term "dialectic of control." See: Anthony Giddens, *A Contemporary Critique of Historical Materialism*. Vol. 1: *Power, Property and the State* (Berkeley and Los Angeles: University of California Press, 1981), pp. 220-226.

30. Nicos Poulantzas, *Political Power and Social Classes*, tr. Timothy O'Hagan (London: New Left Books, 1978), p. 343.

31. Poulantzas, p. 343.

32. Poulantzas, p. 344.

33. Organisation for Economic Cooperation and Development. *Regional Policies: The Current Outlook* (Paris: 1977), pp. 7-58.

34. For a discussion of regional policy in Britain, the determination of "peripheral areas," and the character of industrial development in the regions, see: Great Britain, Reference Division Office of Information, *Regional Development in Britain* (London: John Wiley and Sons, 1972), pp. 425-432. Devon and Cornwall and Northern Ireland of course are "peripheral areas" which fall outside the pattern I have described. Northern Ireland displays rather more complex political affiliations, although it is grossly underdeveloped and extremely reliant on traditional industries (ship building, linen manufacture, marine engineering). Devon and Cornwall fall outside the pattern altogether.

35. For an alternative discussion of the decentralizing strains on bureaucracy from the perspective of post-Weberian theories of organization, see: Nicos P. Mouzelis, *Organization and Bureaucracy: An Analysis of Modern Theories* (Chicago: Aldine Publishing

Co., 1967), pp. 59-62. Drawing on the work of Selznick and Gouldner, Mouzelis discusses the "dialectics" of bureaucracy (as he calls it), from a sophisticated but nonetheless internalist perspective.

36. Weber, *Economy and Society*, 3:1417.

37. Wright, *Class, Crisis and the State*, p. 187.

38. Weber, *Economy and Society*, 3:1394; Wright, pp. 186-188.

39. Claus Offe, "The Theory of the Capitalist State and the Problem of Policy Formation," in *Stress and Contradiction in Modern Capitalism*, ed. Leon N. Lindberg et al. (Lexington, Mass.: Lexington Books, 1977), p. 140.

40. Offe, p. 136.

41. Offe, p. 140.

42. See: Giddens, *Historical Materialism*, p. 223, for a discussion of the dialectic of control in the labor process itself.

Chapter Two

1. NCB, Memoranda Circulated within Industrial Relations Department on Power Loading, August, 1966.

2. NCB, Memorandum to General Purposes Committee on Interpretation of the National Power Loading Agreement, October, 1966.

3. Ibid. See also: NCB, Memorandum on National Power Loading Agreement as it influences the Position of Craftsmen, November, 1966.

4. NCB, Memorandum on Reduction of Effort, [November] 1966.

5. NCB, Memorandum and Brief for General Purposes Committee Meeting on the NPLA, January, 1967.

6. Roger Lumley, "A Modified Rules Approach to Workplace Industrial Relations," *Industrial Relations Journal* 10:4 (Winter 1979-80), 49.

7. Alan Fox and Allan Flanders, "The Reform of Collective Bargaining: From Donovan to Durkheim," *British Journal of Industrial Relations* 7:2 (1969), 151-180. It should be noted that Fox has left the Oxford school and has since leveled serious criticism in their direction. See subsequent work by Fox, including "Collective Bargaining, Flanders and the Webbs," *BJIR* 8:2 (1975), and especially, *Beyond Contract: Work, Power and Trust Relations* (London: Faber, 1974).

8. Fox and Flanders, p. 162.

9. Ibid., p. 173.

10. See: Royal Commission on Trade Unions and Employers' Associations 1965-1968, *Report* (Cmnd. 3623, HMSO 1969), chs. 2-3, 14.

11. See: William Brown, "A Consideration of 'Custom and Practice,' " *BJIR* 10:1 (1972), 42-44.

12. Ibid. See also: A.N.J. Blain and John Gennard, "Industrial Relations Theory: A Critical Review," *BJIR* 7:3 (1970), 392-395. The article provides an excellent overview which influenced my treatment of the Oxford approach.

13. M. G. Wilders and S. R. Parker, "Changes in Workplace Industrial Relations 1966-1972," *BJIR* 13:1 (1975), 22.

14. Michael Terry, "The Inevitable Growth of Informality," *BJIR* 15:1 (1977), 86. Terry makes a persuasive argument for the necessity and permanence of informal bargaining procedure.

15. Lumley, p. 49.

16. See: Kevin Hawkins, "The Future of Collective Bargaining," *Industrial Relations Journal* 10:4 (Winter 1979-80).

17. For an excellent brief summary of these efforts see: Lumley, pp. 49-51.

18. Brown, pp. 46-48.

19. In addition to Brown and Terry, see: H. A. Clegg, *The System of Industrial Relations in Great Britain* (London: Basil Blackwell, 1970); E. J. Hobsbawm, "Custom, Wages and Work Load in the Nineteenth Century," in *Labouring Men* (London: Weidenfield and Nicholson, 1964); E. H. Phelps and S. V. Hopkins, "Seven Centuries of Building Wages," *Economica* 1955, cited in Brown; J.E.T. Eldridge, "The Demarcation Dispute in the Shipbuilding Industry: A Study in the Sociology of Conflict," in *Industrial Disputes: Essays in the Sociology of Industrial Relations* (London: Routledge and Kegan Paul; New York: Humanities Press, 1968); and Stephen Hill, "Norms, Groups and Power: The Sociology of Workplace Relations," *BJIR* 12:2 (1974), 213-235. Stephen Hill comes closest to my perspective (p. 231) when he writes: "[A]ny real understanding of industrial relations must give considerable weight to the generation of rules in the bottom levels of the firm, whether by work group bargaining or by the individuals and other employee collectivities. The structure of workplace social relations is critical for this rule-creation and must therefore remain a primary focus of analysis."

20. Terry (pp. 83-84) argues that an informal rule may be particularly influential because the workers feel more responsible for its formulation.

21. Anthony Giddens, "Functionalism: *Après la lutte*," *Social Research* 43:2 (Summer 1976), 353.

22. Max Horkheimer, *Critical Theory: Selected Essays*, tr. Matthew J. O'Connell and others (New York: The Seabury Press, 1972), pp. 58-59.

23. Giddens, *New Rules of Sociological Method* (London: Hutchinson, 1976), p. 104.

24. Paul DiMaggio, "Review Essay: On Pierre Bordieu," *American Journal of Sociology* 84:6 (May 1979), 1462. See: Pierre Bourdieu, *Outline of a Theory of Practice*, tr. Richard Nice (New York: Cambridge University Press, 1977).

25. My use of the concept of structure as a system of generative rules (and resources) and my approach to the colliery studies owe much to the recent work of Giddens. See, in addition to his works already cited: *Central Problems in Social Theory: Action Structure and Contradiction in Social Analysis* (Berkeley: University of California Press, 1979).

26. John H. Goldthorpe, "Industrial Relations in Great Britain: A Critique of Reformism," *Politics and Society* 4:4 (1974), 428-429. I am not, however, convinced of the importance of Goldthorpe's distinction between "remunerative" and "symbolic" power.

27. Ibid., p. 429.

28. I am of course influenced here by Max Weber's account of types of authority and bases of legitimacy. I use the expression "de facto capacity of compliance" to focus on that aspect of *Herrschaft*, in Weber's terminology, which involves actual compliance or noncompliance with commands (exercises of power) as distinct from the motives for obedience or belief in the legitimacy of authority. See: Max Weber, *The Theory of Social and Economic Organization*, edited and with an Introduction by Talcott Parsons (New York: Macmillan, Free Press, 1964), pp. 152-153; 324-328.

29. It should be obvious that I place myself within the Marxist tradition, but also clear that my emphasis on day-to-day work relations and sources of conflict—and not on long-term tendencies or fundamental explanations of the behavior of the working class—requires a departure from much of the recent work in this field. In Britain, traditionally, Marxist scholarship which is directed at understanding industrial and labor processes has come out of a

rich tradition of empirical social history. Thus the Marxist literature includes impressive, amply documented accounts of the historical evolution of the working class as such and of the labor process in particular industries. There is a literature which examines the relations and divisions between working class fractions which are directly or indirectly conditioned by the development of capitalism. A second tradition in British research into the labor process—the theoretical work of Marxist economists—is growing rapidly. As yet, however, work has been limited primarily to exegetical applications of Marx's categories to contemporary capitalist industry. For reasons of focus and due to space limitations, I have chosen not to address this literature directly, despite its growth since I began this study.

For those who wish to consider this approach, perhaps the most powerful recent contribution to the tradition of Marxist social history in Britain is John Foster's *Class Struggle and the Industrial Revolution* (New York: St. Martin's, 1975). See also more classical works such as Hobsbawm, *Labouring Men* and E. P. Thompson, *The Making of the English Working Class* (New York: Random House, Vantage Books, 1966). For insight into the newer tradition in labor process theory, see, for example: Conference of Socialist Economics (CSE), *The Labour Process and Class Strategies* (London: Stage One, 1976). CSE has, I believe, made a very important contribution to the study and practical application of Marxist economics in Britain, but the published materials have not yet been as exciting as the conferences and working groups set in motion by CSE. The most serious effort to apply Marxist economics in industrial relations is Richard Hyman's *Industrial Relations, A Marxist Introduction* (London: Macmillan, 1975). In my view Hyman fails to break much new ground. The Work Relations Group in the U.S., which developed from a series of workshops at the Institute for Policy Studies in Washington D.C., has provided an excellent starting point for Marxist research into the issues which are traditionally termed industrial relations. See a report prepared by Jeremy Brecher, "Uncovering the Hidden History of the American Workplace," *Review of Radical Political Economics* 10:4 (Winter 1978), 1-23.

30. See: Michael D. Bayles, "The Function and Limits of Political Authority," in *Authority: A Philosophical Analysis*, ed. R. Baine Harris (Alabama: University of Alabama Press, 1976), pp. 101-106.

31. This definition follows Weber's approach, which is ex-

plained clearly by Samuel H. Beer, "Modern Political Development," in *Patterns of Government*, 3rd ed., ed. Samuel H. Beer et al. (New York: Random House, 1973), pp. 17-20.

32. See: Charles E. Lindblom, *The Intelligence of Democracy: Decision Making Through Mutual Adjustment* (New York: The Free Press, 1965).

33. Michael Burawoy, *Manufacturing Consent: Changes in the Labor Process under Monopoly Capitalism* (Chicago and London: University of Chicago Press, 1979), p. 65.

34. Burawoy, p. 63.

35. Richard Edwards, *Contested Terrain: The Transformation of the Workplace in the Twentieth Century* (New York: Basic Books, 1979), p. 162.

36. See: Jack Barbash, "Collective Bargaining and the Theory of Conflict," *BJIR* 18:1 (1980), 84-85.

37. See the discussion of power relations in Sherwood Colliery, Chapter Five below.

Chapter Three

1. Robert Nelson Boyd, *Coal Pits and Pitmen* (London: Whittaker and Co., 1895), pp. 11-26; T. S. Ashton and Joseph Sykes, *The Coal Industry of the Eighteenth Century*, rev. 2d. ed. (Manchester: Manchester University Press, 1964), pp. 70-99.

2. Boyd, pp. 17-21; Ashton and Sykes, pp. 70-72.

3. Ashton and Sykes, p. 75.

4. Ibid., pp. 135-136.

5. Ibid., p. 84.

6. NUM Durham Area, *Changes in Wages in the Durham Coal Trade 1871-1953 and Historical Record 1869-1953* (Durham: n.p., 1954), pp. 7-23.

7. E. Welbourne, *The Miners' Unions of Northumberland and Durham* (Cambridge: Cambridge University Press, 1923), pp. 159-176.

8. Ibid.

9. J.W.F. Rowe, *Wages in the Coal Industry* (London: P. S. King and Son, 1923), pp. 34-35.

10. W. W. Kirby, *The British Coalmining Industry 1876-1946: A Political and Economic History* (London: Macmillan, 1977), p. 13. See also: Rowe, pp. 119-120.

11. Rowe, pp. 39-102.

12. Kirby, p. 15.

13. NCD, Memorandum on National Wages Policy and Previous Methods of Wage Regulation and Control, July, 1941.

14. Ibid.

15. Ibid.

16. Ibid.

17. See: John H. Goldthorpe, "Industrial Relations in Great Britain: A Critique of Reformism," *Politics and Society* 4:4 (1974), 435-438.

18. NCB, Brief on Wages Policy 1947-1974, January, 1974.

19. Memorandum on Systems of Remuneration in the Coal Mining Industry, August, 1951.

20. Ibid.

21. Ibid.; NCB Memorandum on Control Over Price Lists and Piecework, August, 1951.

22. NCB, Memorandum on Systems of Remuneration.

23. Ibid. See also: NCB, General Purposes Committee, Memorandum on Wages Policy for Industrial Employees, March, 1949; NCB, Working Party on Wages Policy, Note by Member on the Regulation of Wages in Accordance with Productivity, July, 1951.

24. H. F. Bulman and R.A.S. Redmayne, *Colliery Working and Management* (London: Crosby Lockwood and Son, 1925), p. 306.

25. Interview with G. L. Atkinson, Area Industrial Relations Officer, Northeast Area Headquarters, Team Valley, Gateshead, 18 January 1977.

26. Ibid.

27. See: A. R. Griffin, *Coalmining* (London: Longman, 1971), p. 10.

28. See: "Mining Equipment: The Projected Expansion in Coal Production," *Financial Times* (London), 8 July 1974.

29. Interview with NCB officials and mining engineer, Northeast Area Headquarters, Team Valley, Gateshead, 8 July 1974.

30. Griffin.

31. E. L. Trist et al., *Organizational Choice* (London: Tavistock, 1963), p. 31.

32. Dave Douglass, *Pit Life in County Durham: Rank and File Movements and Workers' Control*, History Workshop Pamphlets, No. 6 (Oxford: Ruskin College, n.d.), p. 11.

33. Interview by Artist Project, Peterlee, Mr. McManners, n.d.

34. Douglass, *Pit Talk in County Durham: A Glossary of Miner's Talk Together with Memories of Wardley Colliery Pit Songs and Piliking*, History Workshop Pamphlets, No. 10 (Oxford: Truex Press, n.d.), p. 54.

35. Douglass, *Pit Life*, p. 13.

36. Trist, p. 34.

37. See: G. L. Atkinson, "Who'll Draw the Last Cavil?" (mimeographed, 1972), p. 5.

38. G. C. Greenwell, *A Glossary of Terms Used in the Coal Trade of Northumberland and Durham* (London and Derby: Bembrose and Sons, 1888; reprint ed., with an introduction by Thomas Robertson, Newcastle: Frank Graham, 1970), p. 17.

39. Trist, p. 35.

40. See: Douglass, *Pit Life*, p. 18.

41. Ibid., pp. 16-27.

42. NCB, Supplemental Agreement to the Revision of the Wages Structure Agreement of 29 April 1955 [NPLA], Schedule Clause 6.

43. A. R. Griffin, *The Miners of Nottinghamshire 1914-1944: A History of the Nottinghamshire Miners' Union* (London: George Allen and Unwin, 1962), p. 18.

44. William Harold Lazonick, "Marxian Theory and the Development of the Labour Force in England" (Ph.D. dissertation, Harvard University, 1976), pp. 206-207.

45. Interview with NCB officials, North Nottinghamshire Area Headquarters, Edwinstowe, 15 April 1976.

46. Lazonick, p. 208.

47. See: Griffin, *The Miners of Nottinghamshire*, pp. 18, 39, 53-55, 97-100; also, the discussion of Thoresby Colliery, Chapter Five below.

48. Interview at Edwinstowe, 4 June 1976.

49. In the colliery anthropologies which follow, systems of production are described as they were during the course of my main field research (between 1974 and 1977). Present-tense constructions should be read accordingly. Of the ten collieries studied, four have closed: Rainton Adventure (July 1978); Eden and Teversal (July 1980); and Boldon (1982). The Boldon and Teversal closures generated some controversy between the NUM and NCB; the others represented clear cases of exhaustion of coal reserves. Late in 1982, Sacriston is nearing exhaustion.

Chapter Four

1. For an excellent discussion of Harvey see: Dave Douglass, *Pit Life in County Durham: Rank and File Movements and Workers'*

Control, History Workshop Pamphlets, No. 6 (Oxford: Ruskin College, n.d.), pp. 86-92.

2. Ibid., p. 12.

3. Douglass, *The Miners of North Durham*, Socialist Union Pamphlet, No. 3 (Dunscroft, Yorkshire: Socialist Union Press, n.d.), p. 3.

4. For a general account of trade patterns in the industry during this period see: W. W. Kirby, *The British Coalmining Industry 1880-1946: A Political and Economic History* (London: Macmillan, 1977), ch. 1.

5. J[ohn] Carney, J[ames] Lewis, and R[ay] Hudson, "Coal Combines and Interregional Uneven Development in the UK," in *Alternate Frameworks for Analysis*, ed. D. B. Massey and P.W.J. Batey (London: Pion, 1977).

6. For a more extensive discussion of the colliery closure program see: Joel Krieger, "British Colliery Closure Programmes in the North East: From Paradox to Contradiction," in *Analysis and Decision in Regional Policy*, ed. I. G. Cullen (London: Pion, 1979), pp. 219-232.

7. A. E. Allen, *A Commemoration: DMA—1869-1969* (Durham: DMA, 1969), pp. 4-5.

8. Interview with NUM officials, Durham Area Headquarters, Red Hill, Durham, 19 January 1977.

9. Ibid.

10. Interview with NUM officials, Northeast Area Headquarters, Team Valley, Gateshead, 18 January 1977.

11. Ibid.

12. Ibid.

13. Interview at Team Valley, 20 December 1976.

14. Douglass, *Pit Life*, p. 12.

15. All quotations attributed to members of the Boldon Lodge are from a series of interviews conducted on 7 August 1974, 8 August 1974, and 15 November 1976 at Boldon Colliery, Durham.

16. All quotations attributed to NCB officials at Boldon Colliery are from a series of interviews conducted on 15 November 1976 at Boldon Colliery, Durham.

17. NCB, North Durham Area, Industrial Relations Department, Summary of Durham Wages District County Power Loading Agreements, n.d.

18. The two pre-NPLA wage structures—the traditional cavilling/marra structure and the DPLA—will be considered as a sin-

gle, undifferentiated wage structure. This simplification is based on the assumption that men who worked under the DPLA had previously been influenced by the generative rules of the cavilling/ marra structure.

19. A letter addressed to Dr. W. Reid, chairman of the Durham Divisional Coal Board, from A. Hester, secretary of the Durham County Mining Federation Board, in 1963, underscores the tendency for disputes to recur over manpower at Boldon, under the DPLA as well as the NPLA. Hester wrote to Reid: "We have received complaints from our members at Boldon of a shortage of adult labour; power loading faces are being worked without full teams of men, and stonemen are being placed on these faces to the detriment of their own work. There is strong feeling at local level that a chance should now be given to those who were transferred from Boldon some two years ago to return and help to alleviate the position." See: Delegates Notes 1962-1965, Correspondence Concerning Manpower Profile for 1964.

20. All quotations attributed to members of the Sacriston Lodge are from a series of interviews conducted on 16 November 1976 at Sacriston Colliery, Durham.

21. All quotations attributed to NCB officials at Sacriston Colliery are from a series of interviews conducted on 16 November 1976 at Sacriston Colliery, Durham.

22. *Early riding* refers to the practice of leaving work (riding up in the cage) before the completion of the full shift time.

23. NCB, Sacriston Colliery, Pneumatic Pick Hewer's Cavilling Rules, February, 1964.

24. NCB, Northeast Area, Sacriston Colliery, Bargain for Brockwell S.O. 1 Gates, n.d.

25. Interview at Team Valley, 20 December 1976.

26. Ibid.

27. NCB, Northeast Area, Sacriston Colliery, Victoria to Brockwell Fore Drift and Main Intake, March, 1976.

28. The agreement stipulates that additional yards up to the 9.96 square yards per manshift for hewers (which represents the "basic"—preincentive—task) be included in the incentive calculation whenever "geological conditions or mechanical breakdowns beyond their control" intervene to make workers' achievement of the incentive increment impossible.

29. All quotations attributed to members of the Eden Lodge are

from a series of interviews conducted on 31 July 1974 and 11 November 1976 at Eden Colliery, Durham.

30. All quotations attributed to NCB officials at Eden Colliery are from a series of interviews conducted on 11 November 1976 at Eden Colliery, Durham.

31. E. L. Trist et al., *Organizational Choice* (London: Tavistock, 1963), p. 77.

32. It is interesting to note that from the perspective of at least one variant of group theory, the failure of the composite longwall experiment at Eden could be predicted by reference to the character of the incentive structure, the size of the work group, and the intransigence of the "free rider" problem. Of course, the variations in systems of production in the ten selected collieries in Durham and Nottingham could not be explained in this way. See: Mancur Olson, *The Logic of Collective Action: Public Goods and the Theory of Groups* (Cambridge: Harvard University Press, 1973), chs. 1-2.

33. Interview at Team Valley, 8 August 1974.

34. Interview with NCB area official at Eden Colliery, Durham, 31 July 1974.

35. Compare the response of Sherwood men to redeployment under conventional longwall systems, Chapter Five below.

36. Interview with NCB area official, 31 July 1974.

37. The £12.20 figure represents the NPLA rate for the highest underground job category. It is understood that the basic task rate under this agreement would vary commensurately with NPLA increments.

38. NCB, Northeast Area, Eden Colliery, Incentive Agreement for Composite Work and Pillar Extraction, August, 1976.

39. Ibid.

40. Interview with NCB area officials at Red Hill, 4 July 1974.

41. Interview with NCB area official, 31 July 1974.

42. Ibid.

43. Interview with Joe Oxley, Boldon Colliery, 7 August 1974.

44. All quotations attributed to members of the Rainton Lodge are from a series of interviews conducted on 23 November 1976 at Rainton Colliery, Durham.

45. All quotations attributed to NCB officials at Rainton Colliery are from a series of interviews conducted on 29 July 1974 and 23 November 1976 at Rainton Colliery, Durham.

46. Lodge minutes were kindly made available to me by a member of the Rainton Lodge executive.

47. Interview at Sacriston Colliery, 16 November 1976.

48. Douglass, *Pit Life*, p. 12.

49. Interview at Team Valley, 21 October 1976.

50. Ibid.

51. Ibid.

52. All quotations attributed to members of the Horden Lodge are from a series of interviews conducted on 9 December 1976.

53. All quotations attributed to NUM area officials are from a series of interviews at Durham Area Headquarters, Red Hill, Durham, 19 January 1977.

54. Douglass, *Pit Talk in County Durham: A Glossary of Miner's Talk Together with Memories of Wardley Colliery Pit Songs and Piliking*, History Workshop Pamphlets, No. 10 (Oxford: Truex Press, n.d.), pp. 52-53.

55. Ibid., p. 66.

56. R. Page Arnot, *A History of the Miners Federation of Great Britain.* Vol. 2: *The Miners: Years of Struggle* (London: George Allen and Unwin, 1953), pp. 15-23.

Chapter Five

1. Interview with NCB officials, North Nottinghamshire Area Headquarters, Edwinstowe, 22 April 1976.

2. R. G. Searle-Barnes, *Pay and Productivity Bargaining: A Study of the Effect of National Wage Agreements in the Nottinghamshire Coalfield* (Manchester: Manchester University Press, 1969), p. 19.

3. A. R. Griffin, *The Miners of Nottinghamshire 1914-1944: A History of the Nottinghamshire Miners' Unions* (London: George Allen and Unwin, 1962), p. 91. My treatment of Spencerism and the events which mark the development of the NMA is based largely on Griffin's book and on conversations with the author at North Nottinghamshire Area Headquarters, Edwinstowe, 24 March 1976 and 22 April 1976.

4. Griffin, p. 92.

5. Searle-Barnes, p. 23.

6. Interview with NUM officials, Nottingham Area Headquarters, Berry Hill Lane, Mansfield, 13 April 1976.

7. Interview at Edwinstowe, 15 April 1976.

8. Interview at Edwinstowe, 22 April 1976.

9. Interview at Edwinstowe, 22 April 1976.

10. Interview at Edwinstowe, 15 April 1976.

11. All quotations attributed to members of the Thoresby Branch are from a series of interviews conducted on 30 June 1976 and 26 August 1976 at Thoresby Colliery, Nottingham.

12. Griffin, p. 249.

13. Searle-Barnes, p. 26.

14. NCB, Operation of Divisional Power Loading Agreement: Report of Investigating Team, January, 1961.

15. Details concerning specific measures taken by the Thoresby Branch are based on personal and private notes of branch meetings kindly made available to me by Alf Anchors, NUM Branch Secretary, Thoresby Colliery, Nottingham.

16. Searle-Barnes, p. 66.

17. Interview with NCB Colliery officials, Thoresby Colliery, 28 June 1976.

18. NUM Nottingham Area, Minutes of the Executive Committee Meeting, 19 March 1974.

19. NCB, "Sherwood Colliery" (mimeographed [1962]), pp. 4-6.

20. Ibid., p. 7.

21. Ibid.

22. Ibid.

23. NCB, "Sherwood Colliery" (mimeographed [1974]), p. 1. The document includes handwritten emendations of the manpower and productivity figures for the 1974-1976 period.

24. Interview at Edwinstowe, 15 April 1976.

25. All quotations attributed to members of the Sherwood Branch are from a series of interviews conducted on 16 July 1976 and 1 August 1976 at Sherwood Colliery, Nottingham.

26. NCB, "Sherwood Colliery" [1962], p. 5.

27. NCB, Supplemental Agreement to the Revision of the Wages Structure Agreement of 20th April 1955 [NPLA], Schedule Clauses 5 and 6.

28. Searle-Barnes, p. 141.

29. NUM Nottingham Area, Minutes of Meetings of the Executive Committee and of the Council, September and August, 1975.

30. Ibid.

31. Ibid.

32. Ibid.

33. NCB, Public Relations Department, "Get It All Together as a Skilled Miner" [1976].

34. All quotations attributed to NCB officials at Bevercotes Colliery are from a series of interviews conducted on 21 July 1976 and 26 July 1976 at Bevercotes Colliery, Nottingham.

35. NCB East Midlands Division, "Bevercotes Colliery," n.d.

36. NUM Nottingham Area, 1966 Minutes, Report of Delegates to the Annual Conference of the Labour Party, Summary of Statement made by Mr. S.W.G. Ford (President) to the press following the meeting of the NEC on 13 October 1966.

37. All quotations attributed to members of the Bevercotes Branch are from a series of interviews conducted on 13 August 1976 at Bevercotes Colliery, Nottingham.

38. NUM, Annual Conference 1966, Report of the National Executive Committee, p. 30.

39. NUM Nottingham Area, Minutes of a Special Meeting of Branch Officials and Committee Members, 16 May 1966.

40. NUM Nottingham Area, Minutes of Meeting of the Special Executive, 9 May 1966. NUM Nottingham Area, Minutes of a Meeting of the Special Executive, 17 August 1966.

41. NUM, Annual Conference 1966.

42. NUM Nottingham Area, 1966 Minutes, Summary of Statement by S.W.G. Ford.

43. NUM Nottingham Area, Minutes of the Executive Committee Meeting, 14 November 1966.

44. NUM Nottingham Area, 1967 Minutes, letter from W. Paynter to A. Martin, 20 January 1967, Minutes of Council Meeting, 23 January 1967.

45. NCB, Bevercotes Colliery, Wages and Conditions of Service—Industrial Grades Other Than W.P.I.S. Underofficials and Canteen Workers, Attendance at Work, Clauses 10-14.

46. Ibid., Hours, Clause 15.

47. Ibid., Scope, Clause 20.

48. NUM Nottingham Area, Minutes of Executive Committee Meeting, 8 April 1968.

49. NUM Nottingham Area, Minutes of Executive Committee Meeting, 8 December 1969.

50. NUM Nottingham Area, Minutes of Council Meeting, 23 February 1970.

51. NUM, Annual Conference 1970, Report, p. 29.

52. NCB, North Nottinghamshire Area, Face Data Bank, Weekly Listing of Face Performance.

53. NUM Nottingham Area, Minutes of Council Meeting, 28 February 1966.

54. NCB, North Nottinghamshire Area, Action Programme, Bevercotes Colliery, April, 1976.

55. Griffin, p. 257.

56. Ibid.

57. "The Real Question Behind the Miners' Coalfield Ballot," *The Financial Times* (London), 10 December 1976, p. 16.

58. Griffin, p. 258. My treatment of the events at Harworth in 1935-36 is based on Griffin's account as supplemented by discussions with a former Harworth miner on 21 July 1976 at Bevercotes Colliery, Nottingham. All quotations attributed to a former Harworth miner are from this interview.

59. All quotations attributed to members of the Harworth Branch are from a series of interviews conducted on 13 July 1976 at Harworth Colliery, Nottingham.

60. Interview at Edwinstowe, 15 April 1976.

61. Ibid.

62. The Nottinghamshire District Disputes Board, Record of Disputes between Contract Workers on the Conveyor Faces at Harworth Colliery and Barber, Walker and Co. Ltd., 10 July 1945.

63. Interview with NCB officials, North Nottinghamshire Area Headquarters, Edwinstowe, 22 April 1976.

64. NCB, North Nottinghamshire Area, Face Data Bank, Weekly Listing of Face Performances.

65. Interview at Edwinstowe, 15 April 1976.

66. Ibid.

67. Ibid.

68. Ibid.

69. "Ballot Support for Executive Over Landwith," in *Miner: Voice of the National Union of Mineworkers* (March/April 1976), p. 1.

70. All quotations attributed to members of the Teversal Branch are from a series of interviews conducted on 28 June 1976, 2 July 1976, and 9 August 1976 at Teversal Colliery, Nottingham.

71. Assessment of the Optimum Performance of the Double-Ended Conveyor-Mounted Trepanner on 4s Face, Waterloo Seam, Teversal Colliery, and the Manpower Required to Maintain This Optimum Performance in Compliance with the 1957 Nottinghamshire Power Loading Agreement (mimeographed, n.d.).

72. This illustration is based on actual contract statements kindly given to me (and explained) by Cyril Barksby, NUM Branch Secretary, Teversal Colliery, Nottingham.

73. Details concerning specific measures taken by the Teversal Branch in response to the threat of closure are based on personal and private notes of branch meetings kindly made available to me by Dave Minett, a Teversal collier.

74. Interview at Edwinstowe, 17 December 1976.

Chapter Six

1. See: Lucio Colletti, "Lenin's *State and Revolution,*" in *From Rousseau to Lenin: Studies in Ideology and Society,* tr. John Merrington and Judith White (New York and London: Monthly Review Press [1973]). References from Lenin's *State and Revolution* are from: *Selected Works in Three Volumes,* Moscow, 1967, as cited in Colletti.

2. Colletti, p. 222; Lenin, Vol. II, p. 357.

3. Göran Therborn, *What Does the Ruling Class Do When it Rules?* (London: New Left Books; New York: Schocken Books, 1978), p. 25 (italics deleted).

4. Therborn, p. 36.

5. Colletti, p. 222.

6. Colletti, p. 225; see Lenin, Vol. II, pp. 339-343.

7. See *Programme Commun de Gouvernement* (Paris: Flammarion, 1973), particularly Part Three, Chapter 4, "L'administration."

8. Colletti, p. 220.

9. See: NUM, Report of Special Conference held at Congress House, London, 18 February 1966 (London: n.p., 1966), pp. 2-12; Ian Rutledge, "Changes in the Mode of Production and the Growth of 'Mass Militancy' in the British Mining Industry, 1954-1974," *Science and Society* 41:4 (Winter 1977-1978), 414–449; R. H. Heath, "The National Power-Loading Agreement in the Coal Industry and Some Aspects of Workers' Control," in *Trade Union Register,* ed. Ken Coates, Tony Topham, and Michael Barratt Brown (London: The Merlin Press, 1969), pp. 191-192; and David Douglass, "The Miners on Strike," *Radical America* 8:5 (September-October 1974), 97-104.

10. This condition of a single national agreement for underground workers was met with the introduction of the Third National Daywage Structure in June 1971, whereby men on non-

power-loaded faces and development drivages, and men working elsewhere underground were brought into the same agreement as face workers.

11. Rutledge, pp. 415-419; Douglass, "The Miners on Strike," pp. 102-108. See also: Arthur Scargill, "The New Unionism," *New Left Review* 92 (July-August 1975), 8-10.

12. See, for example: NCB, Letter from Member of Industrial Relations Department to South Wales Regional Official, January, 1974.

13. Ibid. See also: "Putting the Future to the Vote," *Financial Times* (London), 31 October 1977.

14. NCB, *Management News* 9:5 (February 1974), 435.

15. "Coal Incentives Vital, Warns Ezra," *Financial Times* (London), 25 June 1977.

16. Joel Krieger, "Britain: Phased Out by Phase Three?" *Working Papers for a New Society* (March-April 1978), 17-19.

17. "Coal Board Expects £7M-£10M Profit," *Financial Times* (London), 21 April 1978.

18. NCB, North Nottinghamshire Area, Effects of Incentive Scheme.

19. Ibid.

20. NCB, *Report and Accounts 1979/80*, p. 15.

21. Interview at Team Valley, 20 August 1980.

22. Interview with Joe Whelan, Nottingham Area Headquarters, Berry Hill Lane, Mansfield, 5 August 1980.

23. Interview with Dave Douglass, Dunscroft, Yorkshire, 14 August 1980.

24. "£ — and Nowt Else!" *Yorkshire Miner*, July 1980.

25. Interview at Edwinstowe, 5 August 1980.

GLOSSARY

BORD AND PILLAR MINING: A system of mining in which a single miner per shift or a small work group excavate small square or rectangular bords of coal, leaving (at least temporary) pillars beyond to support the roof.

BUTTY: A sub-contractor; mainly limited to the Midlands and North Wales.

CAVILLING: A system of allocating working positions by lottery; limited to Durham and Northumberland.

CHOCKS: Roof supports, whether built of timber in a square crosswise pattern or, as is increasingly likely, made of steel and part of an adjustable hydraulic system.

CUTTING: The undercutting of coal along the face by use of a machine, an operation which supplants hewing as the initial "getting" activity.

DEPUTY: NCB official responsible for safety in a particular mining district; the deputy often oversees production more generally.

FILLING: The operation of shoveling the undercut coal onto the conveyor belt which runs along the face.

GAFFERS: Pit managers and other supervisory personnel (often pejorative).

HEWING: Traditional operation for "winning" or "getting" coal; involves breaking into and dislodging coal with hand or pneumatic pick, digging it out, and shoveling it onto conveyor or into tubs.

LONGWALL MINING: A system of mining in which a number of workers labor along a continuous coal face, typically eighty yards or longer.

MARRA: In Durham and Northumberland, a work mate; traditionally, marras often shared a common paynote, coordinated their labor collectively, and developed close bonds.

PULLING: Operation of moving roof supports and conveyor forward; involves both breaking down and resetting chocks.

PUTTING: The operation of conveying tubs to and from the filler, traditionally often with the help of a pit pony; the operation applies in this form to traditional single place working (as in the bord and pillar system).

RIPPING (CAUNCHWORK OR STONEWORK): The task of dislodging stone and setting arches to provide a roadway or gateway where the tunnel meets the edge of the face; generally considered the most dangerous and skilled job underground.

BIBLIOGRAPHY

PRIMARY SOURCES

National Coal Board

At Hobart House I reviewed the complete set of files maintained by the Wages Branch of the Industrial Relations Department for the period 1965-1976. These materials concerned the negotiation and implementation of the NPLA, the Wilberforce Enquiry during the national strike of 1972 and the Enquiry into Pay Relativities which followed the strike of 1974, and annual wage negotiations from 1971-1976. The sources are divided according to their location and arranged chronologically within each division. Sources are arranged alphabetically by colliery or NCB department.

HOBART HOUSE

NCB. *Report and Accounts 1979/80.*
NCB Public Relations Department. "Get It All Together as a Skilled Miner." [1976].
NCB. Letter from Member of Industrial Relations Department to South Wales Regional Official. January, 1974.
NCB. *Management News* 9:5 (February, 1974).
NCB. Brief on Wages Policy 1947-1974. January, 1974.
NCB. Memorandum and Brief for General Purposes Committee Meeting on the NPLA. January, 1967.
NCB. Memorandum on Reduction of Effort. [November], 1966.
NCB. Memorandum on National Power Loading Agreement as it influences the position of Craftsmen. November, 1966.
NCB. Memorandum to General Purposes Committee on Interpretation of the National Power Loading Agreement. October, 1966.
NCB. Memorandum circulated within Industrial Relations Department on Power Loading. August, 1966.

NCB. Note of a Meeting with Representatives of the NUM, Held in Hobart House. March, 1966.

NCB. Note of a Meeting between Representatives of the NUM and NCB. March, 1966.

NCB. Memorandum by Member of Industrial Relations Department for General Purposes Committee on NPLA. March, 1966.

NCB. Exchange of Correspondence between Yorkshire Division Industrial Relations Department and Yorkshire Area NUM Executive. March, 1966.

NCB. Brief on National Power Loading Agreement for Meeting with NUM Executive. March, 1966.

NCB. Brief for General Purposes Committee on the NPLA. March, 1966.

NCB. Memorandum within Industrial Relations Department on Inclusion of Craftsmen on Fully Mechanized Longwall Faces. February, 1966.

NCB. Extract from Minutes of Meetings between NCB and NUM Negotiators. January, 1966.

NCB. Draft of NPLA. January, 1966.

NCB. A Note of a Meeting between NCB Negotiators and National Officials of the NUM. January, 1966.

NCB. Memorandum within Industrial Relations Department over Implications of the Standstill and its Extension. November, 1965.

NCB. Exchange of Memoranda among Members of the Industrial Relations Department. November, 1965.

NCB. Exchange of Correspondence between Members of the NCB Industrial Relations Department and the NUM Executive. November, 1965.

NCB. Draft Memorandum from Member of the NCB Industrial Relations Department to Board Members and Area General Managers on Control of EMS. [November, 1965].

NCB. Exchange of Correspondence between Member of the NCB Industrial Relations Department and the NUM Executive. September, 1965.

NCB Industrial Relations Department. Brief for Informal Meeting with NUM. September, 1965.

NCB. Memorandum from Industrial Relations Department to Divisional Industrial Relations Directors. August, 1965.

NCB. Memorandum within Industrial Relations Department on Power Loading Arrangements. June, 1965.

NCB. Exchange of Correspondence between Members of the NCB Industrial Relations Department and the NUM Executive. June, 1965.

NCB. Notes of Conversations between Representatives of the NCB and the NUM. March, 1965.

NCB. Note on ROLFs and Power Loading. March, 1965.

NCB. Operation of Divisional Power Loading Agreements: Report of Investigating Team. January, 1961.

NCB General Purposes Committee. Brief on National Power Loading Agreement. December, 1960.

NCB. Memoranda within Industrial Relations Department on NPLA. June, 1960.

NCB Industrial Relations Department. Brief for Other Departments on NPLA. June, 1960.

NCB. Brief for the Board's Side of the National Power Loading Joint Committee. October, 1959.

NCB. Exchange of Correspondence between Member of the NCB Industrial Relations Department and the NUM Executive. September, 1959.

NCB Industrial Relations Department. Minutes of a Meeting of Representatives of the Board and the NUM. June, 1959.

NCB. Supplemental Agreement to the Revision of the Wages Structure Agreement of 20th April, 1955.

NCB. Discussion Paper by Two NCB Staff Officials to Wages Policy Committee. [March], 1953.

NCB. Summary of Minutes of Wages Policy Committee. January, 1953.

NCB. Memorandum to Wages Policy Committee on Standardization of Daywage Gradings. January, 1953.

NCB. Memorandum Comparing Earnings in the First Quarter 1951 with the First Quarter 1947. [1951].

NCB. Memorandum on Systems of Remuneration in the Coal Mining Industry. August, 1951.

NCB. Memorandum on Control Over Price Lists and Piecework. August, 1951.

NCB Working Party on Wages. Draft Interim Report on Second NUM Wages Claim 1951. August, 1951.

NCB. Memorandum on National Wages Policy and Previous Methods of Wage Regulation and Control. July, 1951.

NCB. Draft Report on National Wages Policy. July, 1951.
NCB. Five Day Week Agreement of 5 May 1947.

DURHAM

NCB Computer Services. Northeast Area. Weekly Face Results.
NCB. Northeast Area. Eden Colliery, Incentive Agreement for Composite Work and Pillar Extraction. August, 1976.
NCB. North Durham Area. Industrial Relations Department Summary of Durham Wages District County Power Loading Agreements. n.d.
NCB. Rainton Colliery. Weekly Productivity Data.
NCB. Northeast Area. Sacriston Colliery, Bargain for Brockwell S.O. 1 Gates. n.d.
NCB. Sacriston Colliery. Memo from Colliery Manager to Area Headquarters on Incentive Agreements. n.d.
NCB. Sacriston Colliery. "Pneumatic Pick Hewer's Cavilling Rules." February, 1964.
NCB. Northeast Area. Sacriston Colliery, Victoria to Brockwell Fore Drift and Main Intake. March, 1976.

NOTTINGHAM

NCB. North Nottinghamshire Area. Effects of Incentive Scheme. n.d.
NCB. North Nottinghamshire Area. Action Programme Bevercotes Colliery. April, 1976.
NCB. East Midlands Division. "Bevercotes Colliery." n.d.
NCB. Bevercotes Colliery. Wages and Conditions of Service—Industrial Grades Other than W.P.I.S. Underofficials and Canteen Workers, Attendance at Work. n.d.
NCB. Harworth Colliery. Weekly Output Calculations.
NCB. North Nottinghamshire Area. Face Data Bank, Weekly Listing of Face Performance 1967-1972.
NCB. "Sherwood Colliery." [1974]. Mimeographed.
NCB. "Sherwood Colliery." [1962]. Mimeographed.
NCB. Sherwood Colliery. Weekly Performance Charts Arranged by Task and Face.
NCB. Assessment of the Optimum Performance of the Double-Ended Conveyor-Mounted Trepanner on 4s Face, Waterloo Seam, Teversal Colliery, and the Manpower Required to Maintain this Optimum Performance in Compliance with the 1957 Nottinghamshire Power Loading Agreement. n.d.
NCB. Teversal Colliery. Contract Statements, 1951. Passim.

NCB. Teversal Colliery. Surveyor's Reports and Colliery Output Weekly Summaries.

National Union of Mineworkers

NATIONAL

NUM. Rules, Model Rules, Standing Orders. [1974].
NUM. Annual Conference 1970. Report. [1970].
NUM. Annual Conference 1966. Report of the National Executive Committee. [1966].
NUM. Report of Special Conference held at Congress House, London, 18 February 1966. [1966].

DURHAM

NUM Durham Area. *Changes in Wages in the Durham Coal Trade 1871-1953 and Historical Record 1869-1953*. Durham: n.p., 1954.
DMA. Correspondence Concerning Manpower Profile for 1964. Delegates Notes 1962-1965.
NUM Durham Area. Rainton Lodge minutes, 1969-1974. Passim.

NOTTINGHAM

NUM Nottingham Area. Minutes. 1966-1974.
NUM Nottingham Area. Power Loading Agreement 19th August 1957 (with Amendments to June, 1958). [1958].
NUM Nottingham Area. Rules and Standing Orders. 1976.
NUM Nottingham Area. Teversal Lodge minutes, 1976. Passim.
NUM Nottingham Area. Thoresby Lodge minutes, 1965-1974. Passim.

Miscellaneous

The Nottinghamshire District Disputes Board. Record of Disputes between Contract Workers on the Conveyor Faces at Harworth Colliery and Barber Walker and Co. Ltd. 10 July 1945.

SECONDARY SOURCES

Alexander, K.J.W. "Wages in Coalmining since Nationalization." *Oxford Economic Papers* 8:2 (June 1956).
Allen, E. *A Commemoration: DMA—1869-1969*. Durham: DMA, 1969.
Arnot, R. Page. *A History of the Miners Federation of Great Britain*.

Vol. 2: *The Miners: Years of Struggle.* London: George Allen and Unwin, 1953.

Ashton, T. S. and Sykes, Joseph. *The Coal Industry of the Eighteenth Century,* rev. 2d. ed. Manchester: Manchester University Press, 1964.

Atkinson, G. L. "Who'll Draw the Last Cavil?" (mimeographed). 1972.

"Ballot Support for Executive Over Langwith." *Miner: Voice of the National Union of Mineworkers.* March/April 1976.

Barbash Jack. "Collective Bargaining and the Theory of Conflict." *British Journal of Industrial Relations* 18:1 (1980).

Barnard, Chester. *The Function of the Executive.* Cambridge: Harvard University Press, 1938.

Barratt Brown, M[ichael]. "Determinants of the Structure and Level of Wages in the Coal-Mining Industry Since 1956." *Oxford Institute for Economics and Statistics* 29:2 (May 1967).

Bayles, Michael D. "The Functions and Limits of Political Authority." In *Authority: A Philosophical Analysis.* Edited by R. Baine Harris. Alabama: University of Alabama Press, 1976.

Beacham, A. "The Present Position of the Coal Industry." *Economic Journal* 60 (1950).

Beer, Samuel H. "Modern Political Development." In *Patterns of Government.* 3rd ed. Edited by Samuel H. Beer, Adam B. Ulam, Suzanne Berger, and Guido Goldman. New York: Random House, 1973.

Berkovitch, Israel. *Coal on the Switchback: The Coal Industry Since Nationalisation* with a Foreword by Sir Derek Ezra. London: George Allen and Unwin, 1977.

Blain, A.N.J. and Gennard, John. "Industrial Relations Theory: A Critical Review." *British Journal of Industrial Relations* 7:3 (1970).

Blau, Peter M. and Scott, W. Richard. *Formal Organizations.* San Francisco: Chandler Publishing Company, 1962.

Bourdieu, Pierre. *Outline of a Theory of Practice.* Translated by Richard Nice. New York: Cambridge University Press, 1977.

Boyd, Robert Nelson. *Coal Pits and Pitmen.* London: Whittaker and Co., 1895.

Brecher, Jeremy. "Uncovering the Hidden History of the American Workplace." *Review of Radical Political Economics* 10:4 (Winter 1978).

Brown, William. "A Consideration of 'Custom and Practice.' " *British Journal of Industrial Relations* 10:1 (1972).

Bulman, H. F. and Redmayne, R.A.S. *Colliery Working and Management*. London: Crosby Lockwood and Son, 1925.

Burawoy, Michael. *Manufacturing Consent*. Chicago and London: University of Chicago Press, 1979.

Butler, R. J. "Relative Deprivation and Power: A Switched Replication Design Using Time Series Data of Strike Rates in American and British Coal Mining." *Human Relations* 29:7 (1976).

Carney, J[ohn]; Lewis, J[ames]; and Hudson, [Ray]. "Coal Combines and Interregional Uneven Development in the U.K." In *Alternate Frameworks for Analysis*. Edited by D[oreen] B. Massey and P.W.J. Batey. London: Pion, 1977.

Clegg, H. A. *The System of Industrial Relations in Great Britain*. London: Basil Blackwell, 1970.

"Coal Board Expects £7M–£10M Profit." *The Financial Times* (London), 21 April 1978.

"Coal Incentives Vital, Warns Ezra." *The Financial Times* (London), 25 June 1977.

Colletti, Lucio. *From Rousseau to Lenin: Studies in Ideology and Society*. Translated by John Merrington and Judith White. New York and London: Monthly Review Press (1973).

Conference of Socialist Economists. *The Labour Process and Class Strategies*. London: Stage One, 1976.

Crozier, Michel. *The Bureaucratic Phenomenon*. Chicago: University of Chicago Press, 1964.

DiMaggio, Paul. "Review Essay: On Pierre Bordieu." *American Journal of Sociology* 84:6 (May 1979).

Douglass, Dave. "The Miners on Strike." *Radical America* 8:5 (September-October 1974).

————. *The Miners of North Durham*. Socialist Union Pamphlet No. 3. Dunscroft, Yorkshire: Socialist Union Press, n.d.

————. *Pit Life in County Durham: Rank and File Movements and Workers' Control*. History Workshop Pamphlets, No. 6. Oxford: Ruskin College, n.d.

————. *Pit Talk in County Durham: A Glossary of Miner's Talk Together with Memories of Wardley Colliery Pit Songs and Piliking*. History Workshop Pamphlets, No. 10. Oxford: Truex Press, n.d.

Downs, Anthony. *Inside Bureaucracy*. Boston: Little, Brown, 1967.

Edwards, Richard. *Contested Terrain: The Transformation of the Work-place in the Twentieth Century.* New York: Basic Books, 1979.

Eldridge, J.E.T. *Industrial Disputes: Essays in the Sociology of Industrial Relations.* London: Routledge and Kegan Paul. New York: Humanities Press, 1968.

Foster. John. *Class Struggle and the Industrial Revolution.* New York: St. Martin's, 1975.

Fox, Alan. "Collective Bargaining, Flanders and the Webbs." *British Journal of Industrial Relations* 8:2 (1975).

———. *Beyond Contract: Work, Power and Trust Relations.* London: Faber, 1974.

Fox, Alan, and Flanders, Allan. "The Reform of Collective Bargaining: From Donovan to Durkheim." *British Journal of Industrial Relations* 7:2 (1969)

Galbraith, John Kenneth. *The New Industrial State.* Boston: Houghton Mifflin, 1967.

Giddens, Anthony. *A Contemporary Critique of Historical Materialism.* Vol. 1: *Power, Property and the State.* Berkeley and Los Angeles: University of California Press, 1981.

———. *Central Problems in Social Theory: Action, Structure and Contradiction in Social Analysis.* Berkeley: University of California Press, 1979.

———. *New Rules of Sociological Method.* London: Hutchinson, 1976.

———. "Functionalism: *Après la lutte.*" *Social Research* 43:2 (Summer 1976).

Goldthorpe, John H. "Industrial Relations in Great Britain: A Critique of Reformism." *Politics and Society* 4:4 (1974).

Great Britain. Laws, Statutes, etc. *Coal Industry Nationalisation Act,* 1946. 9 and 10 Geo. 6.

———. National Board for Prices and Incomes, Report No. 12. *Coal Prices.* Cmnd. 2919, HMSO, February 1966.

———. Reference Division Office of Information. *Regional Development in Britain.* HMSO, 1974.

Greenwell, G. C. *A Glossary of Terms Used in the Coal Trade of Northumberland and Durham.* London and Derby: Bembrose and Sons; reprint ed., with an introduction by Thomas Robertson, Newcastle: Frank Graham, 1970.

Griffin, A[lan] R. *Coalmining.* London: Longman, 1971.

———. *The Miners of Nottinghamshire 1914-1944: A History of the*

Nottinghamshire Miners' Union. London: George Allen and Unwin, 1962.

Habermas, Jürgen. *Legitimation Crisis*. Translated by Thomas McCarthy. Boston: Beacon Press, 1973.

Hawkins, Kevin. "The Future of Collective Bargaining." *Industrial Relations Journal* 10:4 (Winter 1979-80).

Heath, R. H. "The National Power-Loading Agreement in the Coal Industry and Some Aspects of Workers' Control." In *Trade Union Register*. Edited by Ken Coates, Tony Topham, and Michael Barratt Brown. London: The Merlin Press, 1969.

Hill, Stephen. "Norms, Groups and Power: The Sociology of Workplace Relations." *British Journal of Industrial Relations* 12:2 (1974).

Hobsbawm, E[ric] J. *Labouring Men*. London: Weidenfield and Nicholson, 1964.

Horkheimer, Max. *Critical Theory: Selected Essays*. Translated by Matthew J. O'Connell and others. New York: The Seabury Press [1972].

Hyman, Richard. *Industrial Relations: A Marxist Introduction*. London: Macmillan, 1975.

Kirby, W. W. *The British Coalmining Industry 1870-1946: A Political and Economic History*. London: Macmillan, 1977.

Krieger, Joel. "British Colliery Closure Programmes in the North East: From Paradox to Contradiction." In *Analysis and Decision in Regional Policy*. Edited by I. G. Cullen. London: Pion, 1979.

————. "Britain: Phased Out by Phase Three?" *Working Papers for a New Society* (March-April 1978).

Lazonick, William Harold. "Marxian Theory and the Development of the Labour Force in England." Ph.D. dissertation, Harvard University, 1976.

Lenin, V. I. *Selected Works in Three Volumes*. Moscow, 1967.

Lindblom, Charles E. *The Intelligence of Democracy: Decision Making through Mutual Adjustment*. New York: The Free Press, 1965.

Lumley, Roger. "A Modified Rules Approach to Workplace Industrial Relations." *Industrial Relations Journal* 10:4 (Winter 1979-80).

Manners, Gerald, and others. *Regional Development in Britain*. London: John Wiley and Sons, 1972.

March, James G. and Simon, Herbert A. *Organizations*. New York: John Wiley and Sons, 1958.

Merton, R. K. "Bureaucratic Structure and Personality." In *Reader in Bureaucracy*. Edited by R. K. Merton and others. New York: Free Press, 1952.

Meyer, Marshall W. *Change in Public Bureaucracies*. Cambridge: University Press, 1979.

Michels, Robert. *Political Parties*. Glencoe, Illinois: The Free Press, 1949.

"Mining Equipment: The Projected Expansion in Coal Production." *The Financial Times* (London) 8 July 1974.

Mouzelis, Nicos P. *Organization and Bureaucracy: An Analysis of Modern Theories*. Chicago: Aldine Publishing Co., 1967.

Niskanen, W. A. *Bureaucracy and Representative Government*. Chicago: University of Chicago Press, 1971.

Offe, Claus. "The Theory of the Capitalist State and the Problem of Policy Formation." In *Stress and Contradiction in Modern Capitalism*. Edited by Leon N. Lindberg and others. Lexington, Mass.: Lexington Books, 1977.

Olson, Mancur. *The Logic of Collective Action: Public Goods and the Theory of Groups*. Cambridge: Harvard University Press, 1973.

Organization for Economic Cooperation and Development. *Regional Policies: The Current Outlook*. Paris, 1977.

Perrow, Charles. *Complex Organizations: A Critical Essay*. Glenview, Illinois and Brighton, England: Scott, Foresman, 1972.

Poulantzas, Nico. *Political Power and Social Classes*. Translated by Timothy O'Hagan. London: New Left Books, 1978.

"£ — and Nowt Else!" *Yorkshire Miner*, July 1980.

Programme Commun de Gouvernement. Paris: Flammarion, 1973.

"Putting the Future to the Vote." *The Financial Times* (London) 31 October 1977.

Stinchcombe, Arthur L. "Social Structure and Organizations." In *Handbook of Organizations*. Edited by James G. March. Chicago: Rand McNally, 1965.

————. "Bureaucratic and Craft Administration of Production." *Administrative Science Quarterly* 4 (September 1959).

Reid, G. L.; Allen, Kevin; and Harris, D. J. *The Nationalized Fuel Industries*. London: Heinemann Educational Books, 1973.

[Robinson, Derek]. "British Industrial Relations Research in the Sixties and Seventies" (mimeographed). [1976].

Rowe, J.W.F. *Wages in the Coal Industry*. London: P. S. King and Son, 1923.

Royal Commission on Trade Unions and Employers' Associations 1965-1968. *Report*. Cmnd. 3623, HMSO, 1969.

Rutledge, Ian. "Changes in the Mode of Production and the Growth of 'Mass Militancy' in the British Mining Industry, 1954-1974." *Science and Society* 41:4 (Winter 1977-1978).

Searle-Barnes, R. G. *Pay and Productivity.* Manchester: Manchester University Press, 1969.

Shephard, William G. *Economic Performance under Public Ownership.* New Haven: Yale University Press, 1965.

"The Real Question Behind the Miners' Coalfield Ballot." *The Financial Times* (London), 10 December 1976.

Scargill, Arthur."The New Unionism." *New Left Review* 92 (July-August 1975).

Swidler, Ann. "The Concept of Rationality in the Work of Max Weber." *Sociological Inquiry* 43:1 (Spring 1973).

Terry, Michael. "The Inevitable Growth of Informality." *British Journal of Industrial Relations* 15:1 (1977).

Therborn, Göran. *What Does the Ruling Class Do When it Rules?* London: New Left Books; New York: Schocken Books, 1978.

Thompson, E[dward] P. *The Making of the English Working Class.* New York: Random House, Vintage Books, 1966.

Trist, E[ric] L[andsdowne]; Higgin, J. W.; Murray, H.; and Pollack, A. B. *Organizational Choice.* London: Tavistock, 1963.

Van den Doel, Hans. *Democracy and Welfare Economics.* Translated by Brigid Biggins. Cambridge: Cambridge University Press, 1979.

Weber, Max. *Economy and Society.* 3 vols. Edited by Guenther Roth and Claus Wittich. New York: Bedminster Press, 1968.

————. *The Theory of Social and Economic Organization.* Edited and with an Introduction by Talcott Parsons. New York: Macmillan, Free Press, 1964.

Welbourne, E. *The Miners' Unions of Northumberland and Durham.* Cambridge: Cambridge University Press, 1923.

Wilders, M. G. and Parker, S. R. "Changes in Workplace Industrial Relations 1966-1972." *British Journal of Industrial Relations* 13:1 (1975).

Wright, Erik Olin. *Class, Crisis and the State.* London: New Left Books, 1978.

INTERVIEWS

Interviews are divided between NCB and NUM subjects and further divided by location. Within a particular area, interviews are arranged alphabetically by colliery, with the area officials listed first.

National Coal Board

DURHAM

NCB area officials. Northeast Area Headquarters, Team Valley, Gateshead. 8 July 1974, 30 July 1974, 8 August 1974, 21 October 1976, 20 December 1976, 18 January 1977, 20 August 1980.

NCB area officials for Northeast Area. DMA Headquarters, Red Hill, Durham. 4 July 1974.

NCB area officials for Northeast Area. Eden Colliery, Durham. 31 July 1974.

NCB officials and mining engineer. Northeast Area Headquarters, Team Valley, Gateshead. 8 July 1974.

NCB officials Boldon Colliery. Boldon Colliery, Durham. 15 November 1976.

NCB officials Eden Colliery. Eden Colliery, Durham. 11 November 1976.

NCB officials Rainton Colliery. Rainton Colliery, Durham. 29 July 1974 and 23 November 1976.

NCB officials Sacriston Colliery, Sacriston Colliery, Durham. 16 November 1976.

NCB officials Thoresby Colliery. Thoresby Colliery, Nottingham. 28 June 1976

NOTTINGHAM

NCB area officials. North Nottinghamshire Area Headquarters, Edwinstowe, Mansfield. 24 March 1976, 15 April 1976, 22 April 1976, 4 June 1976, 10 August 1976, 17 December 1976, and 5 August 1980.

NCB officials Bevercotes Colliery. Bevercotes Colliery, Nottingham. 21 July 1976 and 26 July 1976.

National Union of Mineworkers

DURHAM

NUM officials. Durham Area Headquarters, Red Hill, Durham. 19 January 1977.

NUM officials and members Boldon Lodge. Boldon Colliery, Durham. 7 August 1974, 8 August 1974, and 15 November 1976.
NUM officials and members Eden Lodge. Eden Colliery, Durham. 31 July 1974 and 11 November 1976.
NUM officials and members Horden Lodge. Horden Colliery, Durham. 9 December 1976.
NUM officials and members Rainton Lodge. Rainton Colliery, Durham. 23 November 1976.
NUM officials and members Sacriston Lodge. Sacriston Colliery, Durham. 16 November 1976.

NOTTINGHAM

NUM officials. Nottingham Area Headquarters, Berry Hill Lane, Mansfield. 13 April 1976 and 30 July 1976.
NUM officials and members Bevercotes Branch. Bevercotes Colliery, Nottingham. 13 August 1976.
NUM officials and members Sherwood Branch. Sherwood Colliery, Nottingham. 16 July 1976 and 1 August 1976.
NUM officials and members Harworth Branch. Harworth Colliery, Nottingham. 13 July 1976.
NUM officials and members Teversal Branch. Teversal Colliery, Nottingham. 28 June 1976, 2 July 1976, and 9 August 1976.
NUM officials and members Thoresby Branch. Thoresby Colliery, Nottingham. 30 June 1976 and 26 August 1976.

Miscellaneous

Atkinson, G. L. Area Industrial Relations Officer. Northeast Area Headquarters, Team Valley, Gateshead. 18 January 1977.
Douglass, Dave. Dunscroft, Yorkshire. 14 August 1980.
Former Harworth miner. Bevercotes Colliery, Nottingham. 21 July 1976.
Mr. McManners. Peterlee. Interview by Artist Project, n.d.
Oxley, Joe. Boldon Colliery, Durham. 7 August 1974.
Whelan, Joe. General Secretary, Nottingham Area NUM. Nottingham Area NUM Headquarters, Berry Hill Lane, Mansfield. 5 August 1980.

INDEX

Library of Congress Cataloging in Publication Data

Krieger, Joel, 1951-
Undermining capitalism.
Bibliography: p.   Includes index.
1. Coal trade—Government ownership—Great Britain.
I. Title.
HD9551.6.K74   1983   338.2'724'0941   83-42563
ISBN 0-691-07662-6